BRITISH SHIPBUILDING

VOLUME 2 : CLYDESIDE

by NORMAN L. MIDDLEMISS

SHIELD PUBLICATIONS LTD.
NEWCASTLE-UPON-TYNE
GREAT BRITAIN

ISBN 1 871128 11 0

British Library Cataloguing-in-Publication Data.
A Catalogue Record is available from the British Library.

Published by SHIELD PUBLICATIONS LTD.,
7, Verne Road, North Shields, TYNE & WEAR. NE29 7LP.

Printed by Smith Settle, Ilkley Road, Otley.

Cover illustration is a painting of the launch of the liner EMPRESS OF BRITAIN in June,1955 by Her Majesty The Queen. Painted by Arthur McNulty.

View of the Clydeholm yard of Barclay, Curle & Co. Ltd around 1930.
(Strathclyde Regional Archives).

CONTENTS

Two views of the Clyde between the Clydeholm and Linthouse yards showing the narrowness of the river and the consequently steeply angled berths.

INTRODUCTION

This major historical study in three Volumes of all British shipbuilding yards that have built ships during the last hundred years is intended for wide readership. The shipyard welder or painter as well as shipbuilding management will find much of interest here as to achievements, and it will also appeal to seafarers and shiplovers. Since this is the first comprehensive British shipyard study to be published, it is wise at the outset to state what this series attempts to do and what it does not do :-

1. On a historical basis, information is given by river or area sector of the ownership and development of each shipyard, and a full analysis of every type of ship built and for which customers. The British shipbuilding industry was centred on or near sources of coal, iron and steel, with Figure 2 giving comparative percentages for the North East Coast, Clydeside, Belfast, Merseyside and Barrow. It can be clearly seen that the bulk of output came from the first two areas, and this series is thus split into three Volumes :-

Volume I	North-East Coast
Volume II	Clydeside
Volume III	Belfast, Merseyside, Barrow and other Areas.

2. Today there are only three shipbuilding yards left in operation on the Clyde: a Norwegian-owned yard capable of building large merchant ships at Govan, a warship yard at Scotstoun, and a yard at Port Glasgow for small merchant ships. In fact there are only two yards left in the United Kingdom capable of building large merchant ships, with the other at Belfast and both are Norwegian-owned. Thus for the British shipbuilding industry it is very much a case of all 'water under the bridge' and the reasons for the decline from complete supremacy of 81.7% of world market in 1893 to nil in 1993, while deeply interesting, are now largely academic. However it can be quite clearly seen from Figure 1 that the years from 1950 to 1970 were those of crucial decline compared to world competition. United Kingdom output fell in those years from well over 40% to a mere 6% of world output. On the Clyde, the loss of their traditional liner market base to the passenger aircraft and container would not have been fatal if the Geddes recommendations of 1967 for five yards to amalgamate into Upper Clyde Shipbuilders Ltd to beat Japanese competition had not been squandered by 1971. National shipbuilding employment excluding shiprepairing and marine engineering fell by half from 130,000 in 1950 to 65,000 in 1970.

3. This series is written by an independent author with no axe to grind on British shipbuilding, and who has written a dozen books on maritime subjects. He comes from a family whose forebears on both sides of the family worked in British shipyards, and the author himself has worked in a British shipyard. The motive of the author in writing this series is purely to document a proud and great British industry. Now is the time to document while everything is still fresh in the memory of a major industry, whose size on Clydeside can be gauged from the list of closure dates at the end of this introduction. However, this series makes no comment on British shipbuilding practice either from the management point of view, or from the workers and their trades unions point of view.

4. The Clyde river yards are divided into up-river yards and down-river yards with the dividing point being the Renfrew to Yoker ferry. Those yards which only built ships under 500 g.r.t. are not discussed in detail e.g. the Rutherglen yard in east Glasgow which built Clyde paddlers, steam coasters and a few early motor coasters, and the Hay yard at Kirkintilloch on the Forth & Clyde Canal, which built Clyde puffers. A work covering such a large and comprehensive subject as British shipbuilding has to be selective in nature when analysing yard lists. Omissions there most certainly will be, but these will hopefully be few in number, and the author invites constructive comment of a major nature or new research from all readers. Abbreviations are few e.g. brake horse power is b.h.p.; deadweight carrying capacity of a ship is d.w.t.; and gross registered tonnage g.r.t. is a measure of the volume of a ship, which is normally identified by gross tonnage/year of build after the name e.g. 9261/69.

The author wishes to acknowledge the invaluable help and information given by John B. Hill, F. Parks, Anna Robinson, Dr. O'Brien and the staff of Strathclyde Regional Archives, Michael Moss and the staff of Glasgow University Business Archives, the Glasgow Museum of Transport and the Scottish Record Office, and the National Maritime Museum. Thanks are due to the courtesy of the various sources for their kind permission to reproduce photographs, illustrations and yard plans, and these are credited alongside the illustrations, excepting in the case of the photographs on pages 23 to 28 inclusive where UCS records held by Strathclyde Regional Archives are reproduced by courtesy of the Principal Archivist and permission of the Keeper of the Records of Scotland.

Norman L. Middlemiss

Newcastle-upon-Tyne

June, 1994

FIGURE 1.

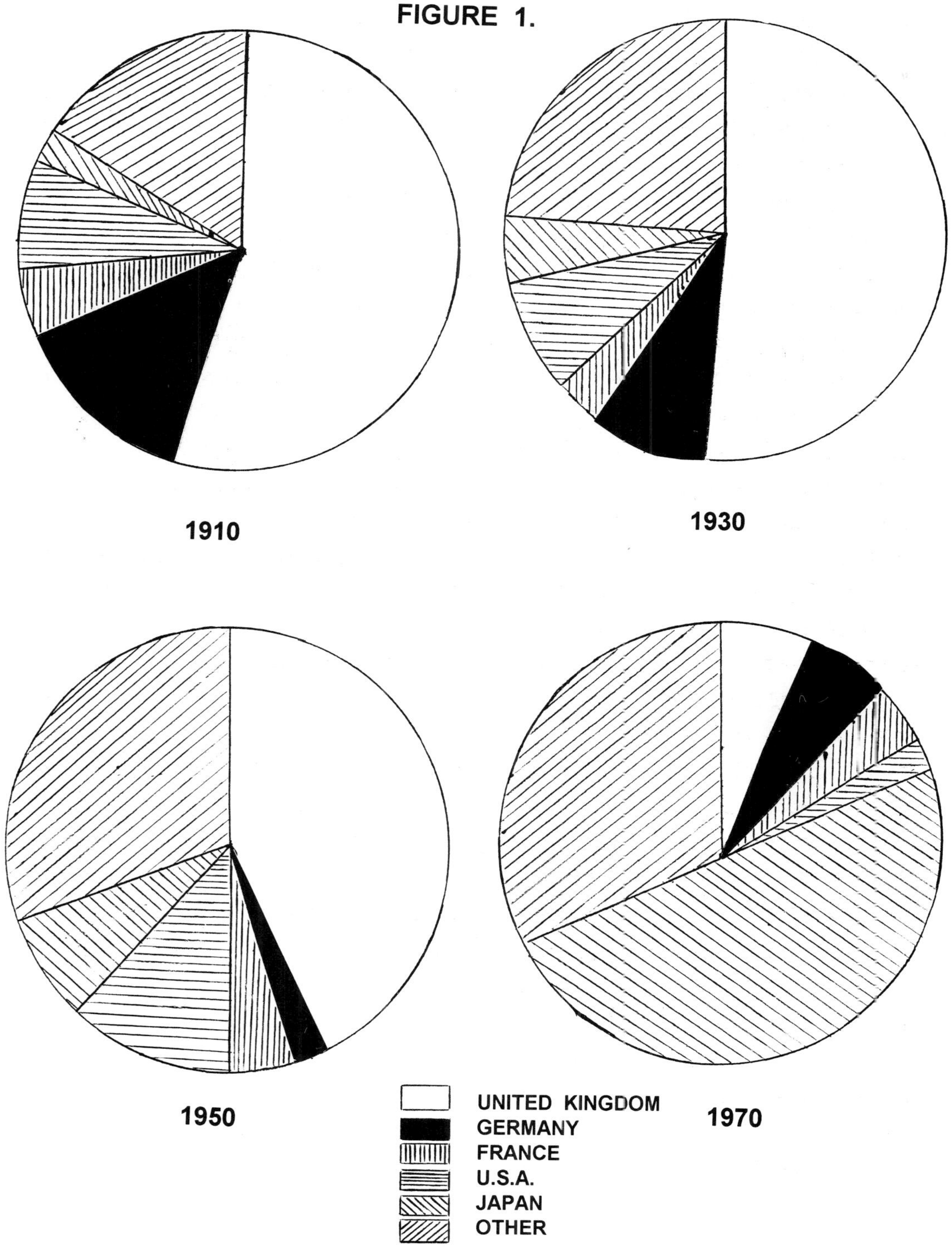

Source: Lloyd's Register Annual Summary of Merchant Ships Launched.

FIGURE 2.

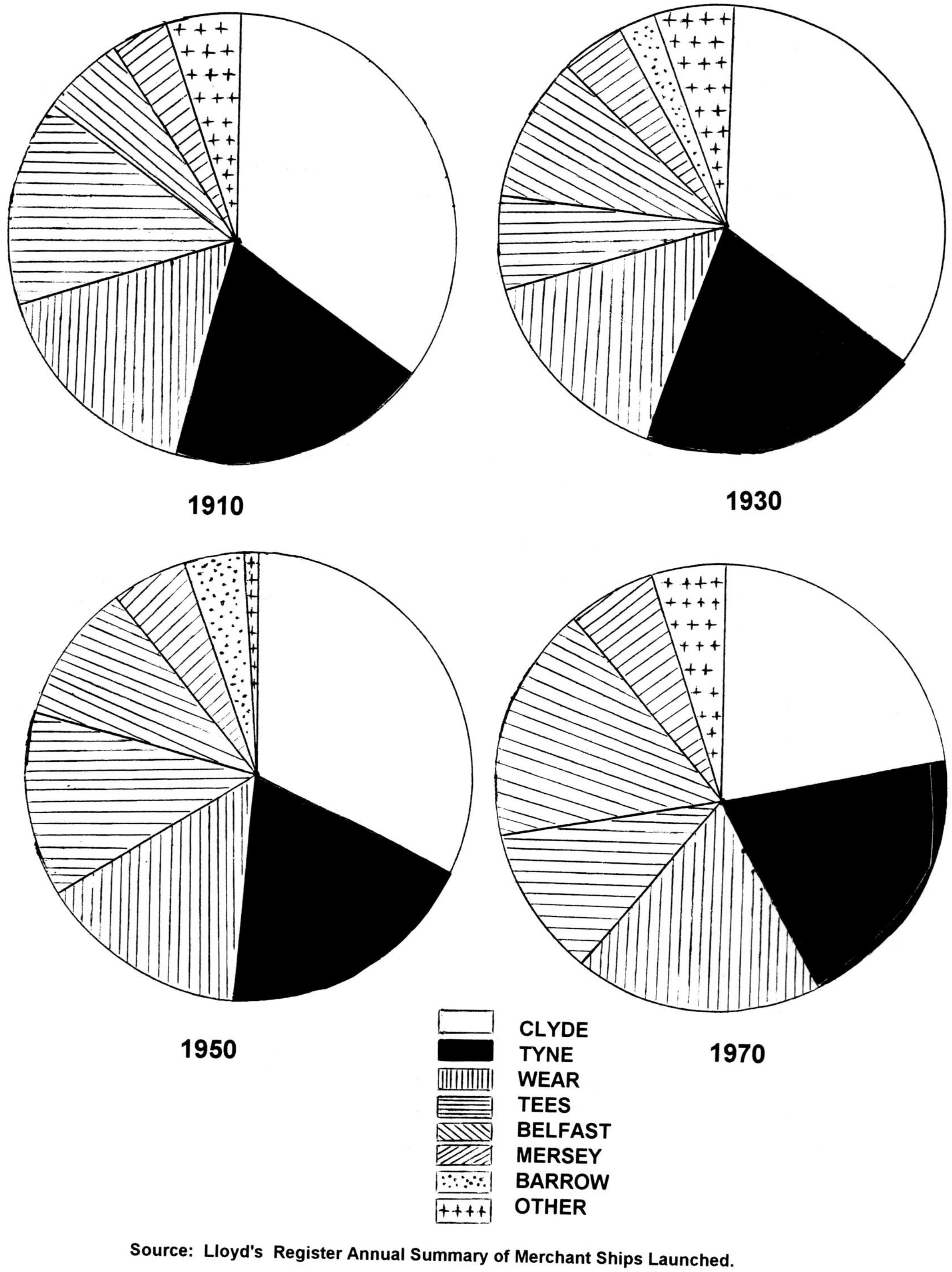

Source: Lloyd's Register Annual Summary of Merchant Ships Launched.

CLOSURE DATES OF CLYDESIDE SHIPBUILDING YARDS

1900 Robert Napier & Sons Ltd, Govan
1900 Taylor & Mitchell, Greenock
1902 T. B. Seath, Rutherglen
1905 W. Beardmore & Co. Ltd, Govan
1912 Mackie & Thomson, Govan
1912 London & Glasgow Eng. & Iron Shipbuilding Co. Ltd, Govan
1912 A. Rodger, Port Glasgow (Bay yard merged with Russell & Co.)
1918 Russell & Co., Port Glasgow (renamed Lithgows Ltd.)
1921 W. Chalmers & Co. Ltd, Rutherglen
1922 Campbeltown Shipbuilding Co. Ltd, Campbeltown
1925 Ross & Marshall Ltd, Port Glasgow
1926 Dunlop, Bremner & Co. Ltd, Port Glasgow (Inch yard)
1927 Murdoch & Murray Ltd, Port Glasgow
1928 Caird & Co. Ltd (Harland & Wolff Ltd), Greenock
1929 John Fullerton & Company, Paisley
1929 Clyde Shipbuilding Co. Ltd, Port Glasgow (Castle yard)
1929 Ailsa Shipbuilding Co. Ltd, Ayr
1931 W. Beardmore & Co. Ltd, Dalmuir
1931 Napier & Miller Ltd, Old Kilpatrick
1931 Ardrossan Dockyard Ltd. (South yard)
1931 R. Duncan & Co. Ltd, Port Glasgow (East yard reopened by Lithgow 1937)
1932 A. MacMillan & Sons Ltd, Dumbarton
1932 Bow, McLachlan & Co. Ltd, Paisley
1935 Lithgows Bay yard
1936 Ayrshire Dockyard Ltd, Irvine
1936 D. & W. Henderson & Co. Ltd, Meadowside
1958 J. & J. Hay, Kirkintilloch (Clyde puffers)
1962 Ardrossan Dockyard Ltd (North yard)
1963 W. Hamilton & Co. Ltd, Port Glasgow (Glen yard merged with Lithgows)
1963 G. Brown & Co.(Marine) Ltd, Greenock (briefly reopened 1981/82)
1963 W. Denny & Bros. Ltd, Dumbarton
1963 Harland & Wolff Ltd, Govan
1964 Blythswood Shipbuilding Co. Ltd, Scotstoun
1964 Simons yard, Renfrew
1964 Lobnitz yard, Renfrew
1964 Fleming & Ferguson Ltd, Paisley (briefly open under new owners until 1969)
1966 Greenock Dockyard Co. Ltd, Greenock (merged with Scotts')
1967 Campbeltown Shipyard Ltd, Campbeltown
1969 Alexander Stephen & Sons Ltd, Linthouse
1973 Brown Clydebank yard (reopened as a rig-builder)
1978 James Lamont & Co. Ltd, Port Glasgow (Castle yard)
1979 Scott & Sons (Bowling) Ltd
1980 Connell Scotstoun yard
1983 Lithgows Kingston/Glen/East yards (reopened as rig-builder)
1984 Scotts' Cartsburn and Cartsdyke yards

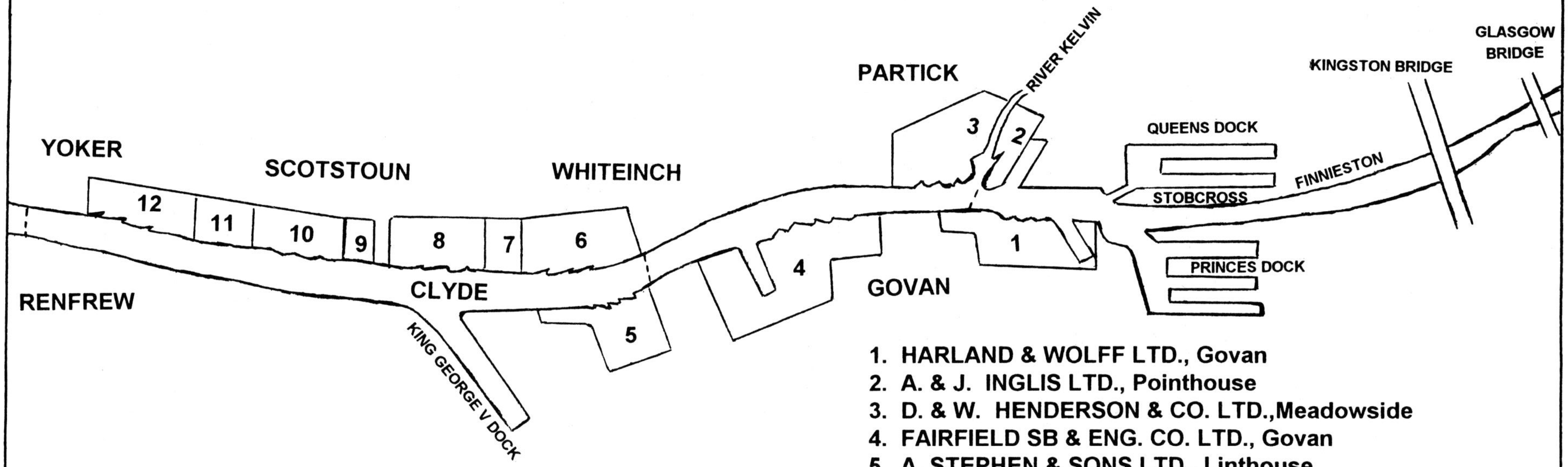

1. HARLAND & WOLFF LTD., Govan
2. A. & J. INGLIS LTD., Pointhouse
3. D. & W. HENDERSON & CO. LTD.,Meadowside
4. FAIRFIELD SB & ENG. CO. LTD., Govan
5. A. STEPHEN & SONS LTD., Linthouse
6. BARCLAY, CURLE & CO. LTD., Clydeholm
7. NORTH BRITISH ENGINE WORKS, Scotstoun
8. C. CONNELL & CO. LTD., Scotstoun
9. HARLAND & WOLFF LTD. DIESEL WORKS, Scotstoun
10. BLYTHSWOOD SHIPBUILDING CO. LTD., Scotstoun
11. YARROW & CO. LTD.
12. BARCLAY, CURLE & CO. LTD, West Scotstoun

FAIRFIELD SHIPBUILDING & ENGINEERING CO.LTD.
UPPER CLYDE SHIPBUILDERS LTD., Govan
GOVAN SHIPBUILDERS LTD.
KVAERNER GOVAN LTD.

The glory days of shipbuilding on the Clyde will never return, however this yard, which was generally acknowledged as the leading yard, is still building ships today. The yard was the creation of John Elder, a brilliant marine engineer who had been trained by Robert Napier at Govan. He pioneered the compound steam engine fitted in the *Brandon* in 1854 while a partner of Randolph, Elder & Company, and this major achievement allowed the steamship to become competitive over long haul voyages. Shipbuilding was started in 1860 at Govan Old yard, and four years later Elder purchased 60 acres of farmland at Fairfield Farm just downstream of this yard in order to lay out the largest integrated shipbuilding/engineering yard in the world.

The Fairfield yard was designed as a six-berth yard with heavily angled slipways due to the narrowness of the Clyde. The slipways were separated from the offices and engine works and the rest of the shipyard by a long shop parallel to the river containing the platers, frame and joiners shops. Thus the materials which formed the bulk of ship construction at that time were nearest to the building berths, and a fitting-out basin of 5.5 acres with a 270 feet wide entrance was excavated at the west end of the yard. The first ship was launched in 1868 when all production was transferred to the new Fairfield yard, but sadly John Elder was only able to see the first four ships launched from the yard before his death in September,1869 aged 45 years. In his will he left the yard to his widow, and in 1870 a new company, John Elder & Company, was formed by John Francis Ure, the brother of Mrs. Elder, and William Pearce as shipbuilding partner, and J.L.K. Jamieson as engineering partner. The full extent of John Elder's shipyard was completed in 1871, and by 1874 the new engine and boiler works had been added. His name lived on in the iron-hulled passenger/cargo-liner *John Elder* 3832/70 for the Pacific Steam Navigation Company, the first of a dozen ships of this size for this company delivered during the next four years and ending with *Iberia* 4671/74. When Ure and Jamieson retired from the yard, William Pearce was left to carry on alone.

The three decades from 1870 until the turn of the century saw the yard expand its liner company clientele, and some long-term and prolific associations were formed e.g. Donald Currie and his Castle Line to South Africa had 14 ships built starting with *Kinfauns Castle* 3507/79 and ending with *Kildonan Castle* 9664/99 with *Garth Castle* 3705/81 named after his estate in Perthshire. Norddeutscher Lloyd of Hamburg had 17 ships built starting with *Elbe* 4897/81 and ending with *Weimar* 4245/90; and the British & African Steam Navigation Co. Ltd with services to West Africa took 15 coastal ships e.g. *Gambia* 1880/75. The Far East and Australasian trades were important to the yard with the following ships and companies :-

ORIENT	5386/79	Orient Line
AUSTRAL	5588/82	"
ORMUZ	6117/86	"
OMRAH	8291/99	"
TONGARIRO	4163/83	New Zealand Shipping Co. Ltd
AORANGI	4163/83	"
RUAPEHU	4163/83	"
KAIKOURA	4474/84	"
RIMUTAKA	4474/85	"
CHINA	4940/89	China Mail Steamship Corp.
KUMANO MARU	4655/00	Nippon Yusen Kaisha,Japan
CHUSAN	3590/74	Shanghai Steamship Co. Ltd

However it was the Transatlantic passenger trade and the building of Blue Riband record breakers that occupied the mind of William Pearce as the best way of advertising the skill of Clydeside workers to the general public. The Guion Line with American finance, although operating under the British flag out of Liverpool, placed orders for three iron-hulled express liners completed as *Arizona* 5147/79, *Alaska* 6932/81 and *Oregon* 7375/83. They were propelled by powerful Fairfield-designed three-cylinder compound engines acting on three cranks, and all three captured the Blue Riband record crossing time. They were not commercial successes, however, as their bunker spaces were too large at the expense of steerage passenger space, and *Oregon* was sold to Cunard Line after only a few crossings of the Atlantic. Cunard also ordered their own record breakers from the yard, *Umbria* 7718/84 and *Etruria* 7718/84, and both achieved record times in 1887. This twin-funnelled pair were built of steel and were single screw with similar engines to the Guion Line trio and had accomodation for 550 first-class and 800 steerage passengers. However not all Atlantic liners were designed as record breakers e.g. *Normannia* 8249/90 for Hamburg-Amerika Line.

The Fairfield Shipbuilding & Engineering Co. Ltd was formed in 1886 led by Sir William Pearce, who had also represented Govan as Member of Parliament since 1885. On his death in 1888 at the age of 55 years he was succeeded by his son Sir William G. Pearce and in the following year the yard was financially reconstructed as a public company although the Pearce family held the majority of shares. The next pair of Cunard Line record breakers firmly established the Fairfield yard in the minds of the general public as builders of express liners. They were ordered in 1891 and were the largest liners of their day when *Campania* 12950/93 was launched by Lady Burns on 8th September,1892 as the first of the pair, her keel having been laid in September,1891. The pair had two sets of triple expansion engines each featuring five cylinders and three cranks, and *Campania* captured the Blue Riband one month after her entry into service in April,1893. Her sister *Lucania* 12952/93 was completed in September,1893 and also captured the Blue Riband one month after her entry into service. Their passenger complement was 550 first-class, 280 second-class and 1000 steerage passengers.

The yard also developed a good reputation for building steam yachts during this period and a dozen were built including three named *Lady Torfrida* for British owners, including the Pearce family. However it was the large Russian yacht *Livadia* that caused a stir with the general public in that she was almost circular in hull design ! The Czar of Russia, Alexander II, stipulated that she must make 14 knots in service and thus a model was built with this unusual hull shape and tested on Loch Lomond. She was 235 feet long and almost as wide with the widest part below the waterline, with three funnels placed athwartships across her widest point. Tens of thousands of people turned out to see her launched and after her fitting-out, with furnishings and appointments costing half a million pounds and her saloon mounted on gimbals, she duly made 15.75 knots on trials.

The yard also developed a good reputation for building coastal and cross-Channel packets for the Zeeland Steamship Company of Holland; the Liverpool & North Wales Steamship Co. Ltd; London,Brighton & South Coast Railway Company; London & East Coast Express Steamship Service Ltd; Isle of Man Steam Packet Co. Ltd; and the London,Chatham & Dover Railway Co. Ltd. The first cross-Channel steamer for the latter company was built to an unusual specification, she had to maintain a 'one-hour-each-way' service every day for a month or else she would not be accepted into service. Despite some tense crossings with *Victoria* 940/86 only just beating the hour on the stopwatch, she was accepted and two twin-funnelled Fairfield Channel packet paddle steamers followed for this owner, *Empress* 1084/87 and *Calais-Douvres* 1065/89, both capable of speeds over 20 knots.

The first triple-expansion steam engine built in the yard to the design of A.C. Kirk, Engine Works Manager, was installed in 1874 in the compound-engined *Propontis* of 2083 grt previously completed by Elder in 1864, and although her boilers as originally designed were not satisfactory, it was not long before improved triple-expansion engines from the yard were in service. However they were normally used when economy in fuel was needed rather than increased power, and the first of these to be fitted in a deep-sea vessel was designed by Kirk and lifted aboard the *Aberdeen* 3658/82, built by Robert Napier & Sons in the nearby Govan East yard for Aberdeen Line service to Australia and China. It is ironic that the Fairfield yard, a pioneer in steam engines, did not build its last sailing ship until the 1890s, with the barques *Chiltonford* 2348/92 and *Chelmsford* 2347/93.

When orders were scarce during the periodic shipping slumps, the Admiralty brought work to the yard. The cruiser *Nelson* was the first contract in 1878 and a further eleven cruisers and six 30 knot torpedo boat destroyers had been built by 1902. These included the protected cruisers *Diadem* and *Argonaut* of 1897/98 and the larger armoured cruisers *Cressy, Aboukir* and *Good Hope* of 1900/01 fitted with 9.2" guns. In 1902 the yard won its first order for a battleship for the pre-Dreadnought *Commonwealth* of the 12" gun King Edward VII class, completed in 1905. In March,1904 the large armoured cruiser *Cochrane* of the Warrior class was laid down and she was completed in 1907. In March,1906 the keel of the battlecruiser *Indomitable* was laid down and she was completed in 1908, and was joined in the fleet by the similar *New Zealand* in 1912. Two further cruisers completed the pre-war naval programme with *Glasgow* (1910) and *Undaunted* (1914).

Armoured cruiser CRESSY of 1901

Sir William G. Pearce, Chairman of the yard, was a founder of the famous shipping company Canadian Pacific Steamships Ltd, and thus a special building relationship developed with the Fairfield yard after the turn of the century. The first Canadian Empresses to be built by the yard were the twin-funnelled *Empress of Britain* 14188/06 and *Empress of Ireland* 14191/06, followed by the three-funnelled *Empress of Russia* 16810/13 and *Empress of Asia* 16909/13 for their Pacific service. Four further small ferries were built for service in British Columbia. The elegant

Transatlantic liner *Furst Bismarck* 8336/05 for the Hamburg-Amerika Line had interiors by Glasgow's famous son Charles Rennie Mackintosh, better known for the artistic decoration in the Willow tearooms in Sauchiehall Street. Further liners and troopships from the yard at this time were :-

HARDINGE	5434/00	Bengal Govt. troopship
PANAMA	5464/02	Pacific Steam Nav. Co. Ltd
VICTORIA	5967/02	"
ORONTES	9023/02	Orient Line
ARMADALE CASTLE	12972/03	Union-Castle Mail S.S. Co. Ltd
DURHAM CASTLE	8499/04	"
HELIOPOLIS	10897/07	Egyptian Mail S.S. Co. Ltd
CAIRO	10864/07	"
OTWAY	12077/09	Orient Line
BALMORAL CASTLE	13361/09	Union-Castle Mail S.S. Co. Ltd
GLOUCESTER CASTLE	8007/11	"
MAUNGANUI	7527/11	Union S.S. Co. Ltd,New Zealand
LLANSTEPHAN CASTLE	11348/14	Union-Castle Mail S.S. Co. Ltd
CALGARIAN	17521/14	Allan Line, Glasgow

ARMADALE CASTLE of 1903

In 1907 the yard had passed into the control of a consortium on the death of Sir William G. Pearce. The Chairman and Managing Director then became the naval architect Dr. Francis Elgar, who was succeeded in 1909 by Alexander Gracie, the son of a shepherd from the hills to the west of the Clyde, and who had served his apprenticeship in Glasgow. He later served on Lord Fisher's advisory committee for the Navy. He continually updated the yard with new machinery, and in 1911 a hammer-head crane was erected on the east side of the fitting-out basin in time to complete the liners *Gloucester Castle* and *Maunganui*. A large shareholding had also been taken in 1905 in the Coventry Ordnance Works jointly with John Brown &

The fitting-out basin in May,1929 showing ARANDORA STAR, the cruiser NORFOLK and EMPRESS OF CANADA. Note the West Yard berths at top left. (Scottish Record Office)

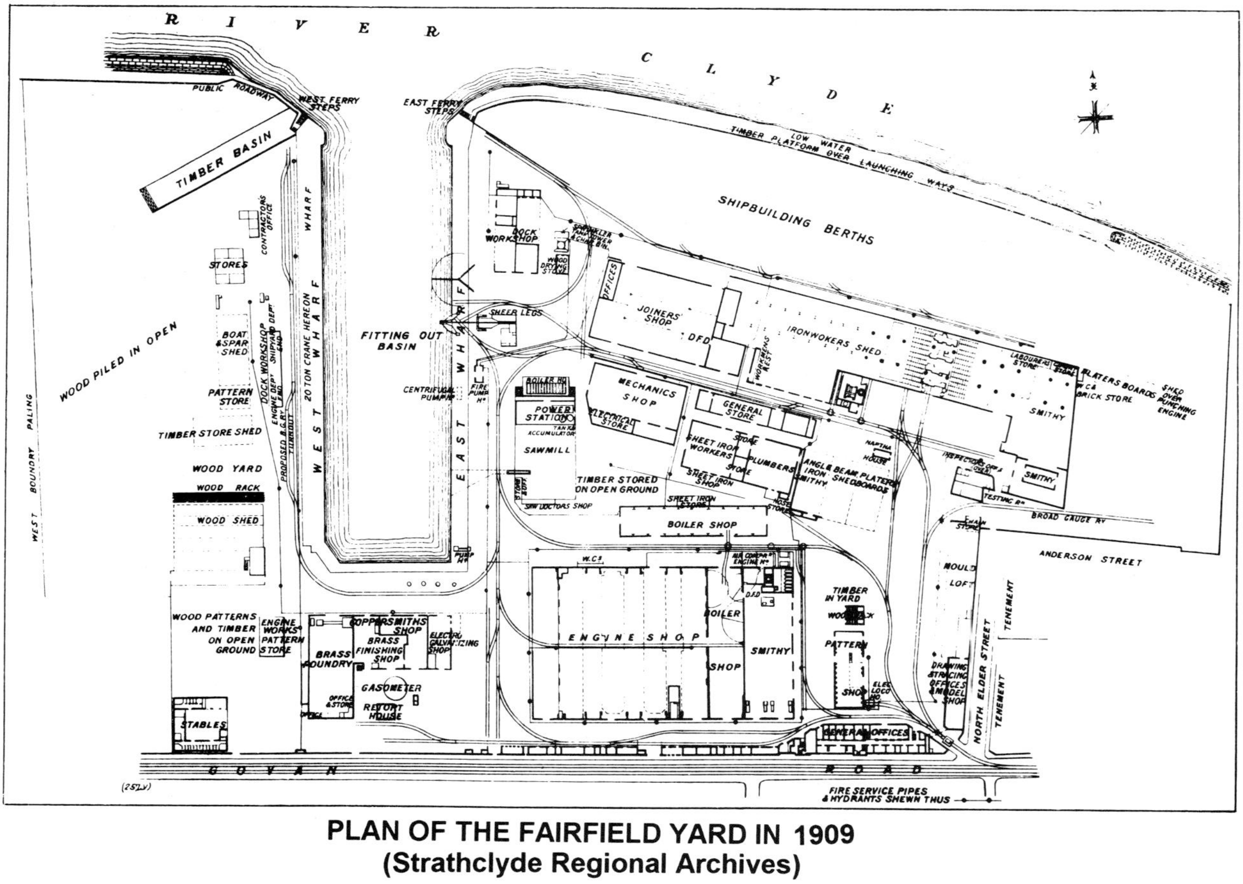

PLAN OF THE FAIRFIELD YARD IN 1909
(Strathclyde Regional Archives)

Co. Ltd, and Cammell Laird & Co. Ltd to secure supplies of naval ordnance from the factory in Coventry. This was to prove invaluable when the yard was switched over entirely to naval construction at the start of the Great War.

The large total of 50 warships with a total displacement tonnage of 144,777 tons was built by the yard during this war, their engines amounting to more than a million horse power. The battleship *Valiant* had been laid down in early 1913 and was ready for action in February,1916, with the battlecruiser *Renown* completing from keel laying to trials in even faster time of just over 18 months from receipt of order in January,1915. She was launched in January,1916 and completed in September of that year, her order and that of sister *Repulse* from John Brown came only after the British success with battlecruisers off the Falkland Islands in January,1915. Three cruisers *Cardiff* (1917), *Carlisle* (1918) and *Colombo* (1918) and 24 destroyers and nine submarines, a train ferry for service to the Continent and minor craft completed the total. A single merchantman was built during the war, having been launched for the Union Steamship Co. Ltd of New Zealand as *Aotearoa* she was completed as the armed merchant cruiser *Avenger* in 1916. Two standard 'AO' type tankers were completed at the end of the war, followed by the similar Norwegian tanker *Tiger* 5655/20 and the cable ship *Lady Denison-Pender* 1984/20 for the Eastern Telegraph Co. Ltd.

In 1919 a large block of shares in the yard came onto the market following the death of Lady Pearce, widow of Sir William G. Pearce, and were purchased by the Northumberland Shipbuilding Co. Ltd of Howdon on Tyneside (See Volume 1), with finance from London merchant bankers Sperling Group. The Northumberland consortium grew to be the largest shipbuilding grouping in the world, with the Fairfield yard now headed by R.A. Workman of shipbuilders Workman,Clark & Co. Ltd, Belfast - another Group member. The expectation of a boom in merchant construction after the enormous war losses led to the construction of four new berths in a new West Yard on the other side of the fitting-out basin. These four new berths were served by an overhead gantry and two of the berths were entirely under cover. In fact, a primitive covered berth had existed on the west side of the fitting-out basin since 1912 and had been used to build *Ermine* 1836/12 for Burns Line. This berth was re-equipped during the war to build submarines, and then in January,1919 the Fairfield Board authorised the expenditure of £70,000 to develop these berths. However they were only in use for ten years, a victim of the severely depressed freight rates of the 1920s and 1930s.

Six high-class liners were ordered from the yard in 1920, two for Canadian Pacific, two for Anchor Line of Glasgow, and two for Donaldson Line of Glasgow. The severe slump of 1921 caused work on three of these to be suspended

AORANGI of 1925 (top) was the first quadruple-screw diesel-engined passenger liner in the world; EMPRESS OF JAPAN (middle) of 1930 was renamed EMPRESS OF SCOTLAND by Canadian Pacific in 1942; TRANSYLVANIA of 1925 (bottom) of Glasgow-based Anchor Line.

indefinitely, but resumed when an order was received for a seventh liner in 1923. This seventh liner was completed as the twin-funnelled *Aorangi* and was notable for her engines, being the first quadruple-screw diesel-engined passenger ship in the world. She was given Sulzer engines after licences were acquired to build both Sulzer and Doxford engines. The seven liners were :-

EMPRESS OF CANADA	21516/22	Canadian Pacific
MONTROSE	16401/22	"
TUSCANIA	16991/22	Anchor Line, Glasgow
TRANSYLANIA	16923/25	"
ATHENIA	13465/23	Donaldson Line, Glasgow
LETITIA	13475/25	"
AORANGI	17491/25	Union S.S. Co. Ltd,New Zealand

The yard also won in 1926 the contract to re-engine with turbines the ex-German liner *Tirpitz*, which had been renamed *Empress of Australia* in 1922 on purchase by Canadian Pacific. The order book was then maintained by four new four-masted passenger ships for Bibby Line for their Burma service, specifying Sulzer double-acting engines, whereas Houlder Brothers and Shaw,Savill & Albion specified Sulzer single-acting engines when they ordered a total of five refrigerated meat carriers :-

SHROPSHIRE	10550/26	Bibby Line,Liverpool
CHESHIRE	10550/27	"
STAFFORDSHIRE	10650/29	"
WORCESTERSHIRE	11452/30	"
UPWEY GRANGE	9130/25	Houlder Brothers
DUNSTER GRANGE	9494/28	"
EL ARGENTINO	9501/28	"
TARANAKI	8285/28	Shaw,Savill & Albion Co. Ltd
KARAMEA	8281/28	"

Canadian Pacific came back to the yard for three ferries for British Columbia service and completed during 1928/30, as well as an order for the three-funnelled twin-screw liner *Empress of Japan* 26032/30. She was launched on 17th December,1929 and completed in June,1930 and was powered by six steam turbines fed by six boilers and had accomodation for 1100 passengers. Shortage of Admiralty orders in the 1920s did not help the yard, with only two three-funnelled 'County' class cruisers completed, *Berwick* in February,1928 and *Norfolk* in June,1930. One of the very few tramps built by the yard was completed in 1928 for Court line as *Rossington Court* 5425/28. Two Solent paddle steamers were completed in 1930 as *Southsea* 825/30 and *Whippingham* 825/30, leaving the order book at only two paddle steamers and two destroyers. The former were completed as *St. Seiriol* 1586/31 for the Liverpool & North Wales Steamship Co. Ltd, powered by four steam turbines and able to carry 2500 day trippers, and the famous twin-funnelled Clyde paddler *Jeanie Deans* 635/31 with triple expansion engines. The destroyers were completed as *Dainty* and *Delight* of 1932/33, when the yard was then reduced to surviving on refit and maintenance work. Massive unemployment gripped the whole of Govan town, and the new West Yard was closed and then demolished in 1934. Sir Alexander Kennedy of the Sperling Group was now Chairman of the yard but with slender financial resources from the lean 1920s, and the bankruptcy of the Anchor Line of whom the yard were creditors, he eventually had to accept a take-over offer from the Port Glasgow yards of Sir James Lithgow and his brother Henry in 1935. No ships were built in 1933, but the Admiralty brought forward an order for the destroyer depot ship *Woolwich* at the end of the year, and the Clyde paddler *Mercury* 620/34 brought jobs to a few men. Freight rates started to rise again in 1935 and shipbuilding got back into gear at Govan when orders for a total of four passenger liners were received from Bibby Line and the local reconstructed Anchor Line.

The Anchor Line pair were for their Indian service and received the first Doxford oil engines to be built at the yard since a Doxford licence was taken out in the early 1920s, and they were completed as *Circassia* 11170/37 and *Cilicia* 11172/38. The Bibby Line pair were for their Burma service and had Sulzer double-acting diesel engines, and were completed as *Derbyshire* 11660/35 and the troopship *Devonshire* 11300/39. A worsening European political scene saw the Admiralty building up its strength with one 'Town' class cruiser launched on 24th March,1937 as *Liverpool* and completed during 1938, as well as the detroyers *Garland* (1936), *Gipsy* (1936), *Gurkha* (1938), *Maori* (1938), *Juno* (1939) and *Kelvin* (1939). Grandstand views of launches from the yard could now be obtained from the new Meadowside Granary, directly opposite the yard on the north bank and opened in 1937.

The yard was again switched over to naval construction at the start of World War II, as had happened in the Great War. The battleship *Howe* had been laid down in June,1937 at the end of Treaty limitations and she was in service in August,1942, the aircraft-carrier *Implacable* was launched by H.M. The Queen and was in service during August,1944 followed by the smaller carrier *Theseus* in 1946. The cruisers *Phoebe* (1940), *Bellona* (1943) and 24 destroyers, two sloops and three large tank landing craft and minor craft made up the total displacement tonnage of 113,738 tons propelled by some 1.5 million horsepower. Orders for a large aircraft-carrier and many destroyers were cancelled at the end of the war, with one incomplete cruiser afloat and laid-up indefinitely. The last of five 'Battle' class destroyers from the yard did not complete until July,1947.

Damage to Govan town and the Fairfield yard from air-raids was lighter than at Clydebank, and the yard was then engaged in the reconversion of a dozen armed merchant cruisers to resume their normal peace-time service; three for Canadian Pacific, two for Anchor Line, four for Bibby Line and one for Union-Castle Line. During the post-war years the yard was switched back to building merchant ship replacements e.g. cargo-liners some with sizable passenger accomodation :-

BEAVERCOVE	9824/47	Canadian Pacific
CALEDONIA	11255/47	Anchor Line
WARWICKSHIRE	8900/47	Bibby Line
LEICESTERSHIRE	8908/49	"
DORIC	10674/49	Shaw,Savill & Albion Co. Ltd
ENGLISH STAR	9996/50	Blue Star Line
SCOTTISH STAR	9996/50	"
SIRA	9538/53	Gorrissen & Klaveness,Norway
SIMOA	9516/53	"
SJOA	9866/54	"
S.A. MERCHANT	9866/55	Safmarine, South Africa
CIUDAD DE MEDELLIN	4219/51	Flota Mercante SA,Colombia
CIUDAD DE BARQUISIMETO	4219/51	"
QUEENSLAND STAR	10657/57	Blue Star Line
SHROPSHIRE	7244/59	Bibby Line
YORKSHIRE	7218/60	"
LANCASHIRE	7034/63	"
GLENOGLE	11537/62	Glen Line
GLENFALLOCH	11537/62	"

and to the ever-escalating size of tankers and ore-oil carriers :-

BOMI HILLS	17881/52	Gorrissen & Klaveness,Norway
ENDURO	17878/52	"
CHATEAUGAY	18019/54	"
MOISIE BAY	17999/55	"
FREE STATE	19614/56	Gorrissen & Klaveness, Norway
CUYAHOGA	19600/57	"
BRITISH REALM	18571/52	British Tanker Co. Ltd
ATLANTIC BARON	12874/53	Livanos,Greece
ATLANTIC BARONESS	12875/53	"
TABOGA	12137/54	Soc. Tropica de Carga S.A.
BRITISH ENERGY	23124/58	British Tanker Co. Ltd
IRISH HAWTHORN	12168/58	Irish Shipping Ltd
IRISH BLACKTHORN	12169/59	"

FAIRFIELD YARD PRE - 1960

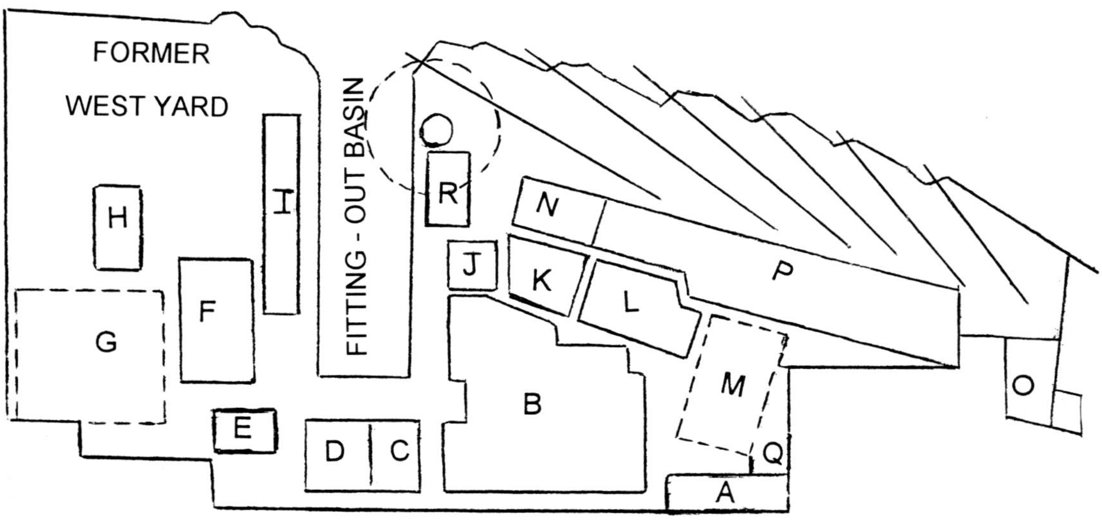

A. OFFICES
B. ENGINE WORKS
C. BRASS FOUNDRY
D. COPPER SHOP
E. PATTERN STORE
F. SAWMILL
G. TIMBER YARD
H. CANTEEN
I. OUTFITTING SHOP
J. POWER STATION
K. MECHANICS SHOP
L. SHEET METAL WORKERS
M. STEEL STOCKYARD
N. JOINERS SHOP
O. SLIDING WAYS
P. PLATERS SHOP
Q. MOULD LOFT
R. CARPENTERS SHOP

FAIRFIELD YARD ALTERED FOR PREFABRICATION

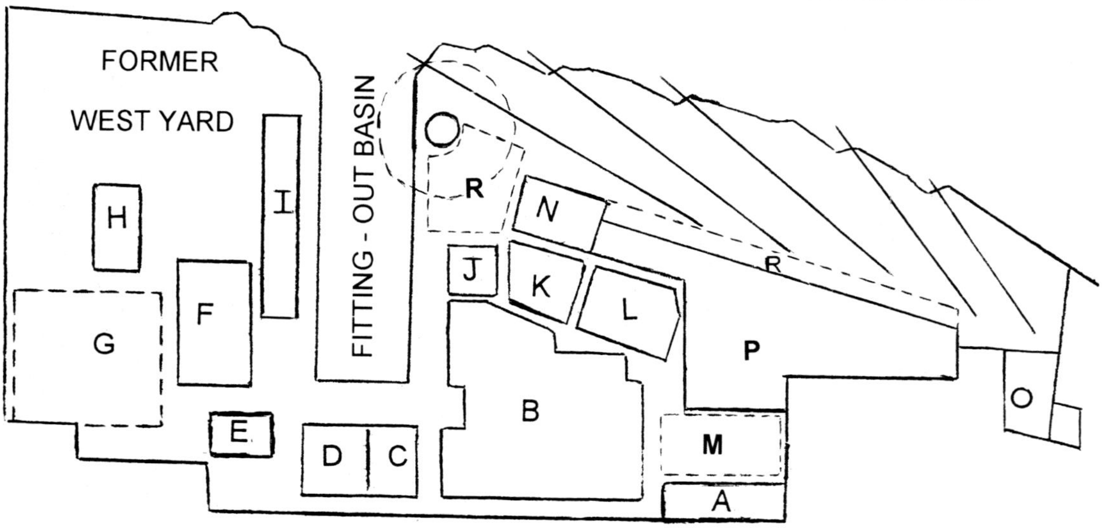

A. - O. AS ABOVE
P. PREFABRICATION SHOP / MOULD LOFT
R. ASSEMBLY STORAGE

The launch of the bridge-forward Great Lakes trader LEECLIFFE HALL on 18th May,1961 for the Hall Corporation of Canada. She was completed in August,1961.

GLENFALLOCH on launch day at the Fairfield yard in July, 1962.

The launch of the cargo-liner LANCASHIRE on 7th May,1963 for Bibby Line.

The launch of the tanker BRITISH GUARDSMAN on 12th December,1962 for the British Tanker Co. Ltd.

The launch of the Mediterranean ferry NILI on 11th August, 1964 for Zim Israel Line.

The launch of the bulker CLUDEN on 25th September, 1964 for Jardine, Matheson & Co. Ltd.

NORDIC HAWK	23124/59	Nordic Tankships,Denmark
SHELL ARAMARE	21840/59	Shell Venezuela
SHELL NAIGUATA	21840/60	"
BRITISH GUARDSMAN	32083/63	British Tanker Co. Ltd
BRITISH COMMODORE	38288/67	"

The last two classic liners built by the yard were completed as *Empress of Britain* 25516/56 for Canadian Pacific with H. M. The Queen as sponsor in June,1955, and the troopship *Oxfordshire* 20586/57 for Bibby Line. The propelling machinery of both liners was double reduction Parsons geared turbines, fed by two Foster-Wheeler superheat boilers and one reheat boiler, the latter using the new Fairfield reheat system first tried in the *Empress of Britain*. The Canadian Pacific liner needed to be ice-strengthened for navigation on the St. Lawrence and had a heated and glazed crow's nest on the navigation mast for observation of ice. She was of almost all-welded construction and aluminium was used for her funnel and much of her superstructure, and she could carry 150 first-class and 900 tourist class passengers.

The Admiralty eventually decided to complete the laid-up cruiser launched during the war with a hangar replacing her 6" gun turrets, and she was accepted into service as *Blake* during 1960. The Daring class destroyer *Delight* (1953) had been followed by the frigates *Chichester* (1958) and *Lincoln* (1960); with two 'County' class guided missile cruisers completing as *Fife* (1966) and *Antrim* (1970) during the next decade, as well as the tank landing ship *Sir Lancelot* (1965). These were the last warships completed by the yard, which then kept to merchant construction under new owners. At the beginning of the decade the yard completed the cable ship *Alert* 6413/60 for H. M. Postmaster, and the Great Lakes bulk carrier *Leecliffe Hall* in 1961 with a length of 711 feet for the Hall Corporation of Canada. The yard order book then received a welcome boost of ten ships from an unexpected customer, however to those workers with a knowledge of yard history it was not that unusual - an order for ten Turkish ferries for service on the Bosphorus and a repeat of a similar order placed sixty years earlier ! The first of these was *Kuzgunck* 810/62 and the remainder were completed during the next twelve months.

The yard had been heavily run down by the long war years and the subsequent years of merchant ship replacement building and was long overdue for modernisation. It was brought into the age of prefabrication by first reorganising the fitting-out shops, and then converting the six-berth yard into one with five larger berths only (See shipyard plan). Concrete roadways 40 feet wide were built between each of the berths and 80-ton travelling cranes installed to lift prefabricated assemblies. Finally in 1960 the erection of new steelwork shops was begun, and when eventually completed stretched the full length of the yard, a distance of over 1000 feet, with further reorganisation of the steel stockyard behind. In 1963 the engineers David Rowan & Co. Ltd,Glasgow were acquired, and their works was integrated with the Fairfield engine works as Fairfield - Rowan Ltd. The benefits of prefabrication were seen in speeded-up building times of the Zim Israel Mediterranean ferry *Nili* 7851/65, and the ill-fated turbo-electric New Zealand ferry *Wahine* 8948/66 (lost while entering Wellington harbour from Picton during a cyclone on 10th April,1968), and the bulkers *Australian City* 18621/64, *Eastern City* 18620/65 and *Cluden* 22341/65 for British owners. However the cost of yard rebuilding at £3M had been too much for the yard's owners Lithgows Ltd, and they were forced to put the yard into receivership at the launch of the tanker *British Commodore* on 15th October,1965.

Many difficulties still faced the yard and British shipbuilding as a whole at this time with its exceptionally bad track record in low productivity and bad management / trade union relationships. The yard was saved from closure when the Labour Government stepped in and offered support together with trade union finance, setting-up Fairfields (Glasgow) Ltd, while initiating a very worthy and long overdue attempt to use production control techniques to give higher productivity. This was badly needed to counter international competition particularly from Japan, and also covered better communication by managers to the workers, new ways of handling disputes, and systematic methods for hiring and terminating temporary workers instead of the degrading spectacle of the selection process at the yard gates in the morning. These revolutionary improvements were hammered out into agreements over three years at the Fairfield yard, which were eventually incorporated into the Employment Protection Acts of 1977.

Meanwhile in Glasgow, the engine works could not be saved and Fairfield - Rowan Ltd closed during 1966. Orders for two bulkers for Reardon Smith of Cardiff were completed as *Atlantic City* 27029/67 and *Indian City* 27018/67, however one of a two-ship order was cancelled by P & O, to whom the yard had been offered for purchase in the late 1950s and early 1960s but had been turned down. This pair had originally been part of a five-ship order with British and Japanese yards, however after the launch of the bulker *Duhallow* 25368/66 on 26th October,1965 work was allowed to continue with British Government support and she was completed in March,1966, but the second order was then switched by the shipowner to a Japanese yard.

The Geddes Report had recommended mergers of British yards into Groups to try and ward off Japanese competition, and the Upper Clyde yards of Fairfield, Clydebank, Connell, Stephen and Yarrow combined into Upper Clyde Shipbuilders

Ltd in 1968. The Fairfield yard then became the Govan yard of UCS, completing the large container ship *Jervis Bay*, launched on 3rd May,1969 for the Australian service of Overseas Containers Ltd. She had a length of 746 feet and a beam of 100 feet and could carry 1530 containers of which 304 were refrigerated for the meat trade. Her two Swedish-manufactured Stal-Laval geared turbines gave her a service speed of 23 knots. Bulk carriers completed included *Welsh City* and *Cornish City*, both 10798/69, *Temple Bar* 13545/70, and the 'Cardiff' class *Vancouver City* 16644/70, *Prince Rupert City* 16639/70, *Fresno City* 16639/70, *Norse Pilot* 17187/71 and *Norse Marshal* 17187/71. Diversification into two surveying ships for the United States Navy, *Harkness* and *Chauvenet*, and into large suction dredgers of 432 feet in length of which three were built, *Pacifique*, *Delta Bay* and *Estato da Guanabara*, did not prevent Upper Clyde Shipbuilders Ltd from going into receivership in 1971. An expensive top-heavy management structure, low productivity, and the failure of the five yards to work together had produced huge debts for UCS Ltd. The resultant 'work-in' at Fairfield and heavy political pressure led to a new company being set-up in 1972 to run the yard, Govan Shipbuilders Ltd.

The success of the 'Cardiff' class of bulkers in attracting further British and overseas orders, together with a large order for 19 'Kuwait' class cargo-liners from the United Arab Shipping Co. Ltd, a grouping covering the fleets of four Arab nations, led to a period of security for the Govan yard Altogether 27 out of 31 'Cardiff' class bulkers were built at Govan and the remainder are now listed :-

NEW WESTMINSTER CITY	16704/74	Reardon Smith,Cardiff
TACOMA CITY	16704/72	"
PORT ALBERNI CITY	16692/72	"
IRISH PINE	16704/73	Irish Shipping Ltd
IRISH MAPLE	16704/73	"
IRISH OAK	16704/73	"
IRISH LARCH	16704/73	"
GOLDEN ANNE	16628/73	World Wide Shipping Ltd
GOLDEN ORIOLE	16628/73	"
NORSE TRADER	16681/74	Cardigan Shipping Co. Ltd
CAMARA	16822/75	East Asiatic Co.,Denmark
CINCHONA	16822/75	"
CAPE ORTEGAL	16646/76	Lyle Shipping Co. Ltd,Glasgow
CAPE RODNEY	16646/76	"
BARON NAPIER	16646/76	H. Hogarth,Glasgow
BARON PENTLAND	16646/76	"
DONA HORTENCIA II	16244/76	Northern Lines Inc,Manila
DON SALVADOR III	16244/76	"
DONA MAGDALENA	16244/77	"
DONA PAZ	16244/77	"

Fifty ships were completed on the Clyde to the two standard designs shown here, the 'Cardiff' class bulker (above), of which 31 units were built, and the 'Kuwait' class of cargo-liner, of which 19 units were built. Pictured are DONA PAZ of 1977 and AL MUHARRAQ of 1978.

LORD BYRON	16421/81	Jebsen U.K. Ltd
LORD JELLICOE	16421/81	"

In addition, three of the 'Cardiff' class were built at the former Connell yard and one at Clydebank. *Dona Paz* was launched by Lord Mountbatten on 18th January,1977, and the last of the class in the above list was completed as *Lord Curzon.* The other main class of ship from the Govan yard was the 'Kuwait' class of cargo-liner for the United Arab Shipping Co. Ltd, and thirteen out of nineteen ordered were built at Govan between 1974 and 1978 with Arab names such as *Al Salimiah* 15543/74 and *Ibn Sina* 15387/77, with the remaining six built at the former Connell yard, then operating as Scotstoun Marine Ltd, a subsidiary of Govan Shipbuilders Ltd.

On the nationalisation of British shipbuilding on 1st July,1977 Govan Shipbuilders Ltd became a member of British Shipbuilders Ltd. The late 1970s saw the major portion of a Polish order for bulk carriers go to Clyde yards, and Govan built four of 16500 dwt and three of 4400 dwt, one of the latter being a sub-contract from the Robb-Caledon yards, with the last delivery being in June,1980. Orders were also received for three very large bulkers of 67400 dwt, two from C.Y. Tung of Hong Kong and one from James Fisher Ltd of Barrow. The first of the Tung pair, *Pacific Patriot*, had an unfortunate launch in January,1982 in that she rammed the quay on the other side of the river, causing severe damage to rudder and sternpost and necessitating her tow from the river to Belfast for repairs. Her sister *Pacific Peace* was launched without incident one month later by Princess Alexandra, but welding problems in both ships prompted Tung to request 100% welding inspection, delaying their completion by several months. The third sister was completed as *Sir John Fisher* 37811/83.

Two sister container ships of *Jervis Bay*, completed at the yard in 1969, arrived at the yard in 1981 to be re-engined with diesel engines instead of their more expensive to run turbines. *Moreton Bay* and *Discovery Bay* had their turbines replaced to suit the slower service speed requirements of the time to give substantial fuel savings. Three Great Lakes grain carriers of 35300 dwt were then completed as *Canada Marquis, Selkirk Settler* and *Saskatchewan Pioneer*, all 21269/83; followed by three bulkers *El Conqueror* 19248/83, *Lakenes* 25956/84 and *Loftnes* 25904/84, the last pair for Jebsen. The first of three 22000 dwt super-colliers for service on the North-East Coast was launched on 7th March,1985 as *Sir Charles Parsons*, followed by *Lord Citrine* and *Lord Hinton*, all were in service by early 1986.

Work started in Autumn,1985 in laying the keel of a large passenger ferry for the North Sea Ferries services from Hull to Rotterdam. *Norsea* 31785/87 was

Aerial views of the yard in the 1980s and 1990s.

KVAERNER GOVAN LTD. 1994 YARD PLAN

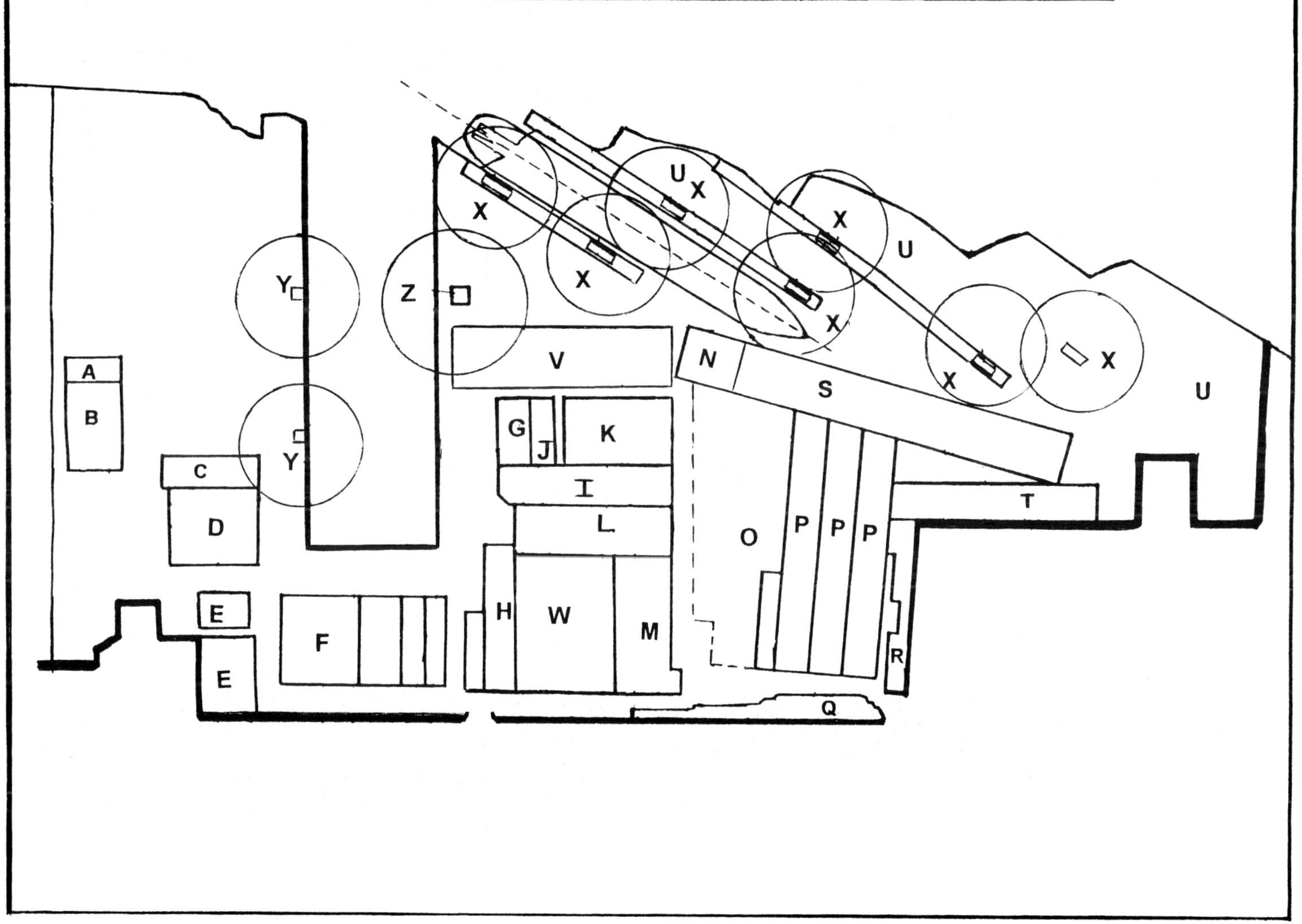

A. CANTEEN
B. TRAINING SCHOOL
C. STORES
D. SAWMILL / TIMBER STORAGE
E. PIPE STORAGE
F. PIPE SHOP
G. OUFIT OFFICES
H. UNIT HALL
I. BLACKSMITHS SHOP
J. ELECTRICIANS SHOP
K. MAINTENANCE SHOP
L. SHEET METAL WORKERS
M. STORES
N. JOINERS SHOP
O. STEEL STOCKYARD
P. STEEL PREPARATION BAYS
Q. MAIN OFFICE
R. OFFICES
S. PREFABRICATION HALL
T. ASSEMBLY HALL
U. ASSEMBLY STORAGE
V. GAS TANK ASSEMBLY HALL
W. SPECIAL FABRICATION SHOP
X. 80 - TON CRANES
Y. 25 - TON CRANES
Z. 200 - TON HAMMERHEAD CRANE

launched on 9th September,1986 and completed in 1987 at a cost of £40M and can carry 1250 passengers and 850 cars at a service speed of 16.5 knots from twin Sulzer 9-cylinder diesels and twin Sulzer 6-cylinder diesels driving highly skewed propellers.

The yard was taken back into private ownership during 1988 as Kvaerner - Govan Ltd, being sold to Kvaerner Industries A/S, Norway with a small yard at Floro in Norway for £6M. This was part of an alleged secret deal by the British Government with the European Economic Commission which also temporarily saved the Greenock engine works of Clark - Kincaid Ltd, but saw the obliteration of all of the Sunderland shipbuilding capacity in return for £45M of grants from the EEC to that town. Kvaerner have since updated the yard with a £30M investment in design facilities and a new assembly hall, where LPG tank units are assembled on low loaders and wheeled out to the berths, leading to a 30% reduction in building times. Two Chinese container ships, *Tai He* 35963/89 and *Pu He* 35963/90, were followed by a series of four liquid petroleum gas carriers e.g. *Helice* 34974/91 and *Havis* 35101/93 for Norwegian owners. The first of four chemical tankers of 37500 dwt was named as *Jo Selje* and launched by H. M. The Queen and completed in October,1993. This chemical tanker and three to follow have a double skin with a two metre separation and 40 out of her 52 tanks are made of stainless steel. The yard made a small profit during 1993, the first for thirty years, and the 1550 workers have work until early 1996 , including the hull of a Royal Navy helicopter ship.

A good aerial photograph of the yard in October,1993 showing the new tank assembly hall (left centre); further recent views of the yard appear on the next two pages. (Author)

ALEXANDER STEPHEN & SONS LTD.

This company had a history almost as long as Scotts' of Greenock with ships being built from 1750 at Burghead on the Moray coast, Aberdeen, and then Dundee. A yard was then opened in 1853 at Kelvinhaugh in Glasgow on the north bank of the river for shipbuilding and repair work. Alexander Stephen, born 1832, then purchased the 32 acre Linthouse estate in 1869 on the south bank of the river opposite Whiteinch and one mile downstream from his Kelvinhaugh yard. The Linthouse estate had beautiful grounds and a mansion house built around 1825 in the middle, which was retained and converted into an office. It also housed the general and rivet store in the basement with the billiard room becoming the model-makers shop! A five hundred feet long platers shed was built across the middle of the estate and faced the eight angled berths. A three-storey building was erected at the west end of the yard to house the spar shed on the ground floor, joiners shop on the second floor and draughting/mould loft on the upper floor. The blacksmiths shop, plumbers shop, painters shop, sheet-iron and tinsmiths shop were built on the eastern side of the yard, with houses for 120 workers and their families in the south-eastern corner. The conversion of the estate was nearing completion in the summer of 1870, with the first steamer being launched on 24th November,1870 as *Glendarroch* 1509/70 for William Ross of Glasgow to trade through the newly - opened Suez Canal to India.

Shipbuilding at Kelvinhaugh then ceased, while mostly speculative building of barques and sealers continued at Dundee until 1894. A sistership for William Ross was launched in December,1870 as *Glensannox* 1500/70 while five ships were launched during 1871, when the engine and boiler works were constructed on the eastern side of the yard. The first set of engines and boilers were lifted aboard the steamer *Nelusko* 2279/73 at the end of 1872 and she was launched in January, 1873. The lifting was accomplished by a large overhead travelling crane across the berths, with the engines and boilers taken by rail to between two of the berths, from where the crane lifted, carried and lowered them into the ship under construction. Larger ships could now be constructed e.g. *California* 3434/72 and *Ethiopia* 4004/73 for Anchor Line. Barques continued to be built such as *Pleione* 1092/76 for Shaw,Savill & Albion Co. Ltd, and *Wanganui* 1077/77 for the New Zealand Shipping Co. Ltd, and other owners, with the last barque being *Afon Cefni* 2066/92 for Hughes of Menai Bridge. Quotations for the more expensive but lighter steel hull were given from 1880, with the first steel steamer completed during 1882.

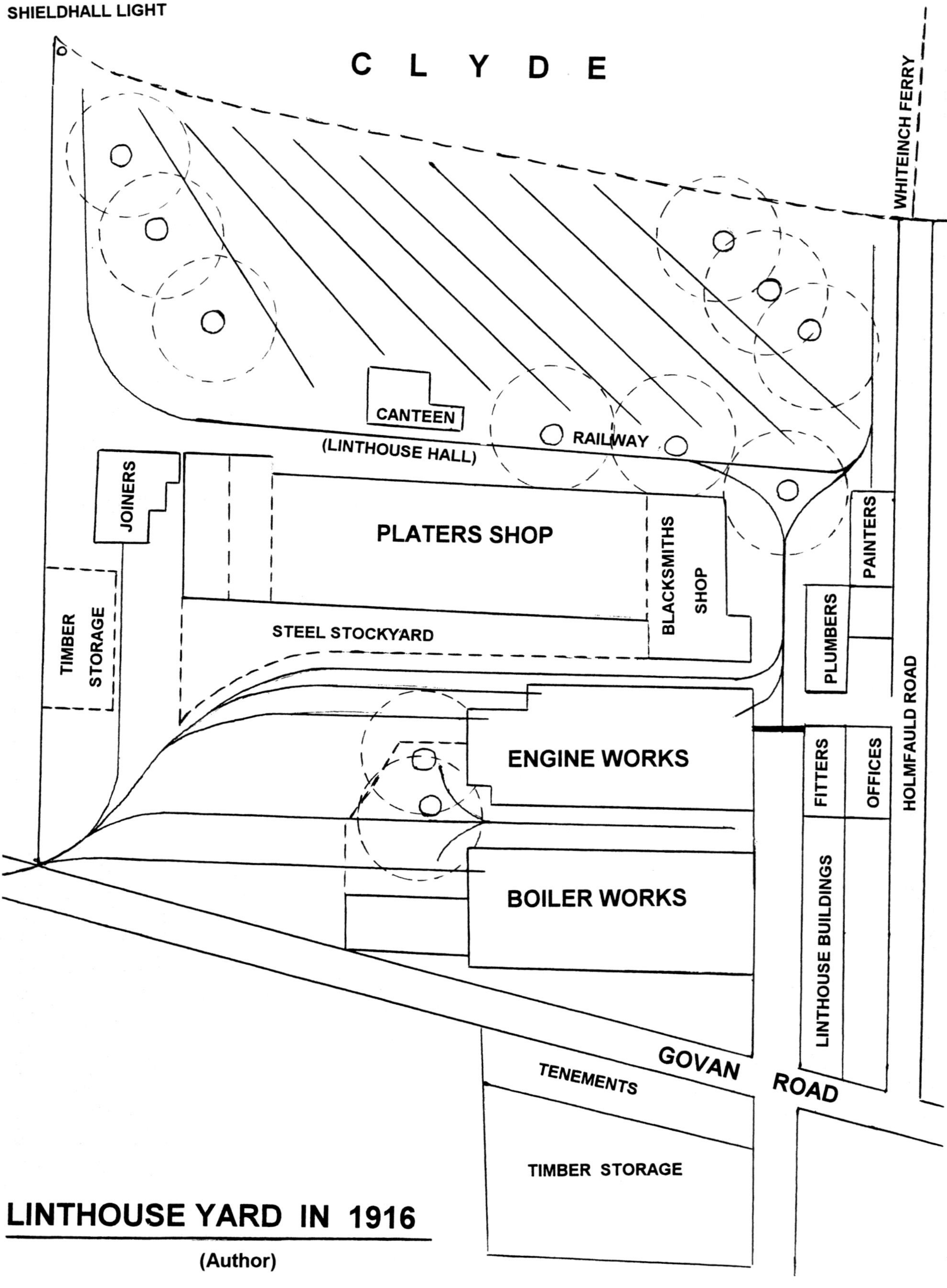

LINTHOUSE YARD IN 1916

(Author)

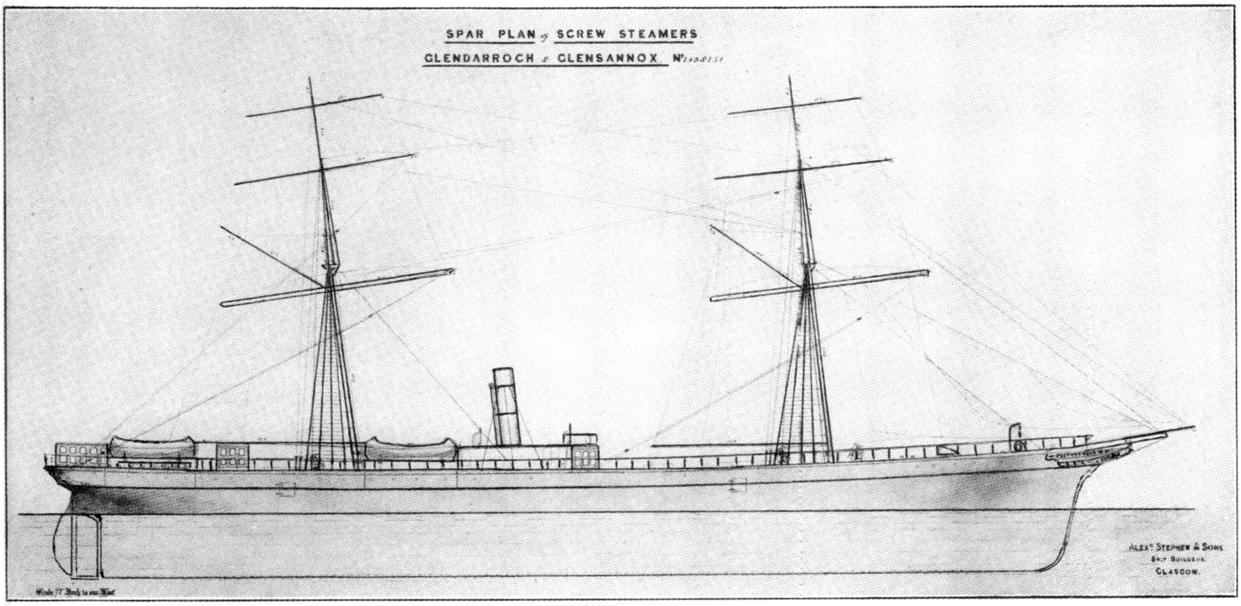

Spar Plan (above) of the first two steamers built at Linthouse, GLENDARROCH and GLENSANNOX of 1870. (Alex. Stephen & Sons Ltd)

View of the yard showing liner ETHIOPIA for Anchor Line (left) and Mansion House (right) used as the yard office. (Alex. Stephen & Sons Ltd).

A major customer of this period was Charles Cayzer and his Clan Line of Glasgow with ten iron steamers built between 1878 and 1883 for services to India and South Africa. The first pair cost £34,000 each with payments being one-third in cash during construction, with Alexander Stephen financing the other two-thirds by Bills of Exchange redeemable within three years. They were completed as *Clan Alpine* 2080/78 and *Clan Fraser* 2083/78, with Alexander Stephen having to offer further financial help until Clan Line was trading at a profit. The Deutsche Transatlantique D/S of Hamburg took five large iron steamers, *Herder* 3494/74, *Lessing* 3496/74, *Wieland* 3507/74 and *Gellert* 3536/76 with the fifth sold to P & O and completed as *Nepaul* 3536/74 - the first from the yard for the famous liner company; while the White Cross Line of T.C. Engels of Antwerp took *Pieter de Connick* 3310/81.

A major disaster occurred at Linthouse on 3rd July, 1883 at the launch of the small steamer *Daphne* of 449 tons, which resulted in the loss of 124 workers lives. Some two hundred workmen were aboard her when she slid down the ways, paused briefly and then rolled over quickly to port, trapping the majority of the workers below decks. This was the worst tradegy in British shipbuilding history, and the enquiry had far-reaching ramifications, restricting the number of men aboard at launch to only a very few men essential for the securing of the vessel. The coaster was later righted, raised and eventually completed as *Rose* at the end of 1883.

The first steamer for a local customer, Maclay & McIntyre of Glasgow, was completed as *General Gordon* of 1294 grt in September,1885, and led to a major association with the yard with a further 23 steamers completed with the last being *Loch Ranza* 4958/34. The Linthouse yard then gained an excellent reputation for building passenger and passenger/cargo-liners for customers such as British India Line with 19 ships built starting with *Wardha* and *Warora*, both 3920/87; and P & O with 14 ships built including *Mazagon* 4997/94, *Sumatra* 4607/95 and *Syria* 6660/01; and Furness,Withy & Co. Ltd.

Sir Christopher Furness of West Hartlepool had already had *Ulunda* 1789/85, *Damara* 1779/85 and *Baltimore City* 2338/88 built by the yard before he placed orders for his newly formed Chesapeake & Ohio Steamship Co. Ltd in 1893 for Transatlantic services to Newport News. A trio of identical clipper-bowed triple-expansion powered steamers were completed at Linthouse later that year as *Rappahannock, Shenandoah* and *Kanawha*, all of 3886 grt, equipped with a water distillation plant below deck for the many cattle they shipped back across the Atlantic. They were fitted with double derricks and six steam winches, and were rigged as pole-masted steamers with telescopic masts for transit of the Manchester Ship Canal, opened in January,1894. Sir Christopher then formed the Wilsons &

The first large passenger and banana ship from Linthouse, PORT KINGSTON of 1904.

The similar ARIGUANI of 1926 for Elders & Fyffes Ltd.
(Alex. Stephen & Sons Ltd)

Furness - Leyland Line with partners Wilson Line and Leyland Line for a Transatlantic passenger service, and the Linthouse yard built *Idaho* and *Megantic*, both 5531/96, *Alexandria* 6919/97 , *Boadicea* 7057/98 and *Bohemian* 8548/00 for the partners. He also had built at the yard *Halifax City* 2141/94 and *St. John City* 2153/95 and sold on two further large hulls to the Hamburg-Amerika Line and completed as *Bengalia* 7690/98 and *Bethania* 7519/99 of their 'B' class. He also had built for himself at Linthouse the steam yacht *Emerald* of 694 tons in 1903, propelled by three steam turbines and which became the first turbine-powered craft to cross the Atlantic.

Alexander Stephen died in 1899 at his home on the Kelly estate at Wemyss Bay, from where he had travelled to the shipyard in steam yachts built at Linthouse. His first steam yacht from the yard was *Sylvia* of 1882 in which he travelled from his former home at Dunoon to the shipyard as well as for summer Clyde cruising. His next yacht was *Nerissa* of 264 tons in 1885 and his final yacht was *Calanthe* of 429 tons in 1898. A series of five racing yachts was also built at Linthouse for the Stephen family. He was succeeded by his sons Alexander E. Stephen and Frederic J. Stephen as joint managing directors, and they turned the company into one of limited liability in the following year.

The first of twenty six elegant banana boats was completed in 1901 as *Port Morant* 2831/01 for the Imperial Direct West India Line, and carried the first ever cargo of West Indian bananas home from Port Kingston, Jamaica later that year. A larger ship named after that port was completed as *Port Kingston* 7585/04, and the first banana boat for Elders & Fyffes Ltd, which took over the Imperial Direct West India Line, was *Nicoya* 3911/05 followed by another 23 banana ships for this owner with the last being *Chuscal* 6282/62. One-third of the total Elders & Fyffes banana fleet was built at Linthouse.

The main customers of the yard during the twenty years before the start of the Great War were the British India Line; and the local passenger companies of the Allan Line and Anchor Line with their services from Glasgow to New York. *State of California* was the heaviest ship built by the yard so far and was a first-class passenger/cargo ship with saloon accomodation for two hundred passengers and her staterooms were dismantled in winter to give more cargo-carrying space. She was ordered by State Line of Glasgow, however they went into liquidation during her construction and she was taken over by Allan Line :-

British India Line		Allan and Anchor Lines	
BEZWADA	5001/93	STATE OF CALIFORNIA	4244/91
UGANDA	5366/98	TUNISIAN	10756/00
UMTA	5366/98	VIRGINIAN	10754/05

The Transatlantic liner HELLIG OLAV of 1903 for DFDS of Denmark.

TUBANTIA of 1914 was completed for the Amsterdam to Buenos Aires service of Konink. Holland Lloyd. (Alex. Stephen & Sons Ltd)

ABHONA	4066/10	GRAMPIAN	9598/07
ELLENGA	5196/11	HESPERIAN	9599/08
ELLORA	5201/11	MASSILIA	5091/02
ARONDA	4062/12	ANCHORIA	5430/11
TAKADA	6949/14	MEDIA	5437/11
TANDA	6956/14	TUSCANIA	14348/15
UMARIA	5317/14		
UMETA	5312/14		
CHAKLA	3081/14		

The clipper-bowed liners *Miltiades* and *Marathon*, both 6765/03, were built for the Aberdeen Line of George Thompson, and returned to the yard in 1912 to be lengthened by fifty feet, increasing their grt to 7827 tons. The Danish trio of liners *Oscar II* 9956/02, *Hellig Olav* 10072/03 and *United States* 10082/03 for DFDS had accomodation for 1100 passengers on their service to New York, from where President Ford left in December,1915 on *Oscar II* on a peace mission to Europe. The twin-funnelled luxury liners *Gelria* 14053/13 and *Tubantia* 14061/14 for the Amsterdam to Buenos Aires service of Konink. Holland Lloyd were the finest liners from the Linthouse yard of this period, and had followed two smaller liners for the same owner *Hollandia* 7291/09 and *Zeelandia* 7958/10.

Several liners were built for Australasian services e.g. *Makura* 8075/08 for the Union Steamship Co. Ltd of New Zealand, and three for the Australasian United Steam Navigation Co. Ltd in *Wyandra* 4508/02, *Wyreema* 6338/08 and *Levuka* 6129/10, and two for Howard Smith in *Cooma* 3839/07 and *Canberra* 7707/13, and one for the Adelaide Steamship Co. Ltd as *Koombana* 4399/08. Other important customers included Elder, Dempster with six ships of which *Montezuma* 7345/99 was the largest, with five smaller ones for West African services. Cie Belge Maritime had three passenger ships built for their Congo services in *Bruxellesville* 5800/09, *Elisabethville* 7034/10 and *Anversville* 7645/12

The outbreak of the Great War saw a splendid new office block opened at the east of the yard , with the old mansion house serving as a canteen during the war before being pulled down to allow larger ships to be built. The war output consisted of the twin-screw turbine-powered Anchor Line passenger ship *Tuscania* of 14348 grt completed in February,1915, cargo-liners, two banana boats, 16 destroyers and three standard 'AO' type tankers. The turbines for *Tuscania* were the first to be made at Linthouse, as the Parsons turbines for the two earlier turbine-powered ships i.e. the Sir Christopher Furness yacht *Emerald* and the Allan liner *Virginian*, had been built at Wallsend. Work was stopped on the last of ten orders from British India Line for cargo-liners from pre-war days and was eventually completed as *Vasna* 5767/17. The Elders & Fyffes new banana boat *Bayano* 5948/13 returned to the yard soon after the outbreak of war to be converted into a auxiliary cruiser, but she was unfortunately torpedoed and sunk off Portpatrick on her first voyage after conversion, however the twin-screw banana boats *Camito* 6611/15 and *Bayano* 6788/17 were then completed to also carry one hundred passengers in addition to their fruit cargoes. The refrigerated *Princesa* 8731/18 was completed for Houlder Brothers, and one standard 'G' class meat carrier was later completed as *Piako* 8283/20. As with some other Clyde yards, the output also consisted of 480 biplane aeroplanes constructed in a purpose-built new building four hundred feet in length on the east side of the yard. James Stephen was sadly killed in action during the war, but morale was boosted by visits of the King and the Prince of Wales.

The construction of six large passenger liners dominated the Linthouse yard during the next ten years, with two for Anchor Line in *California* 16792/23 with a single cowl-topped funnel and *Caledonia* 17046/25 with three cowl-topped funnels with the first and third being dummies. The construction of *California* was suspended in 1922 for seven months and that of *Caledonia* for over two years due to the post-war slump, however both were completed with oil-fired geared turbine machinery.

CALEDONIA completed in 1925 for Anchor Line was torpedoed and sunk while serving as the armed merchant cruiser H.M.S. SCOTSTOUN in 1940.
(Alex. Stephen & Sons Ltd)

A painting of the P & O liner CHITRAL of 1925 and a British India cargo-liner, both Linthouse-built, at Aden.

The launch of the P & O liner CARTHAGE on 18th August,1931.
Barclay,Curle's yard is on the opposite bank. (Alex. Stephen & Sons Ltd)

Four liners were ordered by Lord Inchcape, Chairman of P & O, with three 'C' class and a larger flagship for their important Bombay service, *Viceroy of India*. Their launch dates were :-

	Launch Date	Sponsor
CHITRAL	27.1.1925	Hon. Elsie Mackay, daughter of Lord Inchcape
CORFU	20.5.1931	Hon. Patricia Mackay, granddaughter of Lord Inchcape
CARTHAGE	18.8.1931	Miss Jean Shaw, granddaughter of Lord Inchcape
VICEROY OF INDIA	15.9.1928	Lady Irwin, wife of the Viceroy of India

Corfu had the misfortune to damage her starboard shell plating while berthing after her launch at the fitting-out quay, but this did not delay her completion date of September,1931. The 'C' class were of around 14500 grt and had accomodation for 400 passengers, while the larger *Viceroy of India* at 19648 grt had accomodation for 683 passengers with 420 crew for her Bombay service, her public rooms being traditional and opulent and she had a very fine promenade deck. All four were twin-screw with *Chitral* having quadruple expansion engines and *Corfu* and *Carthage* were geared turbine-powered. Turbo-electric drive had been specified in the contract awarded in April,1927 for *Viceroy of India* after extensive tank-testing of her design at Teddington. Her turbo-alternators and electric motors were supplied by British Thomson-Houston (later English Electric) and she was given six Yarrow oil-fired water-tube boilers. She achieved 19.8 knots on her trials on 7th March,1929 and was handed over to her owners on the same day. Lord Inchcape also ordered the large twin-screw triple-expansion powered yacht *Rover* 1851/30. She was one of the finest steam yachts ever built in Britain, and her long counter stern and large open spaces made her very popular for dancing and games, with guests having marble bathrooms in every stateroom. She was visited by H.M. The King and Queen during Cowes week in 1930.

Dalgoma of 1923 for British India Line was the first motorship from the yard, powered by two 4-cylinder Stephen - Sulzer oil engines of 3200 bhp and was twin-screw. The following cargo-liners and banana boats were completed during this period : -

NARIVA	8723/20	Royal Mail Line
NATIA	8723/20	"
MATAKANA	8048/20	Shaw,Savill & Albion Co. Ltd
MULBERA	9200/22	British India Line
DALGOMA	5953/23	"
FAMAKA	5815/22	Khedivail Mail S.S. Co. Ltd
FEZARA	5809/23	"

TORTUGUERO	5285/21	Elders & Fyffes
CAVINA	6908/24	"
ARIGUANI	6745/26	"
TUCURINCA	5411/26	"
CHAGRES	5406/28	"
TELDE	2519/27	"
OROTAVA	2518/27	"
NICOYA	5363/29	"
CORRALES	5362/30	"
BRITANNIA	8463/26	Anchor Line
JUMNA	6078/29	Nourse Line
KENYA	9890/30	British India Line
KARANJA	9891/31	"
ORARI	10106/31	New Zealand Shipping Co. Ltd
OPAWA	10107/31	"

In addition, two large twin-screw steam tankers of 16000 dwt were completed for Imperial Oil of Canada in *Victolite* 11410/28 and *Vancolite* 11403/28, as well as the cable-layer *Cable* 1534/24 for the Eastern Telegraph Company, and the tramps *Induna* 5086/25 and *Masunda* 5250/29 for Maclay & McIntyre. Coastal ships included *Toward* 1571/23 for the Clyde Shipping Co. Ltd, and *St. Patrick* 1922/30 for the Great Western Railway Company, and *Taif* and *Talodi*, both 1590/28 for the Khedivail Steamship Co. Ltd.

After the completion of the liner *Carthage* in November,1931 the order book consisted of a small French cargo ship and a yacht for the Stephen family. The French ship left the yard as *Gazcon* in April,1932 and the workforce was paid off and the yard closed for nearly two years. The opportunity had already been taken to reduce the number of berths from eight to six in 1927, and a complete set of new electric cranes was also installed, with the yard then covering 48 acres with a waterfront of 1140 feet not including the neighbouring Shieldhall Quay to the west where out-fitting took place from around 1935. Prior to this out-fitting was done in the Princes Dock, but a lease of Shielhall Quay from the Clyde Navigation Trust was much more convenient and a 120-ton tripod crane and 35-ton mobile crane were installed.

Orders from the Union Steamship Co. Ltd of New Zealand for small cargo ships re-opened the yard, with *Waitaki* of 2212 grt completing in April,1934 followed by seven similar ships over the next four years, the largest of which were *Komata* and *Kurow*, both 3900/38. The Maclay & McIntyre tramp *Loch Ranza* was completed at the end of 1934, followed by the Australian coastal passenger ship *Manoora* of 10856 grt for the Adelaide Steamship Co. Ltd in February,1935. She was followed out to the Antipodes by the smaller passenger ship *Taroona* 4587/35 for Tasmanian Steamers Ltd. Two coastal ships were then completed for the Clyde Shipping Co. Ltd in *Rathlin* and *Beachy*, both 1600/36.

The Admiralty now began to build up its strength and ordered four destroyers *Gallant*(1936), *Grenade* (1936), *Zulu* (1938) and *Sikh* (1938) and two sloops *Mallard* (1936) and *Puffin* (1936). Three cargo-liners were then completed in *Surat* 5529/38 and *Shillong* 5529/39 for P & O, and *Kaipaki* 5862/39 for the New Zealand Shipping Co. Ltd, as well as the twin-screw single-funnelled P & O liner *Canton* of 16033 grt completed in September,1938.

Ships could now be built up to seven hundred feet in length, and the aircraft carrier *Ocean* was to stretch the slipway to its limit with her length of 690 feet and beam of 80 feet, and she was completed early in 1945. Other World War II output included the cruisers *Kenya* (1940), *Hermione* (1941) and *Ceylon* (1943), the fast 38 knot three-funnelled minelayers *Manxman* (1941) and *Ariadne* (1943), 13 destroyers, two sloops, two minesweepers and two tank transport ferries. One cruiser and one 'Battle' class destroyer were cancelled at the end of the war, with *Dunkirk* and *Jutland* of the 'Battle' class completed in 1946/47. Merchantmen completed the tramp *Trevethoe* 5257/40, and five cargo-liners for the Federal S.N. Co. Ltd and New Zealand Shipping Co. Ltd, of which *Nottingham* 8532/41 had the shortest career - being tragically sunk south of Greenland on her maiden voyage only six days after leaving the Clyde in November,1941.

The aircraft carrier OCEAN shortly before her launch in July,1944. (Glasgow University)

Aerial view of Linthouse yard and engine works looking north-west in 1946. (Glasgow University)

Aerial view of Linthouse yard and engine works looking south-east in 1946. (Glasgow University)

View of Linthouse berths in 1949 with Federal S.N. cargo-liner DORSET (right) almost ready for launch. (Glasgow University)

View of fitting-out quays in 1949 with French Line FORT RICHEPANSE (left) and FORT DAUPHIN (right) and banana carrier GOLFITO. (G.Univ.)

Aerial view of Linthouse yard in 1953 showing Greek liner OLYMPIA at the fitting-out quay. King George V Dock is at top right (G. University)

Aerial view of the yard in May,1962 with tanker BRITISH BOMBARDIER ready for launch. (Glasgow University)

Welding was first tried at Linthouse at the end of the war, and by 1950 the existing steelwork facilities were partially rearranged and a new prefabrication shed built to make increased use of welding. Berth cranes were now of 30-ton capacity and welded assemblies of up to this limit were built, with plates being moved by magnets and turned upside down by electrical tilters in readiness for the flame planing machine for plate edges, together with cold bending of frames.

A regular customer in post-war years was the Union Steamship Co. Ltd of New Zealand with orders for 14 of their 'K' class of three-hold motor cargo ships of 5200 dwt, and fitted with a dozen derricks including a 25-ton heavy derrick for the New Zealand to Australia trade. Two high-class liners were built, *Aureol* 13110/51 for the West African service of Elder,Dempster with accomodation for 450 passengers of which 250 travelled first-class, and *Olympia* of 22979 grt launched on 16th April,1953 unnamed as Y636 for Greek Line as a mark of respect to H. M. The Queen, who launched the royal yacht *Britannia* on the same tide at Clydebank. She was completed in October,1953 having attained a speed in excess of her service speed of 21 knots from her four geared steam turbines built by the yard. Two ferries were also built, *Princess of Vancouver* 5554/55 for the British Columbian services of Canadian Pacific, and the Harwich ferry *Avalon* 6706/63 for British Rail. The main product of the Linthouse yard in post-war years was however cargo-liners and banana boats :-

DEVON	9943/46	Federal S.N.
SOMERSET	9943/46	"
HUNTINGDON	11281/48	"
CUMBERLAND	11281/48	"
MATINA	6801/46	Elders & Fyffes
GOLFITO	8736/49	"
CAMITO	8687/56	"
CHANGUINOLA	6282/57	"
CHIRRIPO	6282/57	"
CHICANOA	6283/58	"
CHUSCAL	6282/62	"
KAMPALA	10304/47	British India Line
KARANJA	10294/48	"
FORT RICHEPANSE	5050/49	French Line
FORT DAUPHIN	5050/49	"
DORSET	10108/49	Federal S.N.
CORNWALL	7560/51	"
SURREY	8320/52	"
MIDDLESEX	8320/52	"
RIO BERMEJO	7143/50	Argentine Govt.
DUNEDIN STAR	7322/50	Blue Star Line
CITY OF BEDFORD	7050/50	Ellerman Lines

CITY OF SINGAPORE	7050/51	Ellerman Lines
CITY OF NEWCASTLE	7727/56	"
CITY OF MELBOURNE	9914/59	"
ENTON	6350/52	Birt,Potter & Hughes
PATONGA	10071/53	P & O
WHAKATANE	8726/54	New Zealand Shpg. Co. Ltd
BALLARAT	8792/54	P & O
BENDIGO	8792/54	"
IRMA	4450/54	Bergen Line
CRUX	4429/56	"
FERNVALLEY	4504/55	Fearnley & Eger, Oslo
CASTILIAN	3803/55	Ellerman Lines
DONEGAL	6386/57	Avenue Shpg. Co. Ltd
ANTRIM	6461/62	"
IBERIC	11248/61	Shaw,Savill & Albion Co. Ltd
ZEALANDIC	7946/65	"
MAJESTIC	9117/67	"
BRITANNIC	9097/67	"
PIAKO	7596/62	P & O
DUMURRA	8238/61	Elder, Dempster
MARKHOR	9120/63	Brocklebank Line
MAHOUT	9153/63	"
PORT CHALMERS	12398/68	Port Line
PORT CAROLINE	12398/68	"

Tankers and dredgers were the other commercial ships built by the yard during the 1960s. Five tankers were completed, three for the British Tanker Co. Ltd in *British Fulmar* 11169/59, *British Curlew* 11157/60, and the 725 feet long *British Bombardier* 32138/62 and 54120 dwt, and the longest ship ever built by the yard. Mobil Oil also ordered two tankers of 18000 dwt, completed as *Mobil Apex* and *Mobil Acme*, both 12754/60. The yard also built diesel-electric suction dredgers, including three for Russia in 1965/66, having taken over Simons-Lobnitz Ltd in 1964 with the two famous dredger builders having previously merged in 1957.

The Admiralty had also placed valuable contracts with the yard in post-war years, including the 'Daring' class destroyer *Defender* (1952), the 'Rothesay' class frigate Lowestoft (1961), the 'Tribal' class frigate *Zulu* (1963), and the 'Leander' class frigate *Phoebe* (1966) and *Hermione* (1968) as well as two tank transport and landing ships *Sir Galahad* (1966) and *Sir Geraint* (1967); and the frigate *President Steyn* (1963) was built for South Africa. The Linthouse yard became a constituent member of Upper Clyde Shipbuilders Ltd at the end of 1967, but with orders scarce launched the last ship *Port Caroline* on 16th April,1968 as Y701 and completed in October,1968. After building two 'kit-form' dredgers for re-erection elsewhere the yard was closed and subsequently demolished. The yard had remained Stephen family-owned until almost the end, with Sir Alexander Murray Stephen, grandson of

Alexander Stephen the founder of the Linthouse yard, as the last Chairman. The ship repair and marine engine building activities continued as two independent companies, Alexander Stephen Shiprepairers Ltd and Alexander Stephen Engineering Ltd. The repair company closed at the end of 1976 and was purchased in April,1977 by the newly formed Clyde Dock Engineering Co. Ltd.

The derelict Linthouse yard was acquired by the Scottish Development Agency in April,1987 and demolished except for the engine shop, built in 1872 with cast iron columns and wooden roof. This was painstakingly taken apart and removed to the Scottish Maritime Museum at Irvine and re-erected next to the platers shop of the old Ayrshire Dockyard (q.v.).

Model showing the two bays of the 1872 Linthouse engine shop (below) re-erected as the Main Exhibition Hall of the Scottish Maritime Museum.

(Scottish Maritime Museum)

HARLAND & WOLFF LTD.

This yard on the south side at Govan was the first to be passed when sailing on a pleasure cruise from Glasgow city quays or from the cargo-berths at Yorkhill Quay and Queens Dock on the north side and Princes Dock on the south side. The fitting-out basin was on the east side of the yard, thus new ships could be easily seen from all of these vantage points. The yard was completely rebuilt by Harland & Wolff Ltd, Belfast during the years 1913 to 1917, with ships being launched from the seven berths diagonally up-river towards Yorkhill Quay except for the most easterly berth which launched down-river. The ground where the rebuilding took place had much shipbuilding history and had been occupied by three adjacent yards known as Govan Old yard, Govan Middleton yard and Govan East yard in that order from west to east. The fitting-out basin was dug in the East yard when it was amalgamated with the Middleton yard of the London & Glasgow Engineering & Iron Shipbuilding Co. Ltd in 1905. Harland & Wolff Ltd acquired both these yards from the latter company for £218,000 in 1912, while the Govan Old yard was acquired from Mackie & Thomson in return for four ships being sub-contracted from Belfast to their new yard at Irvine, later known as the Ayrshire Dockyard Co. Ltd. A brief history of the three Govan yards up to this point is now given :-

GOVAN OLD YARD was owned by Mackie & Thomson from 1888 to 1912. William Mackie, formerly Chief Draughtsman at Stephens yard and Robert Thomson built over four hundred coasters and trawlers during this time as well as the four-masted barques *Cedarbank* 2649/92 and *Olivebank* 2647/92 for Andrew Weir, the latter having a long life in the Finnish grain fleet of Gustaf Erikson until becoming a war loss in 1939. The largest steamers from the yard were *Junee* 2218/07 for the Adelaide Steamship Co. Ltd, Australia and *Sea Belle* 2132/06 for Leach & Co. Ltd, London with a whole fleet of coasters built for the General Steam Navigation Company, of which the largest was *Lapwing* 1192/11. The last two ships from the yard in 1912 before the take-over were the Brazilian coastal ships *Taquary* 1943/12 and *Jacuhy* 1951/12 delivered in April and May to the Cia Commercio e Navegacao, Rio de Janeiro.

GOVAN MIDDLETON YARD was known as the 'limited' yard with the London & Glasgow company having been the first limited company on the river in 1864, and built 270 ships between then and 1912. This company had a large number of small shareholders and a good reputation for building both merchant and naval vessels.

The Cunarders *Sylvania* and *Carinthia* of 1895 and the Orient Line *Osterley* 12129/09 were the best-known, and a series of cargo-liners had been built for Glen Line culminating in *Glenlochy* 4654/96 and *Glenturret* 4696/96; with two for the local Donaldson Line in *Kastalia* 4039/97 and *Lakonia* 4686/99; and others for the Indo-China Steam Navigation Co. Ltd including *Lai Sang* 3460/01 and *Nam Sang* 4035/02. Many tramps had also been built including *Goodwin* 4421/95, *Needles* 4697/98 and *Spithead* 4697/99 for the Clyde Shipping Co. Ltd, and *Rutherglen* 4214/06 and *Kassala* 3825/07 for Maclay & McIntyre of Glasgow. The last merchant ship built before the take-over in 1912 was *Indraghiri* 5723/12 for Indra Line of Liverpool owned by T.B. Royden. Warships had included the smaller cruisers *Melpomene, Dido, Isis* and *Hyacinth* of the 1880/90s, leading to the larger four-funnelled protected cruisers *Cumberland, Monmouth* and *Roxburgh* at the turn of the century and fitted with 9.2" guns. The last warships built by the yard before the take-over were the cruisers *Yarmouth* (1911) and *Sydney* (1912), the latter completing fitting-out on the take-over.

GOVAN EAST YARD was operated by Robert Napier & Sons Ltd between 1850 and 1900 and William Beardmore & Co. Ltd between 1900 and 1905. Robert Napier was known as the father of Clyde shipbuilders as nearly all of the subsequent prominent shipbuilders of the river had received their training in the yard. Robert Napier personally supervised his yard until his death in 1876. The pioneer triple-expansion powered *Aberdeen* was built at the yard in 1882, and two of the best-known large ships from the yard was the twin-screw twin-funnelled Orient Line *Ophir* 6800/91, which was used as the Royal yacht by the Duke and Duchess of York during their tour of Australia in 1901, and the cruiser *Gibraltar* of 1890. A series of cargo-liners had been built for the Royal Mail Line culminating in *Tagus* 5545/99 and *Trent* 5525/00, as well as *Kasuga Maru* 3815/98 and *Yawata Maru* 3817/98 for Nippon Yusen Kaisha,Japan, *Eastern* 3586/99 for the Eastern & Australian Steamship Co. Ltd, and a trio of small passenger ships for the Roumanian Government in 1897. Tramps had been built for Glen & Company of Glasgow, the last being *Camperdown* 2554/98. After the yard take-over by William Beardmore in 1900 he used the yard as a 'stop-gap' measure while planning the construction of his huge armaments and shipyard complex at Dalmuir (q.v.) The yard built the cruisers *Berwick* (1903) and *Carnarvon* (1905) , as well as ten merchant ships up to 1905 including *Highland Brigade* 5662/01 for Nelson Line, *Alnwick Castle* 5893/01 and *Berwick Castle* 5883/02 for Union-Castle Line, *Empire* 4496/02 for Eastern & Australian S.S. Co. Ltd, London, the Glasgow sludge carrier

Dalmuir, *Rathlin* 1321/05 for Clyde Shipping Co. Ltd as well as the coaster *Highland Laddie* launched last on 20th April,1905.

Harland & Wolff Ltd took over six existing contracts from the London & Glasgow company in 1912: three 'K' class destroyers, the torpedo depot ship *Woolwich*, the auxiliary cruiser *Sydney* and the passenger/cargo-liner *Evangeline* 4500/12. The first ship to be completed under Harland & Wolff yard numbers was the small passenger tender *Attendant* of 317 tons in August,1913 for Elder, Dempster. The Lancefield engine works at Finnieston also came with the deal, but the first two large Harland & Wollf ships from Govan were towed across to Belfast to have their engines installed. These were the Royal Mail liner *Alcantara* of 1583' grt launched on 30th October,1913 and handed over after trials in May,1914; and the Elder,Dempster liner *Apapa* of 7832grt and launched on 30th September,1914. The latter company also took delivery of *Egba* 4989/14 and *Egori* 4995/14, while the first motor vessel from the yard was *Mississippi* 4717/14 fitted with a B & W oil engine built at Finnieston.

Henry P. Harland became Manager of the yard, which was completely rebuilt during the years 1913 to 1917. New long brick-built platers shops were built on a triangular site to the west of the yard and fronting the river, and involved a contraction of the Govan ferry area, which acquired a smaller concrete slip. The frame shops which were built at the rear of the yard were even longer, with seven new longer berths fitted with gates at the river end to ensure dry working at all stages of the tide and increase their effective lengths. The most easterly berth launched down-river, while the other six launched diagonally up-river towards Yorkhill Quay. New high hammerhead and tower cranes completed this now modern yard, which complemented the Harland & Wolff works at Belfast and was largely used in building the 'overflow' orders for cargo-liners, tramps and tankers from Belfast. The output of triple-expansion steam machinery from the Finnieston works was increased.

The yard made an important contribution to naval construction during the Great War with four monitors built, *Raglan* (1915), *Prince Eugene* (1915), *Erebus* (1916) and *Terror* (1916), six destroyers, three patrol boats and four naval tugs. The twin-funnelled liner *Regina* 16313/18 was built for Dominion Line together with the smaller cargo-only consort *Rimouski* 9281/18; the motorship *Glengyle* 6225/15 and steamer *Glenavy* 5075/15 for Glen Line, and *Millais* 7300/17 and *Marconi* 7402/17 for Lamport & Holt Ltd, and one for White Star Line in *Vedic* 9332/18. Three standard 'A' type tramps and six 'AO' type tankers with engines amidships and the partially-prefabricated 'N' type *War Passion* completed the war total.

The yard built the passenger-liners *Volendam* 15440/22 and *Veendam* 15450/23 for Holland-Amerika Line and mostly cargo-liners during the 1920s, with large orders from Bank Line (21 ships), Glen Line (7 ships) and Pacfic Steam Navigation Company (4 ships). The large floating crane *London Mammoth* was delivered to the Port of London Authority in July,1927 as well as a large floating dock for Argentina. Five fruit ships were then completed for Macandrews & Company, London; four shallow-draught 'Mosquito' tankers for Dutch Shell as well as the fitting-out of the last ship *Behar* 6100/28 from the former Caird (q.v.) yard at Greenock and towed up-river to Govan at the end of 1928.

The completion of the twin-screw motor-driven passenger-liners *Llangibby Castle* 11951/29 and *Dunbar Castle* 10002/30 for Union-Castle Line, and *Highland Hope* 14129/30 for the River Plate services of Nelson Line; and the refrigerated *Westralia* 8107/29 for Huddart,Parker of Australia, and the cargo-liners *Kufra* 2608/29, *Bhutan* 6104/29, *Edward Blyden* 4022/30, *Alfred Jones* 4022/30, *Ganges* 6523/30 and *Somali* 6809/30 left the yard with a very depleted order book. After the completion of the Pacific phosphates carrier *Triona* 4413/31, and the Mersey ferry *Royal Iris II* 607/32 and three small ferries for Bombay during 1932/33 the vast majority of the workforce was paid-off, with Harland & Wolff Ltd putting into effect rationalisation plans for its Clyde yards with the closure of the Meadowside yard of D. & W. Henderson, opposite the Govan yard, in 1935. The dry-dock of this yard was previously used to give Govan-built ships their pre-trial dry-docking, and a repair subsidiary was finally formed in 1936 as D. & W. Henderson Ltd to secure the future of the dry-dock and thus help that of the Govan yard.

An order for a refrigerated cargo-liner for Shaw,Savill & Albion Co. Ltd brought the yard back into life in 1934 and she was launched as *Wairangi* on 9th October,1934 of 10779 grt. She was followed by the first of a series of 16 tankers built before the start of World War II, mostly of 12000 dwt :-

ANADARA	8008/35	Anglo-Saxon/Shell
SAN ARCADIO	7419/35	Eagle Oil
STANDELLA	6197/36	Anglo-Saxon/Shell
SIMNIA	6197/36	"
SITALA	6218/37	"
BRITISH POWER	8334/36	British Tanker Co. Ltd
BRITISH DESTINY	8334/37	"
BRITISH INTEGRITY	8334/37	"
BRITISH SECURITY	8334/37	"
BRITISH FIDELITY	8465/38	"
BRITISH TRUST	8466/39	"
BOARDALE	8334/37	Admiralty
BROOMDALE	8334/37	"

DONAX	8036/38	Anglo-Saxon/Shell
DROMUS	8036/38	"
SAN EMILIANO	8071/39	Eagle Oil

as well as the Australian passenger/cargo-ships *Adelong* 3576/36 for Huddart, Parker, and *Koolama* 4026/38 for the Western Australian Government. The Royal Mail cargo-liner *Lochavon* 9204/38 had a fine array of derricks and steam turbines, whereas *Salacia* 5495/37 for the local Donaldson Line was powered by oil engines.

The World War II construction total of the Govan yard was nineteen ocean-going tankers including three fast Admiralty oilers completed as *Wave King* 8159/44, *Wave Monarch* 8159/44 and *Wave Chief* 8097/46, as well as three smaller fleet oilers *Black Ranger*, *Blue Ranger* and *Brown Ranger,* all 3417/41, and five coastal tankers, three of them for Far Eastern service. Five standard 'Empire' tramps and the cargo-liners *Novelist* 6133/40 for T.& J. Harrison,Liverpool and the sisters *Parima* 7543/44 and *Pilcomayo* 7540/45 for Royal Mail Line, and two large landing craft, which were finished off by John Brown & Co. Ltd at Dalmuir, completed the total.

The yard gave the reconditioning refits to the pre-war *Llangibby Castle*, built by the yard in 1929, and the Shaw,Savill & Albion liner *Mataroa* during 1947, when number seven berth at the extreme end of the yard and next to the fitting-out basin was eliminated to provide more storage space for work-in-progress. This berth had launched smaller ships down-river rather than diagonally up-river as in the remaining six berths. The yard was also upgraded with a new welding shop completed in the early 1950s as welding became more extensive in the large tanker programme of the yard. Sections gradually got larger, and extra tower cranage was purchased from the neighbouring Fairfield yard. The tanker programme was :-

BRITISH KNIGHT	8629/46	British Tanker Co. Ltd
BRITISH RANGER	8575/48	"
BRITISH MARINER	8576/48	"
BRITISH WORKMAN	8575/49	"
BRITISH CAPTAIN	8700/49	"
BRITISH COMMANDER	8700/49	"
BRITISH CONSUL	8655/50	"
LIPARUS	6473/48	Anglo-Saxon/Shell
CAZADOR	6441/49	Shell Argentina
BRATSBERG	8255/50	Borgestad A/S,Norway
BINTA	8162/50	Per Gjerding, Norway
BOLLSTA	16405/51	Fred Olsen, Norway
ILIADE	12801/52	Soc. Navale Delmas Vieljeux
BLANDFORD	12514/53	Blandford Shpg.(Fred Olsen)
BRITTA	12757/53	A.H. Mathiesen, Norway
BRITISH GUNNER	10076/53	British Tanker Co. Ltd

BRITISH SERGEANT	10073/54	"
BELFAST	12744/55	Belships A/S, Norway
ESKFIELD	18851/59	Hunting & Son, Newcastle
BRITISH GULL	11156/60	British Tanker Co. Ltd
NORSK DROTT	18483/61	Norsk Tankers, Denmark
BRITISH OSPREY	11131/62	British Tanker Co. Ltd
BRITISH MERLIN	11132/62	"

together with the following cargo-liners, mostly with accomodation for twelve passengers, and with *Imperial Star* and *Melbourne Star* being twin-screw and given two B & W oil engines, with several of the following list having single B & W oil engines :-

LA HAGUE	4027/47	French Line
LA HEVE	4027/47	"
MORBIHAN	4025/47	"
IMPERIAL STAR	13181/48	Blue Star Line
MELBOURNE STAR	13179/48	"
AMARNA	3422/49	Moss Hutchinson Line
EBRO	5855/52	Royal Mail Line
ESSEQUIBO	5855/52	"
PORT MONTREAL	6843/54	Port Line
WESTERN PRINCE	7917/55	Prince Line
SOUTHERN PRINCE	7917/56	"
ROWANMORE	8495/56	Johnston Warren Line
ESCALANTE	7791/55	Royal Mail Line
TUSCANY	7455/56	"
ALBANY	7299/57	"
THESSALY	7299/57	"
ALARIC	6692/58	Shaw,Savill & Albion
BULIMBA	6796/59	British India Line
BANKURA	6796/59	"
BARPETA	6736/60	"
BAMORA	6744/61	"
BOMBALA	6744/61	"

Two phosphate carriers were completed for the British Phosphate Commission as *Triaster* 9994/55 and *Tri-Ellis* 11760/58 for Pacific service. Three ore-carriers were completed for companies under the management of Common Brothers of Newcastle as *Afghanistan* 11188/57, *Daghestan* 11210/60 and *Iron Age* 11188/58. The last two ships built by the yard were the sister Norwegian bulk carriers of 15000 dwt, *Ringwood* 10860/62 completed in September of that year for Ringdals Rederi A/S, and *Belisland* 10862/63 launched on 26th September,1962 and completed in January,1963 for Belships A/S.

It was announced on 22nd October,1963 that the famous Govan yard was to be placed on a 'care and maintenance basis', and in 1965 the land was sold by Harland & Wolff Ltd to Glasgow Corporation for housing, while the fitting-out basin was sold to Alexander Stephen & Sons Ltd. The site was soon transformed into a housing estate, however the sites of the slipways are still plainly visible as the walkway along the riverfront detours around their river ends.

Aerial view of the Harland & Wolff Ltd Govan yard showing the frame shops and five of the seven berths (bottom right), the triangular-shaped platers shop (centre), and the four-berth Meadowside yard of D. & W. Henderson & Co. Ltd (top right). (Harland & Wolff Ltd)

BARCLAY, CURLE & CO. LTD.

Robert Barclay and Robert Curle became partners in 1845 in a small shipyard at Stobcross with three building berths and two repair slipways. Ten years later they purchased the Clydeholm yard at Whiteinch from J. G. Lawrie, and in 1857 three more partners were taken, including Archibald Gilchrist, whose family was to provide an unbroken chain of management until his great-grandson James Gilchrist as Chairman closed the yard in 1967 some 110 years later. Robert Barclay died in April,1863, and shiprepairing was also moved from Stobcross to Whiteinch in 1874 when the Stobcross land was required for the construction of the new Queens Dock, the first part of which was opened in September,1877. Robert Curle died in 1880 and although the name Barclay,Curle was retained, no further members of the founding families were involved in its management. Barclay,Curle & Company became a limited liability company in 1884.

Some twenty two sailing ships had been completed by the yard by 1870 for the famous City Line of Glasgow, managed by George Smith & Sons. In that year City Line took delivery of their first steamer from the Clydeholm yard, *City of Oxford* 2319/70. Donald Currie had previously had two sailing ships built at the yard in 1867/68 for his Castle Line, and his first steamer *Walmer Castle* 2450/72 was completed by the yard and again propelled by a two-cylinder compound engine built in the yard, and was followed by larger steamers e.g. *Grantully Castle* 3489/79 and *Lismore Castle* 4171/91. The first steel steamers were built in 1880 with *Toledo* 1222/80 for James Currie, brother of Donald Currie, but the yard continued to build steel barques as well as steamers, with the last barques being *Cromdale* 1903/91 for Donaldson, Rose & Co. of Glasgow and *Solway* 1720/95 for J. & J. Rae of Liverpool.

The local Donaldson Line also took delivery of their first steamers *Astarte* and *Marina*, both 1360/70 from the yard and powered by two-cylinder compound engines from the yard engine works. Small paddle steamers for service on the Clyde were also built including *Meg Merrilies* 244/83, *Diana Vernon* 193/85, *Jeanie Deans* 258/84 and *Redgauntlet* 384/95. The last named was launched on 4th April,1895 and had a single diagonal engine of non-compound type by the builder to give her a good turn of speed for service to Craigendoran. The steam yacht *Capercailzie* was completed in 1883 for Sir John Burns, later Lord Inverclyde, and was sold to the Admiralty in 1891, and in 1913 was purchased by Glasgow owners for the *Comet* centenary, but unfortunately sank off Colonsay on her first cruise after refitting.

After the turn of the century larger and more powerful liners and cargo-liners were being ordered by many owners e.g. *Corsican* 11419/07 for the local Allan Line, with *Castalia* 6715/06 for Anchor Line of Glasgow and several others for Gow & Harrison of Glasgow. However the main customers became British India Line and P & O , the two companies amalgamating together in 1914 :-

CHANDA	6168/06	SICILIA	6696/01
CHUPRA	6173/06	SOUDAN	6680/01
CHILKA	3952/10	SARDINIA	6574/02
COCONADA	3958/10	PALERMO	7597/03
EDAVANA	5284/11	POONA	7625/05
ELEPHANTA	5292/11	PESHAWAR	7634/05
BARODA	3172/11	DONGOLA	8090/06
BARATA	3148/12	MOREA	10890/08
BANKURA	3159/12		
BARJORA	3164/12		
BANDRA	3284/14		
BARPETA	3283/14		
BAMORA	3285/14		
NEURALIA	9082/12		
NEVASA	9071/13		
MALDA	7884/13		
MANORA	7875/13		
MASHOBRA	8173/14		
MERKARA	8228/14		

and Ellerman Lines and Union - Castle Line :-

CITY OF DELHI	4448/01	AROS CASTLE	4460/01
CITY OF PARIS	9200/07	CORFE CASTLE	4591/01
CITY OF CHESTER	5413/10	CAWDOR CASTLE	6235/02
CITY OF BARODA	5032/11	CLUNY CASTLE	5147/03
NEWBY HALL	4391/05	COMRIE CASTLE	5147/03
TRAFFORD HALL	5321/05	DOVER CASTLE	8260/04
DENBIGH HALL	4943/06		
WALTON HALL	4932/07		
THORNTON HALL	5524/06		
MELFORD HALL	5514/11		
CITY OF DUNKIRK	5861/12		
CITY OF CORINTH	5879/13		

Many other liner companies were customers e.g. Pacific Steam Navigation Company with *Oriana* 8086/06; Elder,Dempster with *Lake Champlain* 7550/00 and *Lake Erie* 7392/00; Booth Line with *Boniface* 3506/04; Elders & Fyffes with the fruit ship *Miami* 3762/04; Messageries Maritime with *Peiho* 5443/07; Lloyd Sabaudo with the emigrant carriers *Principe di Udine* 7785/08 and *Tomaso di Savoia*

CLYDEHOLM YARD IN 1909

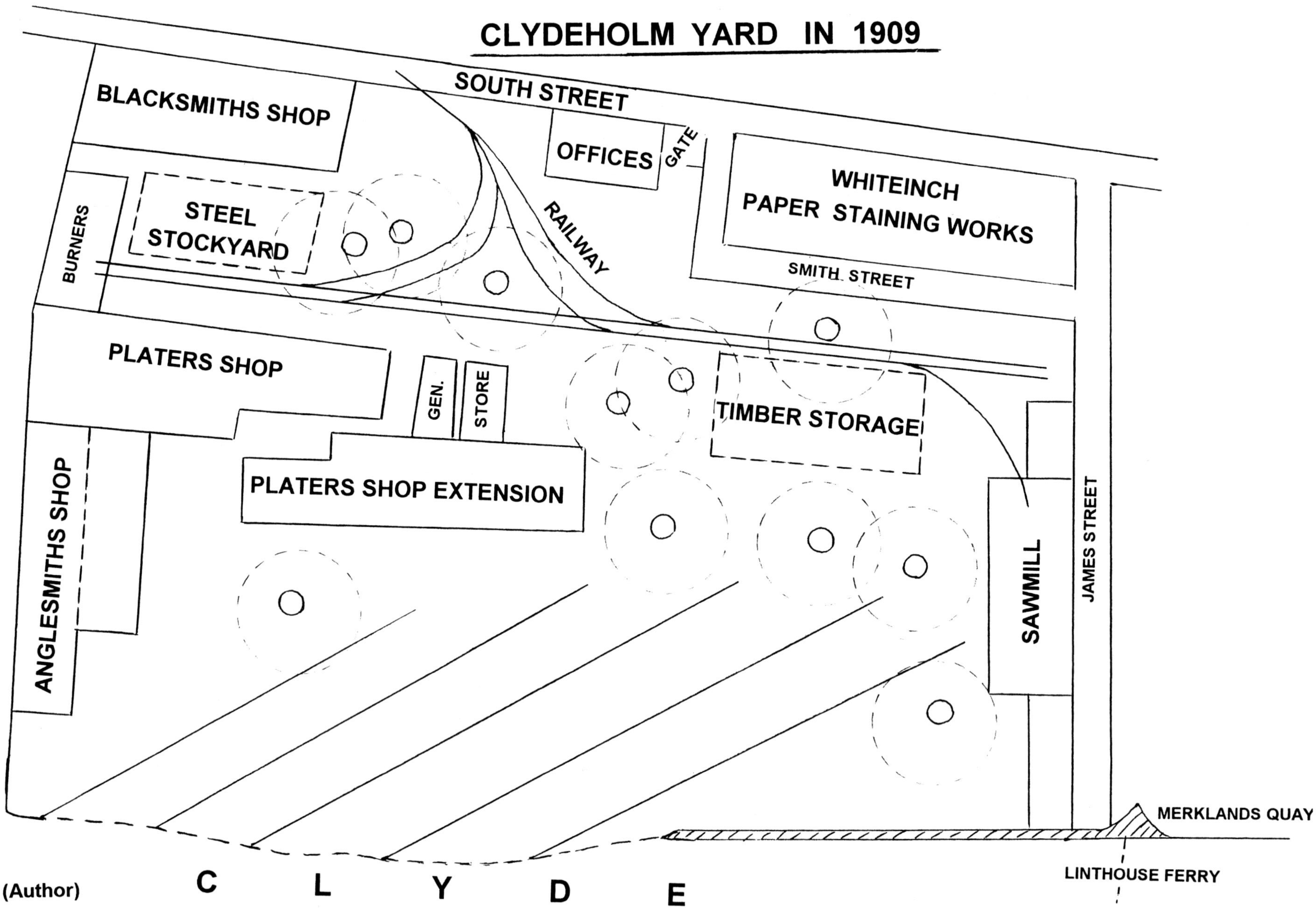

(Author)

7914/07; East Asiatic Co. of Copenhagen with *Bandon* 3487/09, *Chumpon* 3475/09, and *Pangan* 3489/09; and the Russian liners *Russia* 8596/08, *Czar* 6345/12 and *Czarita* 6852/14.

In 1912 control of the five-berth Clydeholm yard equipped with eleven cantilever tower cranes passed to the Tyneside shipbuilder Swan,Hunter & Wigham Richardson Ltd, with the latter eventually holding 99% of the shares, and with three directors from Wallsend sitting on the Clydeholm Board. The yard had in the previous fifty year period before take-over constructed some 409 ships of which 148 were sailing ships, 35 were paddle steamers, and 226 were screw steamers. The Tyneside shipbuilder also gained control of the Elderslie shipyard and dry-docks in West Scotstoun, as well as dry-docks at Govan, the latter purchased in 1902 by Barclay,Curle & Co. Ltd. The Elderslie yard had been purchased by Barclay,Curle & Co. Ltd from John Shearer & Sons Ltd in May,1912, having previously built some 46 small coasters, and extra land was then leased to enlarge the shipbuilding part of the yard into four large berths together with a six hundred feet long fitting-out quay. This yard was to build the excess orders that the Clydeholm yard could not handle and was operational from 1913.

It was British India Line that was to monopolise the building berths after the take-over, taking delivery of seventeen ships prior to the start of the Great War, the largest being the troopships *Neuralia* and *Nevasa*, and Canadian Pacific took delivery of the Transatlantic liners *Missanabie* 12469/14 and *Metagama* 12420/15. A significant vessel from the Clydeholm yard was *Jutlandia* of July,1912 and the first ocean-going British-built motorship in the world. Her oil engine was manufactured at Finnieston, and she followed her sistership *Selandia* completed on 17th February,1912 at the yard of Burmeister & Wain, Copenhagen as the first ocean-going motorship in the world. They were twin-screw ships and propelled by two 8-cylinder B & W diesels of 2500 bhp giving 11 knots service speed at 140 rpm. Following the success of the motorship *Jutlandia* the company purchased the North British Engine Works at Scotstoun later in 1912. This brick and glass-pained building was the height of a five-storey block of flats with a roof shaped roughly like half an octagonal, and had been built at the turn of the century. The company then developed this engine works as their main engine-building plant with a boiler works on the other side of South Street, and closed the Finnieston engine works. In the 1920s with the acquisition by the company of the intervening yards and land between the Clydeholm yard and the North British Engine Works a fitting-out quay was built beside the latter equipped with a 150-ton hammerhead crane to lift engines directly into newly-launched ships.

The combined output of the Clydeholm and West Scotstoun yards during the Great War produced the high total of 57 ships. A dozen merchant ships including the twin-funnelled Canadian Pacfic liners *Melita* 13967/18 and *Minnedosa* 13972/18 sub-contracted from Harland & Wolff Ltd at Belfast, and the British India *Mandala* 8246/15, *Mantola* 8246/16 and *Margha* 8278/17 were in addition to thirty convoy escort sloops, five 'P' class submarine hunters, four river gunboats and six oil tankers including the fast Admiralty oilers *Boxleaf* 7283/16 and *Limeleaf* 7398/16, the latter pair converted from two 'M' class hulls building for British India, and two standard 'AO' type tankers. The diesel-powered *Glenapp* 7374/18 for Glen Line had her oil engine built at the North British Engine Works. A very large number of ships were repaired at Govan and West Scotstoun, the totals being 1000 ships dry-docked and 2244 ships repaired afloat.

During 1919/20 the yards were occupied in building eight war replacement 'G' class meat carriers :-

NERBUDDA	7911/19	British India Line
NUDDEA	7928/19	"
NARDANA	7591/19	"
WOODARRA	7998/19	"
PESHAWAR	7934/19	"
OTAKI	7951/20	New Zealand Shipping Co. Ltd
SALLAND	6547/20	Royal Holland Lloyd
HIGHLAND WARRIOR	6507/20	Nelson Line

the first six being twin-screw ships fitted with two triple expansion engines, and the last two being single-screw ships fitted with turbines. British India then monopolised the yards again :-

CHANTALA	3129/20	British India Line
MASULA	7261/19	"
MUNDRA	7275/20	"
MASHOBA	8324/20	"
MANELA	8303/21	"
MADURA	8975/21	"
MANTOLA	8963/21	"
MATIANA	8965/22	"
MALDA	8965/22	"
DOMALA	8441/21	"
DUMANA	8428/23	"
TAIREA	7933/24	"
TAKLIWA	7936/24	"

Domala and *Dumana* were the first diesel-powered British passenger ships with accomodation for 150 passengers and oil engines by the North British Engine Works, and *Tairea* and *Takliwa* were three-funnelled liners for the Calcutta to Japan service. The twin-funnelled liner *Flandria* 10171/22 was built for Konink. Holland Lloyd, and *Waterland* 6847/22 for Konink Holland Lloyd, as well as the cargo-liners *Melford Hall* 5669/20, *Algerian* 2485/24, *Nigerian* 5343/25, *Kantara* 3236/24 and the Australian mini-liner *Malabar* 4511/25 for Burns,Philp; and the tramps *Hopeland* 4284/23, *Swanley* 4960/24 - fitted with a Maclagan two-stroke double-acting oil engine from the North British Engine Works, and *Inella* 5024/24.

The next shipyard down-river from the Clydeholm yard, the Jordanvale yard, was purchased in 1922 having been closed in February,1921 with 800 men paid-off by the owners Lloyd Royal Belge after building some 25 ships for their own and others accounts since 1916. The yard was purchased by the Australasian Steam Navigation Co. Ltd and then sold to the company in 1922, and was later absorbed into the Clydeholm yard. It had been owned until closure in 1909 by John Reid & Co. Ltd and had built small sailing ships and coasters. In 1916 the British Government allowed the Belgian shipping company Lloyd Royal Belge to reopen the yard to build war replacements for their fleet under the management of Brys & Gylsen Ltd. This yard was then modernised (See Shipyard plan) and increased in size to 7.5 acres to a lay-out designed by Donald Bremner, formerly owner of Dunlop,Bremner at Port Glasgow, who managed the yard until he set-up the new Blythswood yard in October,1919. The Jordanvale yard had its platers shop served by a railway and fed with steel from the plate and angle racks by overhead crane. The joiners shop had a sawmill on the ground floor with the joiners working above, and the engineers shop was well equipped with machinery including lathes, shaping machines, drilling and screwing machines as well as a portable jib crane. Three war standard 'A' tramps, five 'C' types and six engines-amidships standard coasters were then built during and shortly after the war. There were two berths of length 440 feet, one of 330 feet, and two of 250 feet length.

The twin-screw French liners *De La Salle* 8400/21 and *Sinaia* 8567/22 were built at West Scotstoun for Cie Generale Transatlantique and Fabre Line respectively. An order for a pair of twin-funnelled liners from P & O saw an interesting double launch from the yards on Friday 31st October,1924. *Comorin* 15279/25 was launched by the Hon. Mrs Alexander Shaw (Lord Inchcape's eldest daughter) at the Clydeholm yard, followed a few minutes later by *Cathay* 15121/25 from the West Scotstoun yard launched by Viscountess Inchcape. This unique sight was watched in admiration by thousands of Glaswegians as the double launch of these two large liners on the same tide was successfully accomplished. *Cathay*

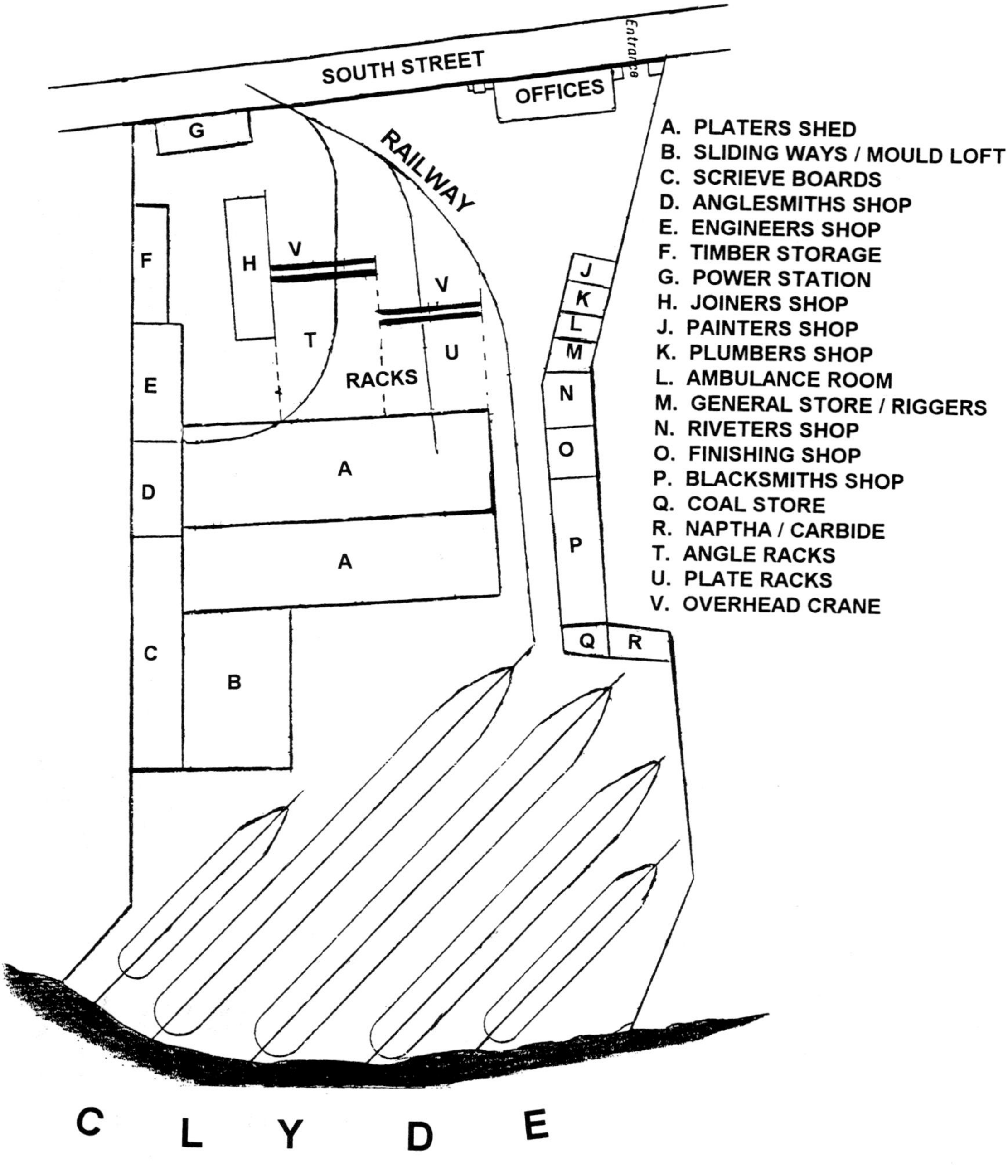

JORDANVALE YARD

(Author)

Three P & O liners from Barclay,Curle: CATHAY of 1925 (top), COMORIN of 1925 (centre) and the troopship ETTRICK of 1939 (bottom).

completed her fitting-out first and ran successful trials in the Firth of Clyde in March,1925 followed by *Comorin* in April,1925. The owners P & O then placed orders with the yards for three cargo-liners completed as *Bangalore* 6067/28, *Burdwan* 6069/28 and Soudan 6677/31. However shipbuilding ceased at the West Scotstoun yard during 1925 due to lack of orders.

Union-Castle Line took delivery of *Llandovery Castle* 10639/25, and Canadian Pacific of *Beaverhill* and *Beaverford*, both 10042/28, British India of *Rajula* 8478/26, and Ellerman Lines of *City of Khios* 5574/25, *City of Stockholm* 5076/25, *City of Wellington* 5733/25, *City of Hereford* 5101/27, *City of Lille* 6588/28 and *City of Barcelona* 5787/30 with the latter fitted with heavy-lift gear for handling and carrying locomotive engines up to 125 tons in weight. She was fitted with a four crank triple-expansion engine in combination with a Metropolitan-Vickers turbo-generator. *Lafian* 3824/28 was built for the West Africa service of United Africa Co. Ltd, and three steam-powered reefers for the West Indian services of Cuyamel Fruit as *Aztec* 5383/29, *Maya* 5383/29, *Toltec* 5399/29 with high bridge and boat decks and flat-plated elliptical counter sterns, with the similar *Contessa* 5324/30 for Vacarro Brothers. Swan,Hunter & Wigham Richardson Ltd also transferred some of the 50 Great Lakes traders built by the Group in the 1920s to the yards, and completed as *Glenburnie* for Glen Line and *Fairlake* and *Fairriver*, both 1940/29, *Coteaudoc* 1975/29, *Sarniadoc* 1940/29, *Sioux* 2197/29 and *Algonquins* 2211/29. The following oil tankers were also completed :-

STORSTEN	5343/26	Rafen & Loennechen, Tonsberg
SOLSTEN	5379/29	"
HAVSTEN	6161/30	"
BUESTEN	5187/28	"
ELSA	5381/28	A/S Oljefart, Norway
ALCIDES	7634/30	I.M. Skaugen, Oslo
NEW ZEALAND	9311/30	E.H. Samuelsen, Oslo
POLARTANK	6356/30	Melsom & Melsom, Larvik
BEAUFORT	5053/28	Blom Blomstad, Norway
NORFOLD	6374/30	J. Rasmussen, Norway
NORVINN	6569/30	"

The largest of these tankers *New Zealand* was on charter to Texas Oil. However with an empty order book in 1931 rationalisation of the yards followed in 1932 with the West Scotstoun yard doing only shiprepair work, with shipbuilding then concentrated at the Clydeholm and Jordanvale yards, with repair work at Govan as well. A second dry-dock was completed and opened at West Scotstoun in 1932. The yards could still build ships up to 700 feet in length fitted with all types of propelling machinery including triple-expansion, turbine and Doxford opposed-piston oil engines and Sulzer diesels. Ships built during the worst years of the Depression included two small motor passenger/cargo-liners for Burns,Philp & Co. Ltd, Sydney in *Macdhui* 4561/31 and *Malaita* 3310/33; with steamer *Gartbrattan* 1811/31 for Gart Line,Glasgow; *Courland* 1325/32, *Merkland* 1469/34 and *Zealand* 1433/36 for Currie Line, Leith; and *Hai Heng* and *Hai Chen*, both 3370/34 for China Merchants Steam Navigation Co. Ltd. The small Norwegian tanker *Moira* 1560/35 for Owren was one of the first examples of an all-welded tanker in the world. However a start was then made on a number of rivetted tramps, cargo-liners, troopships :-

HOPECREST	5099/35	Hopemount Shpg. Co. Ltd
QUEEN ADELAIDE	4937/36	T. Dunlop, Glasgow
QUEEN VICTORIA	4937/36	"
QUEEN ANNE	4937/37	"
DUNKELD	4944/37	R.J. Dunlop, Glasgow
CITY OF BENARES	11081/36	Ellerman Lines
CITY OF BOMBAY	7140/37	"
CITY OF KARACHI	7139/37	"
JHELUM	4038/36	Nourse Line
JOHILLA	4042/37	"
POMONA	3457/38	F. Laeisz,Hamburg
EL MADINA	3962/37	Scindia Line, India
DILWARA	12555/36	British India Line
DUNERA	12615/37	"
ORNA	6779/38	"
BULOLO	6397/38	Burns,Philp, Australia
ETTRICK	11279/39	P & O troopship

The twin-screw *Ettrick* was launched on 25th August,1938 and completed shortly before Christmas of that year and fitted with Doxford oil engines. She could carry 1150 troops on her main and lower mess decks with cabin accomodation for officers and families, and for the families of troops. Three Scandinavian tankers were completed just before the start of hostilities in 1939 as *Britamer* 9986/39, *Polarsol* 10022/39 and *Kongsten* 9596/39 with the latter then being renamed *Athelchief* in October,1939 as a result of an exchange of tankers between Athel Line and one building in Sweden. The five-berth enlarged Clydeholm yard produced fifteen cargo-liners for private account and two fast cargo-liners for Ministry account, seven standard 'Empire' tramps, and the frigates *Loch Alvie* and *Berkeley Castle* and two large transport ferries. The private owners included British India (8), P & O (4), Burns,Philp of Australia (1), Bibby Line (1), and Ellerman Lines (1).

The yard then concentrated in post-war years on building high-class passenger and cargo-liners and modern general cargo ships of up to seven hundred feet in length, including the British India liners *Kenya* 14434/51 and *Uganda*

Two for British India Line with cargo-liner SANGOLA of 1947 (above) having accomodation for 51 passengers, and troopship NEVASA of 1956 having accomodation for 1000 troops and 500 other passengers in three classes.

14430/52 for their East African service, and their troopship *Nevasa* 20527/56. *Kenya* was launched on 28th November,1950 by Lady Currie, wife of the Chairman of British India - P & O and achieved 19.16 knots on her trials on 11th July,1951 and was handed over during the next day to Sir William Currie. The keel of *Uganda* was laid at the end of 1950 and she was launched on 20th January,1952 six months after the *Kenya* entered service. Some of the other yard post-war products were :-

LANDAURA	7289/46	British India Line
SANGOLA	8646/47	"
CITY OF KHARTOUM	9955/46	Ellerman Lines
CITY OF SWANSEA	9959/46	"
CITY OF JOHANNESBURG	8207/47	"
EUCADIA	9912/46	Anchor Line, Glasgow
SOMALI	9080/48	P & O
SOUDAN	9080/48	"
CANNONORE	7065/49	"
COROMANDEL	7065/49	"
BRAESIDE	5867/49	Burns,Philp, Australia
DUMRA	4867/46	British India Line
DARA	5030/48	"
DARESSA	5180/50	"
CARPENTARIA	7268/49	"
CHANDPARA	7274/49	"
CHANTALA	7551/50	"
CHAKDARA	7232/51	"
CHINKOA	7102/52	"
SANTHIA	8908/50	"
MALEKULA	3786/52	Burns,Philp, Australia
WINDSOR	7652/52	Watts,Watts & Co. Ltd
WOKINGHAM	7659/53	"
ARAFURA	8775/54	Eastern & Australian SS Co.
NUDDEA	8596/54	British India Line
NARDANA	8511/56	"
WAROONGA	8753/57	"
WOODARRA	8753/57	"
CITY OF COLOMBO	7739/56	Ellerman Lines
WEYBRIDGE	9221/58	Watts,Watts & Co. Ltd
WIMBLEDON	9223/58	"
TREVAYLOR	6501/59	Hain Line
CITY OF SYDNEY	10242/60	Ellerman Lines
CITY OF CANBERRA	10543/61	"
WILLESDEN	8556/61	Watts,Watts & Co. Ltd
HOPECREST	9858/61	Hopemount Shpg. Co. Ltd
HOPECRAG	9858/63	"
HOPEPEAK	9858/63	"
CITY OF ADELAIDE	10316/64	Ellerman Lines
NAKWA RIVER	7322/65	Black Star Line, Ghana

The launch of UGANDA on 15th January,1952 (BBC Hulton Picture Library)

KENYA on trials in July,1951 (centre), and UGANDA about to dry-dock at Rotterdam (L. Dunn).

PORT BURNIE 8374/66 Port Line

Several tankers of 18000 dwt were also built for Norwegian and British owners, with Melsom & Melsom of Larvik taking *Polarbris* 12552/51, *Polartank* 12651/53, *Polarprins* 12453/55; and Rafen & Loennechen of Tonsberg taking *Hurricane* 12909/59; and Athel Line taking *Athelqueen* 12458/60. Russian fish factory ships were also built e.g. *Georgi Sava Rakovsky* 8556/62, and then the longest berth in the yard was specially extended to take the 775 feet length of the P & O tanker *Opawa* 38896/65 and 65800 dwt. Two large bulk carriers were then built, the first for Czechoslovak Ocean Shipping as *Vitkovice* 24326/66 and 40300 dwt, and the second for Danish owners as *Hamlet* 29256/67 and 52075 dwt. Swan Hunter Shipbuilders Ltd then closed the Clydeholm yard after the completion of the collier *Needwood* 1555/66 for France,Fenwick and *Hamlet* in 1967, with the shiprepairing assets at West Scotstoun acquired by Yarrow in 1975, while the North British Engine Works at Scotstoun became part of British Shipbuilders in 1977. After completion of only a few more marine engines the factory was converted into a guided missile launcher manufacturing plant.

A typical Barclay,Curle cargo-liner CITY OF COLOMBO of 1956 for Ellerman Lines.

CHARLES CONNELL & CO. LTD.

Charles Connell was born in 1822 in Ayrshire the son of John Connell, shipbuilder, and Mary Cuthbert. He served his apprenticeship with Robert Steele of Greenock, building fast sailing ships, and on completion of training he moved to up-river yards, becoming a foreman. He then joined Alexander Stephen as shipyard manager at his Kelvinhaugh yard, after Stephen had observed his very detailed knowledge of ship construction. However in 1861 he decided to start building for his own account at Scotstoun, and his first ship was the small steamer *Palermo* 289/61. His previous experience dealing with Glasgow shipowners now proved useful and he obtained the first of eight orders for sailing ships in the following year for the famous City Line of Glasgow managed by George Smith & Sons, and she was completed as *City of Paris* 990/62. Another early local customer was R. & J. Craig of Glasgow and their *'County'* ships. The China tea clippers *Taitsing* 815/65, *Crusader* 1058/65 and *Spindrift* 1065/67 were followed by twenty iron barques in the 1870s as well as the more famous China tea clipper *Fiery Cross* 1456/78 for J. D. Clink, Glasgow. The last iron barque from the yard was *Lismore* 1598/85 for J. Cornfoot, Glasgow, built on a standard sailing hull with dimensions 270 feet length, 38 feet beam and 23 feet depth, and therebye giving the many production benefits arising from standardisation.

Steamers fitted with compound engines had also been built during this period with seven for the City Line of Glasgow starting with *City of Poonah* 2283/70 and ending with *City of Calcutta* 3873/81, and four for Hall Line in *Speke Hall* 2672/78, *Wistow Hall* 2674/78, *Bretton Hall* 2421/81 and *Werneth Hall* 4104/82; City Line and Hall Line later became part of Ellerman Lines in 1901. Larger iron passenger/cargo steamers followed with *Kansas* 5276/82 for Warren Line, Liverpool, *City of Chicago* 5202/83 for Inman Line, and *Vancouver* 5141/84 for Mississippi Line of Liverpool and were some of the last iron products of the yard. One of the first steel steamers was *Alberta* 2282/83 for the Canadian trade.

The founder was twice married, his first wife being Catherine Bradford, and on his death on 14th February,1884 at Partick he was survived by his second wife, Elizabeth - the daughter of a shipbuilder, and ten children, of which seven were male. Charles B. Connell was the eldest of these and his brothers and half-brothers included William Connell and A. H. Connell. The founder's estate was in excess of £250,000 and included considerable shareholdings in ships, mines, public utilities and schools. He had lived a quiet life, latterly in West Glasgow at Partick, and died at his home in Broomhill Drive.

Charles B. Connell succeeded his father in control of the Scotstoun yard, and continued to build standard sailing barques when he changed to steel with *Balclutha* of 1689 tons and completed in December,1886 for R. McMillan,Glasgow and which is still afloat today and preserved at San Francisco. A further forty steel barques were built on similar dimensions during the next seven years, including five for James Nourse in *Volga* 1817/91, *Arno* 1825/93, *Ems* 1829/93, *Forth* 1829/94 and *Mersey* 1829/94, which later became famous as the White Star Line training ship. Ten barques were built for German owners B. Wencke and Evers & Classen, both of Hamburg; with *Hazelbank* 1660/89 for Andrew Weir; *Marion Ballantyne* 1567/88 for W. Lewis, Glasgow; and the larger barques *Vimeira* 2233/91 for J. Hardie, Glasgow; *Marion Josiah* 2257/92 and *Marion Frazer* 2264/92 for Rogers & Co.,Glasgow; *Hawaiian Isles* 1974/92 for A. Nelson of Honolulu; *Glenclova* 2246/93 for the Dundee Shipowners Co. Ltd; and *Ben Dearg* 2193/94 for Watson Brothers of Glasgow. The last pair were completed in the Autumn of 1894 as *Dudhope* 1930/94 for Charles Barrie & Sons of Dundee and *Whitlieburn* 2006/94 for M. Carswell, Glasgow, and Charles B. Connell invested in four 64ths in each ship.

Many ships were built for local owners, with James Gardiner the best customer with twenty two ships, starting with the sailing ship *Lismore* 1675/85 and ending with the steamers *Glenlyon* 4933/17 and *Glenlee* 4947/17; and also several for Robert Mackill starting with the steamer Liddesdale 2422/87 and including *Evandale* 3775/95 and two that were ordered by Mackill but were completed for DFDS as *Texas* 4446/99 and *Alabama* 4034/99; and also for Bell Bros. & McClelland e.g. *Bellevue* 3814/96. A new customer at this time and one to be of great future importance was T. & J. Harrison of Liverpool and their Charente Steamship Co. Ltd. Their first steel steamer from the yard was completed as *Traveller* of 3042 grt in 1888. Their next ship from the yard, *Capella* of 3115 grt, was purchased on the stocks in 1889 from Rathbone Brothers and completed without renaming. These were followed by larger four-masted quadruple-expansion powered steamers with *Custodian* 9241/00 the largest, with Harrisons becoming the most important customer of Connell with a total of 50 ships delivered, the last being *Inventor* 8813/63.

More long associations were formed by the yard in the liner trades with Nourse Line taking 26 ships for their Indian trades, starting with the barque *Volga* 1817/91 and ending with *Jumna* 9890/62; Ben Line of Leith took thirty ships for their Far East services starting with *Benvorlich* 5193/19 and ending with *Benstac* 12011/68, which was the last ship built by the yard under the Connell family. Indra Line of Liverpool, Brocklebank Line, Asiatic Steam Navigation Co. Ltd were some of the more important liner customers, with Union-Castle Line taking *Gordon Castle*

4406/01. In the twenty years before the start of the Great War the yard built a series of large two-deck cargo-liners of up to 500 feet in length and 12,000 dwt, some powered by quadruple-expansion steam engines giving speeds of 12 knots :-

CRAFTSMAN	6196/97	T. & J. Harrison,Liverpool
COLLEGIAN	7236/99	"
CUSTODIAN	9241/00	"
YEOMAN	7379/01	"
CIVILIAN	7099/02	"
HUNTSMAN	7460/04	"
EXPLORER	7608/10	"
DIPLOMAT	7615/12	"
DEFENDER	8258/15	"
MAPLMORE	7717/98	Johnston Line,Liverpool
PINEMORE	6215/98	"
ROWANMORE	9456/00	"
KNIGHT BACHELOR	6505/94	Greenshields,Cowie,Liverpool
KNIGHT ERRANT	7564/98	"
KNIGHT OF THE GARTER	6655/02	"
KNIGHT OF THE THISTLE	6675/03	"
KNIGHT TEMPLAR	7175/05	"
KNIGHT COMPANION	8631/10	"
INDRA	6057/96	Indra Line, Liverpool
INDRALEMA	6669/01	"
INDRAMAYO	5200/02	"
INDRASAMHA	5297/01	"
INDRAVELLI	5805/97	"
INDRAWADI	5204/02	"
MALAKUTA	7205/14	Brocklebank Line
MAHANADA	7196/14	"
RAJAH	5662/99	Asiatic S.N. Co. Ltd,Liverpool
RAJPUT	5628/00	"
PASHA	5930/02	"
PUNDIT	5917/02	"
SATURNIA	8611/10	Donaldson Line, Glasgow
CATALINA	5296/93	Pinilos & Izquierdo, Cadiz
CADIZ	4218/95	"
BARCELONA	4218/95	"
MERA	4797/01	"
VALBANERA	5090/06	"
BARCELONA	5450/08	"
CADIZ	5437/08	"
AMASIS	4552/96	Kosmos Deutsche D/S,Hamburg
AMMON	4554/96	"
ASSUAN	4793/00	"
VANDALIA	4179/05	Hamburg-Amerika Line
AUGSBURG	4287/96	Deutsche-Australien D/S,H'burg
TEXAS	4446/99	DFDS, Copenhagen

A general view of the Connell berths (above), and (below) the refrigerated cargo-liner CORINALDO for the local Donaldson Line on launch day 7th July, 1949. (Strathclyde Regional Archives)

ALABAMA	4034/99	DFDS

Charles B. Connell, son of the founder, had one son, Charles (later knighted), and two daughters and he purchased the Craigallian estate at Milngavie a few miles to the north of the shipyard and this then became and remained the family home. Several ships were built 'on-spec' and were then managed by the other Connell brothers from Hope Street in Glasgow, including *Kilbride* 3712/01, *Kilbrennan* 3640/03, *Kilchattan* 3758/06, *Kilkerran* 3755/06 and *Killin* 3544/08. A number of steam yachts were built at the yard for the Connell brothers and included *Moneira* and *Athene* of 1895, *Calista* and *Oriana* of 1896 and another *Calista* in 1898.

The four-berth Connell yard was not noted for building passenger ships, and one of the few small examples built was *Stephano* 3449/11 with accomodation for 180 first-class passengers and 60 second-class on the Red Cross Line summer service from St. John's(NF) to Halifax(NS) to New York service of Bowring. In winter she went crusing from New York to the Caribbean, or even helped with the seal kills off Newfoundland, one of the mainstays of the Bowring business at that time.

Output during the Great War consisted of seven sloops for the Admiralty, seventeen cargo-liners for private account, and six standard tramps and tankers. *Shuja* 4932/16 was built for the Bombay & Persia S.N. Co. Ltd, *Betwa* 3819/17 for Nourse Line, *Manaar* 7242/17 and *Maizar* 7293/17 for Brocklebank Line, *Nawab* 5430/15 and *Nizam* 5322/14 for the Asiatic S.N. Co. Ltd, *Glenlyon* 4933/17 and *Glenlee* 4947/17 for James Gardiner of Glasgow, and *Barrister* 3679/15, *Defender* 8258/15 and *Senator* 3670/17 for T. & J. Harrison. The standard ships were three 'A' types completed as *Clan Skene* 5257/19 for Clan Line, *Benvorlich* 5193/19 for Ben Line and *Silarus* 5101/19 for Royal Mail Line; and three 'AO' tankers in *War Prophet, War Singer* and *War Cateran.*

The Connell yard was constrained by South Street in the size of ship that could be built, but was re-equipped with tower cranes during 1919. The yard did not possess a fitting-out quay, with much machinery being Rowan-built and lifted aboard at the Finnieston quay with out-fitting completed in the Glasgow docks. The provision of a fitting-out quay in the 1920s at the adjacent North British Engine Works of Barclay,Curle & Co. Ltd meant that much machinery was ordered from their neighbour and this also eased the fitting-out problem. Three turbine-powered cargo-liners were built for T. & J. Harrison as *Dramatist* 5443/20, *Diplomat* 8240/21 and *Huntsman* 8196/21, but this form of propulsion was not repeated with the next thirteen ships delivered by the yard during the 1920s to their most important customer. A further sixteen ships were delivered to other owners during this decade of difficult trading conditions :-

The Norwegian cargo-liner CORONA is launched for H. M. Wrangell of Haugesund, and she is seen on completion in October, 1949 at the North British Engine Works after installation of her 4 - cylinder Barclay, Curle - Doxford oil engine of 4400 bhp.
(Strathclyde Regional Archives)

BENREOCH	5818/21	Ben Line, Leith
BENARTY	5800/26	"
BENVENUE	5920/27	"
BENMHOR	5920/28	"
BENCRUACHAN	5920/28	"
BENWYVIS	5920/29	"
BENLEDI	5943/30	"
BENLAWERS	5943/30	"
BARON KELVIN	3081/24	H. Hogarth, Ardrossan
MASIRAH	6836/19	Brocklebank Line
MANGALORE	9751/20	"
MAHSEER	7864/25	"
MAIDAN	7861/25	"
NURJEHAN	5450/23	Asiatic S.N. Co. Ltd, London
NURMAHAL	5419/23	"
LAMMER LAW	4971/29	Thomas Law, Glasgow
TRAPRAIN LAW	4976/30	"
ARDANGORM	5200/30	Clark & Service, Glasgow

Benlawers was the last ship delivered before the onset of the Depression, during which the yard was closed for a longer period then any other British shipyard, eight years until the Spring of 1938 when two tramp hulls were laid down for the local J. & J. Denholm Ltd and completed as *Mountpark* and *Wellpark*, both 4648/38. The yard then built *Rothermere* 5356/38 for the local Donaldson Line, *Settler* 6225/39 for T. & J. Harrison, *Bhima* 5280/39 for Nourse Line, and *Baron Semple* 4573/39 for Hogarth.

World War II output consisted of twelve tramps of which eight were of standard design, twelve cargo-liners for private owners Nourse Line (8), Ben Line (3), T. & J. Harrison (1) and the fast cargo-liner *Empire Wilson* 9916/44 for Government account. The first four tramps were built to a Connell design with counter sterns, and the yard also launched at the end of the war a large tank transport ferry, which was not completed but later towed in 1950 to Rio de Janeiro for Brazilian coastal service.

The local tramp company of J. & J. Denholm Ltd then became important to the yard, building replacements for the two pre-war tramps that were lost during the war and given the same names *Mountpark* and *Wellpark*, both 6722/46. Their first motortramp was completed at the yard as *Carronpark* 5358/49 in June of that year and an exact sister followed in April,1951 as *Lylepark* 5269/51. The similar five-hold engines-amidships *Glenpark* 6151/56 of October,1956 had a summer dwt of 10580 tons on a draft of 27 feet, and she was fitted with steel Macgregor hatch covers on the weather deck and conventional wooden covers for the 'tween decks. Her cargo gear consisted of twelve derricks of 5-ton capacity and four of 10-ton

**BENALDER pictured on her launch day 12th September,1949 for Ben Line;
and BENWYVIS pictured on trials in 1967.**

(Strathclyde Regional Archives)

capacity, and she was powered by a 4-cylinder Doxford oil engine of 3500 bhp to give a service speed of 13 knots, and a sister *Broompark* 6100/59 was then delivered.

J. & J. Denholm Ltd also entered the oil trades with two tankers of 18650 dwt from the yard, and jointly financed by Denholm, Connell and their Norwegian charterer. *Norscot* 12709/53 and *Scotstoun* 12722/55 were powered by 6-cylinder Doxford oil engines from the adjacent North British Works of Barclay, Curle & Co. Ltd. Two ore-carriers were also built for the Denholm-managed Scottish Ore Carriers Ltd as *Craigallian* and *Crinan*, both 7088/60, with the former named after the Milngavie estate of Sir Charles and Lady Connell and their son Charles R. Connell. Sir Charles and his son, the latter representing the fourth generation of the family in the yard, made attempts to introduce production control into the Scotstoun yard in 1961/62 by the appointment of a production consultant, however this was not implemented until the building of standard ships was begun when the yard became part of Uppper Clyde Shipbuilders Ltd in 1968. The 16800 dwt general cargo ship *Scotstoun* 11457/64 was then built 'on-spec' for management by Denholm, followed by the first bulk carrier *Mountpark* 21833/65 of 34715 dwt for Denholm ownership.

However cargo-liners was the speciality of the yard and the following examples were built during post-war years :-

BENVORLICH	9767/46	Ben Line, Leith
KALLADA	6607/46	Nourse Line
MARJATA	6652/46	"
MUTLAH	6652/47	"
PURNEA	5340/47	British India Line
FACTOR	6532/48	T. & J. Harrison, Liverpool
CORINALDO	8348/49	Donaldson Line, Glasgow
BENMACDHUI	7845/48	Ben Line, Leith
BENVENUE	7846/48	"
BENCLEUCH	7863/49	"
BENALDER	7877/49	"
TAMESIS	6749/49	W. Wilhelmsen, Oslo
CORONA	5136/49	H. M. Wrangell, Haugesund
GANGES	6724/50	Nourse Line
BETWA	6722/50	"
BENREOCH	10142/52	Ben Line, Leith
TALISMAN	6785/52	W. Wilhelmsen, Oslo
INDUS	7049/54	Nourse Line
FERNMOOR	7082/55	Fearnley & Eger, Oslo
FERNSTATE	9409/58	"
TEMERAIRE	8779/57	W. Wilhelmsen, Oslo
TURANDOT	8788/57	"
TIJUCA	8831/59	"
BENVRACKIE	10302/55	Ben Line, Leith

BENDORAN	10355/56	"
BENLOMOND	10325/57	"
BENLOYAL	11463/59	"
BENGLOE	11282/61	"
BENVALLA	11391/62	"
JUMNA	10051/62	Nourse Line
KOHINUR	10039/63	New Zealand Shipping Co. Ltd
INVENTOR	9171/64	T. & J. Harrison Ltd, Liverpool
BENARMIN	11362/63	Ben Line, Leith
BENDEARG	11902/64	"
BENLEDI	11898/65	"
BENWYVIS	11958/66	"
BENALBANACH	11466/67	"
BENSTAC	12011/68	"

The last in the above list, *Benstac*, was the last ship launched by the yard under Connell family management on 20th November,1967. Tankers had also been built for Norwegian owners with three for W. Wilhelmsen as *Tartar* 11103/51, *Tibetan* 12548/54 and *Turcoman* 12552/54; two for Fearnley & Eger as *Fernstar* 12719/55 and *Fernhaven* 12689/58; one for Bergen Line as *Castor* 11144/51, and one for Jacob Kjode of Bergen as *Hornblower* 11102/51. Two large tankers were then built for the P & O Group and registered under Nourse Line as *Erne* 14244/62 of 20090 dwt and *Foyle* 24549/61 and 39300 dwt.

The early 1960s was not an easy time for the yard, and two small coaster orders had to be taken to ensure continuity, completed as *Saint Aidan* 973/62 for J. & A. Gardner, Glasgow and *Tuskar* 1598/62 for the Clyde Shipping Co. Ltd. Three large bulk carrier orders were then obtained for *Romandie* 21449/65 of 33600 dwt for Suisse - Atlantique A/S, and *Mountpark* 21833/65 of 34715 dwt for Denholm, and *Stonepool* 27049/66 of 45027 dwt for Ropner. This last bulker was of 718 feet in length and was the largest ship built by the yard.

The Connell yard joined Upper Clyde Shipbuilders Ltd effective from 7th February,1968, however this was short-lived and was liquidated during 1971 with the Scotstoun yard becoming part of Govan Shipbuilders Ltd (the former Fairfield yard) during 1972. The yard began trading as Scotstoun Marine Ltd, a subsidiary of Govan Shipbuilders Ltd during 1973. Ships built by the former Connell yard during this turbulent period were the cargo-liners *Bencruachan* 12092/68, *Benlawers* 12989/70 and *City of London* 9792/70; the bulkers *Scotspark* 16792/69, *Glenpark* 16782/71, *Vancouver Island* 16781/72, *Sig Ragne* 11857/71 of the 'Clyde' class, and *Harfleet* 16715/73, *Harfleur* 16715/73 and *Norse Herald* 16682/74 of the 'Cardiff' class.

The first orders secured by Scotstoun Marine Ltd were two reefers of 11160 dwt for management by Denholm as *Loch Lomond* and *Loch Maree*, both 10397/75, followed by two smaller reefers for Geest Line as *Geesthaven* 8030/75 and *Geestcape* 8030/76. The yard then constructed six of the 19 'Kuwait' class cargo-liners under construction for the United Arab Shipping Co. Ltd at Govan, these being *Ibn Abdoun, Ibn Al-Haitham, Ibn Shuhaid, Ibn Zuhr, Al Muharraq* and *Arafat,* and shared in the Polish bulk carrier order by building seven mini-bulkers of 4400 dwt during 1979/80 as *Gniezo II, Sieradz, Wyszkow, Comza, Chorzow, Wielun* and *Warka*. The yard was then closed later in 1980, the Connell family having still remained in business as shipowners and managers.

The 'Cardiff' class bulker NORSE HERALD of 1974.

D. & W. HENDERSON & CO. LTD.

David and William Henderson were two of four famous brothers who were involved in shipping or shipbuilding. The others were Thomas and John, both partners in the famous Glasgow shipping company Henderson Brothers, much better known as Anchor Line. David and William owned an engineering works at Finnieston and in 1873 with help from their shipowning brothers purchased the Meadowside shipyard of Tod and Macgregor. David Tod and John Macgregor were experienced shipbuilders and had established the Meadowside yard in 1847, and counted Cunard Line, Inman Line and P & O among their customers. In 1856 the yard was slightly increased in area by the purchase of the adjacent yard of coaster builder Thomas B. Seath. Tod and Macgregor then sold the shipyard in 1873 for £200,000, a very large sum in those days, to the Henderson brothers.

The Henderson family placed no fewer than 32 orders for Anchor Line ships with the Meadowside yard between 1876 and 1911, together with substantial repair work. The yard was thus locally known as the 'Anchor Line' yard, the first having been *Alsatia* 2766/76 and powered by compound steam engines. All of their ships were named after countries, continents or places ending in 'ia' e.g. *Armenia* 3396/81, *Nubia* 3551/82, *Arabia* 3598/83, *Persia* 3596/83 and *Asia* 3611/84. The first to be built of steel and also the first to be given a triple expansion steam engine was *Anglia* 3287/88. She was followed by larger and similar Anchor Line ships such as *Algeria* 4550/91, but the period of Anchor Line expansion came to a temporary halt with the deaths of all four Henderson brothers between 1892 and 1895. In 1899 their shipowning partnership was dissolved and there was no longer any financial interest in the Meadowside yard, although Anchor Line ships continued to be ordered from the yard at the rate of one or two per year. The shipbuilding yard was incorporated as a limited liability company in 1900 as D. & W. Henderson & Co. Ltd.

There had been, of course, other important customers of the yard such as Lamport & Holt Ltd of Liverpool with 19 ships starting with *Milton* 2679/88 and ending with *Lalande* 7453/20; Maclay & McIntyre of Glasgow with 16 ships starting with *Madura* 2490/94 and ending with *Loch Lomond* 5452/34; Bell Bros. & McClelland, Glasgow with a dozen steamers with names all beginning with 'Bell' e.g. *Bellaisla* 3797/96; Allan Line of Glasgow with *Rosarian* 3204/87, *Monte Videan* 3077/87, *Brazilian* 3204/91, *Mongolian* 4838/91 and *Numidian* 4836/91; and the local Donaldson Line with *Tritonia* 4272/93.

The last sailing ships from the yard were the four-masted barques *Marion Lightbody* 2176/88 for Rogers & Company, Glasgow and *Torrisdale* 2160/92 for J.& A. Roxburgh, Glasgow and the more famous five-masted *France* 3942/90 for A. D. Bordes & Son of Dunkirk and which could carry 6500 tons of cargo. The yard also built some splendid yachts designed by the yard naval architect George Thompson. The schooner yacht *Rainbow* was built in 1898 for C.C. Orr-Ewing, others being the racing yachts *Thistle* (1897), *Valkyrie II* (1893), *Valkyrie III* (1895) which challenged for the America Cup. The most famous of all was *Britannia* of 1893 for the Prince of Wales.

A series of five twin-screw four-masted passenger/cargo-liners of 6200 grt was built for Nippon Yusen Kaisha in 1896/97 as *Kanagawa Maru, Bingo Maru, Hakata Maru, Inaba Maru* and *Wakasa Maru.* Three cargo-liners were completed for the China Mutual S.N. Co. Ltd of Alfred Holt as *Kaisow* 3921/95, *Moyung* 4646/95 and *Teenkai* 4642/95, and Apcar Brothers of Calcutta took the passenger ship *Catherine Apcar* 2727/92 for their service to Japan. At the turn of the century and during the next decade large and important passenger/cargo-liners were built by the yard for the Anchor Line and T. & J. Harrison Ltd of Liverpool :-

ASSYRIA	6370/00	INVENTOR	7679/10
NUMIDIA	6399/00	BOTANIST	7688/12
SCINDIA	5106/00	BENEFACTOR	5511/12
CALABRIA	4376/01	INGOMA	5686/13
PERUGIA	4348/01		
OLYMPIA	5124/02		
COLUMBIA	8292/02		
ITALIA	4806/03		
CIRCASSIA	6732/03		
CALEDONIA	9223/05		
CALIFORNIA	8662/07		
ELYSIA	6374/08		
CAMERONIA	10963/11		

with the most famous of these being the three-funnelled *Columbia,* which was also the first to be twin-screw, and had a passenger complement of 345 saloon, 218 cabin and 740 steerage passengers. The first with two funnels was *Caledonia* and together with the last trio built at the yard had twin screws driven by reciprocating machinery.

The South American passenger trade from New York of Lamport & Holt Ltd received a boost with a liner with refrigerated capacity in *Voltaire* 8615/07. The twin-funnelled *Tabaristan* 3883/07 came from this yard and was the only twin-funneller ever owned by Strick Line, and had followed *Armanistan* 4002/05 from the yard. Local owners continued to place repeat orders for tramps such as *Bellucia* 4368/09 for Bell Bros & McClelland, *Ardanmhor* 4454/07 for the Ardan Steamship Co. Ltd of Clark & Service, *Craigvar* 4415/05 for Biggart,Fulton, and a series of tramps for Maclay & McIntyre culminating in *Kalimba* 4982/14. The last named was more important than might appear at first sight, for her design was used for that of the war standard 'A' type tramps built from 1917 to 1920. Sir Joseph Maclay was appointed Shipping Controller in December,1916 and naturally used the designs and blueprints of his own tramps for these 400 feet long, 52 feet wide and 31 feet deep standard tramps of 5200 grt., the 'B' type only differing in having a second deck. Six 'A' type and three 'B' types were ordered from the Henderson yard, with five of the 'A' type completed for Hain Line e.g. *Tremeadow* and two of the 'B' type completing for Lamport & Holt as *Balfe* and *Balzac*, the latter being the last standard ship completion in March,1920. Two standard 'AO' tankers were also completed as *War Kinsman* and *War Roman*. Merchant ships for private account had also been built e.g. *Herschel* 6293/14 and *Holbein* 6278/15 for regular customers Lamport & Holt Ltd, and *Governor* 5523/15, *Astronomer* 8681/17, *Actor* 5548/17, and *Governor* 5571/18 for T. & J. Harrison Ltd; and the tanker *Lompoc* 7270/14 for Bowring.

In early 1917 the ordinary shares in the Henderson yard and its neighbouring shipyard on the other side of the Kelvin river, A. & J. Inglis (q.v.) were purchased by Harland & Wolff Ltd, Belfast jointly for £397,466. However they were to remain independent and use their own yard numbers until 1919. The Henderson yard with four berths had six vessels under construction for Leyland Line and two for Lamport & Holt when the yard was placed under Harland & Wolff management in 1919. These and other cargo-liners and tramps completed during the 1920s and 1930s until closure of the yard in 1935 were :-

LALANDE	7453/20	Lamport & Holt Ltd, Liverpool
HOGARTH	8109/21	"
DAKARIAN	6426/21	Leyland Line, Liverpool
DAKOTIAN	6426/22	"
DARIAN	6434/22	"
DAYTONIAN	6434/22	"
DAVISIAN	6433/23	"
DELILIAN	6423/23	"
DORELIAN	6300/23	"
ASUKA MARU	7488/24	Nippon Yusen Kaisha, Japan
THISTLEROS	4615/25	Allan,Black, Sunderland
KING JAMES	5065/25	King Line
KING MALCOLM	5064/25	"
MARTHARA	4999/26	Maclay & McIntyre, Glasgow
UGANDA	4966/27	"
NYANZA	4974/28	"

COLONIAL	5108/26	T. & J. Harrison, Liverpool
DIRECTOR	5107/26	"
DESIGNER	5945/28	"
KERMA	4333/28	Strick Line
CELTIC MONARCH	5822/29	Raeburn & Verel, Glasgow
BARON VERNON	3642/29	H. Hogarth, Glasgow
BARON RAMSAY	3650/29	"
WILLIAM WILBERFORCE	4013/30	Elder,Dempster
MACGREGOR LAIRD	4015/30	"
ARDANBHAN	4980/30	Clark & Service, Glasgow
BARON NAPIER	3659/30	H. Hogarth, Glasgow
BARON ERSKINE	3659/30	"
BARON ARDROSSAN	3896/32	"
BARON DUNMORE	3938/33	"
BARON ELGIN	3942/33	"
LOCH LOMOND	5452/34	Maclay & McIntyre, Glasgow
HENZADA	4161/34	P. Henderson, Glasgow
MARTABAN	4161/34	"
BARON RENFREW	3635/35	H. Hogarth, Glasgow
BARON CAWDOR	3638/35	"
SAGANAGA	5454/35	Chr. Salvesen, Leith
INVENTOR	6210/35	T. & J. Harrison, Liverpool

The motortramps *King James* and *King Malcolm* had originally been ordered by Sir William Petersen of Newcastle in a grand scheme to reduce freight rates on the North Atlantic, but after his death in June,1925 they were sold for the knock-down price of £25,000 each to the British Motorship Co. Ltd and managed by King Line. The tanker *Clydefield* 7365/28 was completed for Hunting & Son of Newcastle, as well as ten small cargo-only Cross-Channel ships for the Southern Railway Company of which the last was completed as the first to carry cars across the Channel as *Autocarrier* 822/31. Glasgow owners James & Alexander Brown took the collier *Minmi* 1455/27, and the Clyde Shipping Co. Ltd the ccasters *Eddystone* 1550/27 and *Rockabill* 1392/30, with six coasters for Richard Hughes of Liverpool e.g. *Dorothy Rose* 1600/29, and four colliers for Worms et Cie of Paris e.g. *Chateau Larose* 2047/30, and two steam ferries, *Irwin* and *Goschen*, both 970/29 were built for the Southern India Railway Co. Ltd.

The Meadowside yard could build tramps and cargo-liners more cheaply than the parent Harland & Wolff yard at Belfast, but with thinning order books the only option was sterilisation of berths by selling them to National Shipbuilders Security Ltd. Pressure was applied when the bankers of the yard became no longer willing to finance the yard in March,1935, and D. & W. Henderson & Co. Ltd was placed into receivership on 4th April,1935. The snag was that Harland & Wolff wished to retain the Meadowside dry-dock and fitting-out berth for use by their Govan yard, and a repair subsidiary D. & W. Henderson Ltd was finally formed in 1936 to secure the future of the dry-dock. The last new ship was completed in September,1935 as *Inventor*, and repair work was then undertaken until closure in 1962 when Harland & Wolff Ltd withdrew from the Clyde. Landing craft were built during World War II and the site is now an industrial estate with the dry-docks having been filled in.

The famous three-funnelled Anchor Line COLUMBIA of 1902. (G.Stromier/L.Vogt)

A. & J. INGLIS LTD.

The brothers Anthony Inglis (1813 - 1884) and John Inglis (1819 - 1888) began an engineering business in 1847 at Finnieston, which occasionally involved sub-contracting a hull to one of the thirty or more Clyde yards then operating. The Pointhouse shipyard was opened in 1862 on the east bank of the Kelvin where it joins the Clyde, and its main feature was a patent cradle of length 270 feet which could lift ships from their building position and move them to a launching slipway and slowly release them into the water (See shipyard plan). Their first ship was the iron steamer *Blanche* 255/62 followed by *Cheduba* 660/63 and *Euphrates* 488/63 for William McKinnon, being the first of 45 steamers for their most important customer, British India Line. A mixture of sailing ships, such as the composite *Oberon* 1181/69 and the iron barque *Loch Etive* 1235/77, and iron paddle steamers such as *Ichang* 3090/73, *Shanghai* 3088/73, *Pekin* 3076/73 and *Hankow* 3073/74 for the Yangtze services of John Swire were then built. The first steel steamers built were *Camorta* 2094/80 and *Compta* 2135/81 for British India Line, and other customers for these steamers included Hamburg-Amerika Line; A/S D/S Atlantic, Hamburg; Konink. Paketv. Maats. and the Hong Kong, Canton & Macao Co.

John Inglis (1842 - 1919), son of Anthony, took over after the death of his father in 1884, having married Agnes Denny of the famous Dumbarton shipbuilding family in 1867. He is also remembered as a designer, experimenter - having developed the idea of an integral keel, writer, yachtsman and influential director of the North British Railway Company, for whom many Clyde paddlers were built by the yard. The yard built the first tanker for the Anglo-American Oil Co. Ltd, the British arm of Standard Oil of U.S.A., the latter being very clear in their specifications of nine pairs of tanks in the 4000 dwt *Bayonne* 3294/89, which was launched sideways and followed by *Potomac* 3868/93 of 4700 dwt. A series of a dozen large cargo-liners for British India Line were built as *Taroba* 4686/88, *Tara* 4710/90, *Dunera* 5413/91, *Dilwara* 5444/91, *Matiana* 5264/94, *Onda* 5247/95, *Upada* 5295/99, *Urlana* 5253/99, *Ikhona* 5265/00 and *Itria* 5267/00 and ending with the twin-funnelled *Bangala* 3933/02 and *Bihara* 3935/03. The yard subsequently only built small coastal ships, and the reason for this would appear to have been the loss of their most important customer and a slump in orders. The partnership was made into a limited liability company of the same name in 1905, and continued to build Clyde paddlers for the North British Railway Company e.g. *Marmion* 414/06; and for David Macbrayne with *Pioneer* 241/05 and *Mountaineer* 235/10 and *Prince Edward* 304/11. The contract for the Royal yacht *Alexandra* 2147/07 was the first to be

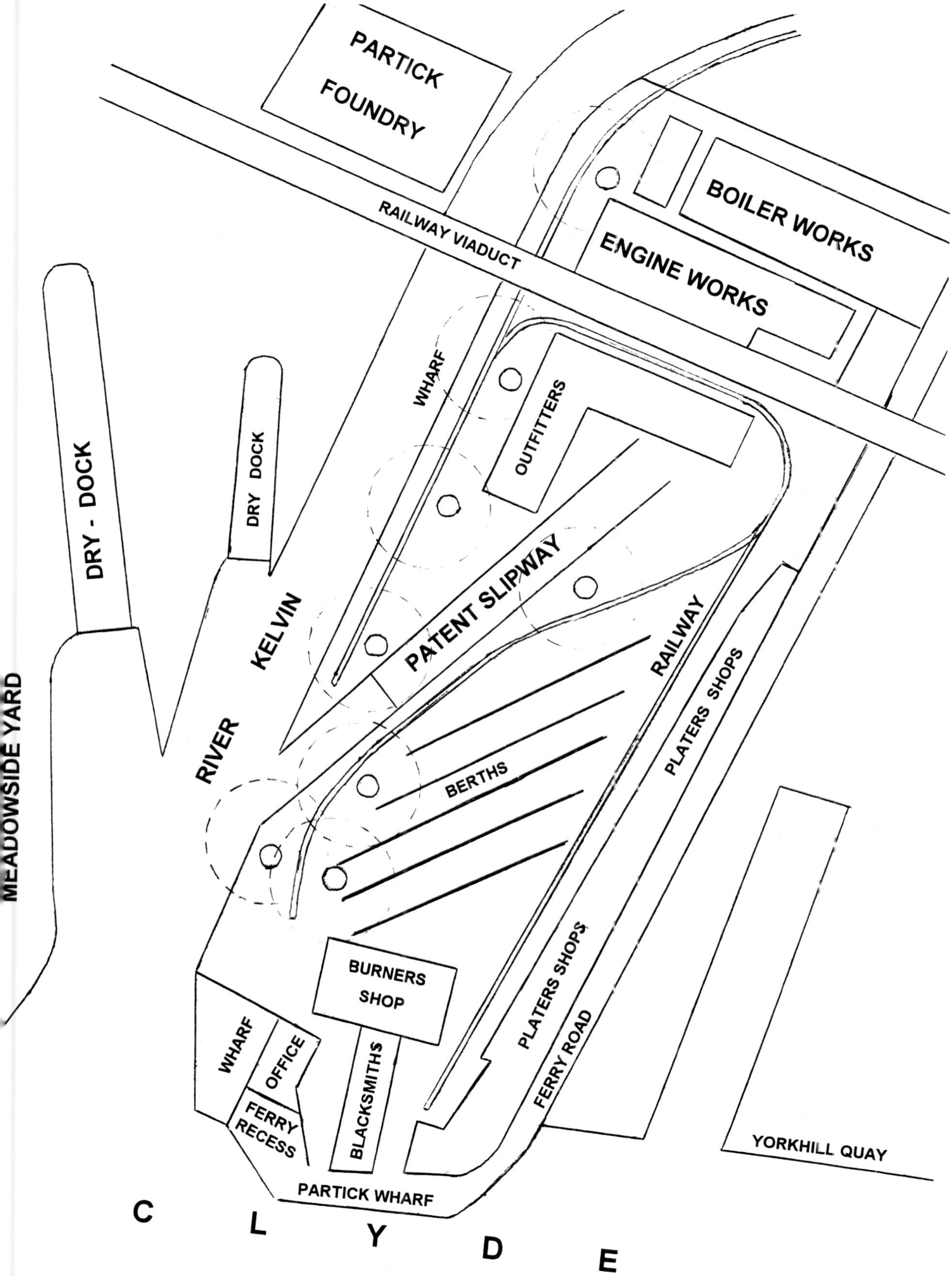

POINTHOUSE YARD OF A. & J. INGLIS LTD. (Author)

given to a private yard, and she was luxuriously appointed and turbine-powered with triple screws and was used extensively in the Mediterranean. The Admiralty placed their first contract in 1911 for the destroyer *Fury* and further destroyers and minesweepers were completed during the Great War.

The ordinary shares in the Pointhouse yard were purchased in early 1917 together with those of neighbour D. & W. Henderson Ltd (q.v.) by Harland & Wolff Ltd, Belfast for £397,466. However both yards were to remain independent and use their own yard numbers until 1919, when the first co-operation took place with the Harland & Wolff yard on the opposite side of the river at Govan with the Govan-built coaster *Coney* 697/19 engined at Pointhouse in March,1919. Three standard 'H' type ship[s were then completed for Macandrews & Co. Ltd in *Arana* 2504/19, *Alvarado* 2464/20 and *Almagro* 2478/20. A series of six coasters was then built for Coast Lines Ltd and their subsidiaries e.g. *Eastern Coast* 1223/22 as well as the cable layer *Cable Enterprise* 943/24 for the Western Telegraph Company. A series of two-deck passenger ferries and one-deck cargo coasters was then completed for service in the Plate region, either on Montevideo to Buenos Aires service or on Parana river services. The shallow-draft passenger ferry *Iguazu* 523/27 was followed by the train ferries *Delfina Mitre* 2235/28 and *Carmen Avellaneda* 2234/29, and by the larger passenger ferries *Ciudad de Ascuncion* 2851/30, *Ciudad de Corrientes* 2854/30 and *Guayra* 1496/30.

The launch of the Argentinean ferry CIUDAD DE CORRIENTES in 1930. (John B. Hill)

GUAYRA (Y873) on right under construction in 1930 at the Pointhouse yard, and also seen at a much later stage in construction (below). (John B. Hill)

The yard suffered badly during the Depression, completing only two lightships, a tug, a trawler and the Clyde paddler *Talisman* 544/35 during the six years from 1930. The paddler was the first direct-acting diesel-electric paddle steamer in the world, and she was followed by the lighthouse tender *May* 491/37 for the Forth service of the Northern Lighthouse Commissioners, replacing an earlier Pointhouse-built Forth tender *Queen o' the May* 270/95, which by that time was the Tyne pilot cutter. Two coasters were then completed, *Cameo* 946/37 for the local William Robertson and *Donaghadee* 662/37 for John Kelly, Belfast, followed by two tugs for the South African Government.

World War II production included the Humber ferry *Lincoln Castle* 598/41, two dry-cargo standard coasters, ten coastal tankers and eight more with diesel-electric engines and fitted-out for service in the Far East, as well as eleven corvettes and nine trawlers for the Admiralty. The first ship built for a commercial owner after the war was probably the most famous from the yard and is still afloat today as the much-loved twin-funnelled paddle steamer *Waverley* of 693 grt completed in June,1947 for Clyde service. This ended in 1974 for her railway owner, and she was then sold to a private preservation society and has been beautifully restored and maintained not only for Clyde excursions but also around Britain.

The Pointhouse yard went on to build 14 whale catchers mostly for Norwegian owners e.g. *Arnt Karlsen* and *Ernst Karlsen*, both 598/49 and *Anders Arvesen* 742/51, tugs for South Africa and Nigeria, coasters for Northern Ireland owners e.g. *Ballylumford* 1242/54, and two seaward defence boats for the Admiralty. Another famous paddler was the Loch Lomond steamer *Maid of the Loch* 555/53, which was built at Pointhouse and then re-erected at Balloch, from where she cruised for thirty years until laid-up. Her deterioration has recently been halted and she has been painted and partially restored. Two Clyde ferries were then completed in *Maid of Argyll* and *Maid of Skelmorlie*, both 508/53.

Associated Humber Lines Ltd then ordered three coasters for their service to Rotterdam, completed as *Wakefield* 1113/58, *Leeds* 1113/59 and *York* 1095/59, and the last ships to be completed at the Pointhouse yard were the hopper dredgers *Cressington* 1431/62 and *Aigburth* 1037/63. The yard had built over five hundred ships and was closed later in 1963 and acquired by Glasgow Corporation in 1965 for redevelopment as a trading estate.

BLYTHSWOOD SHIPBUILDING CO. LTD.

This tanker specialist yard operated successfully for forty years from a five-berth yard at Scotstoun until it could no longer compete for tanker orders due to size restrictions in the early 1960s. Hugh H. Macmillan of the famous Dumbarton ship-building family and Donald Bremner, formerly owner of the Inch yard of Dunlop, Bremner & Co. Ltd at Port Glasgow set-up the above company on 6th October,1919 and began construction of a five-berth yard with slipways of length 500 feet on a greenfield site adjacent to and partly-owned by Yarrows. They were encouraged by five tanker orders placed in the post-war freight boom, however two of these were cancelled in the subsequent slump and another was sold by Harris & Dixon Ltd of London to the British Tanker Co. Ltd. The steam tanker *British Architect* of 11624 dwt was launched in the Autumn of 1922 and completed on 19th December,1922 at a cost of £308,803 as the first ship from the yard. Two similar tankers then followed as *Toco* and *Chuky*, both 7337/22, for the Shendans Steamship Co. Ltd.

The yard was idle during 1923 until construction of three tramps was begun in 1924, two of these for Newcastle tramp owner Robert S. Dalgleish in a comparison exercise with two motortramps from Macmillan of Dumbarton. The Blythswood-built steam tramps were completed in the Autumn of 1924 as *Farnworth* and *Warkworth*, both 4971/24, and the third ship was the motortramp *Silurian* of 11000 dwt, launched on 29th May,1924 and completed on 30th October,1924 for Owen & Watkin Williams of Cardiff. This engines-aft pioneer of the modern bulk carrier was given two 6-cylinder Tosi diesel engines built under licence by Beardmore at Dalmuir to drive twin propellers and give a loaded service speed of 11 knots. She was equipped with all-electric auxiliaries and was the largest deep-sea single deck motorship in the world when completed. She moved down to Dalmuir for engine installation, but most out-fitting of Blythswood - built ships was done at Finnieston and Stobcross quays.

The yard returned to tanker construction in 1925 with the Norwegian tankers *O.A. Knudsen* 9026/25 for Knut Knutsen of Haugesund, and *Storstad* 8998/26 for A.F. Klaveness of Oslo. The yard was acquired by the Northumberland Shipbuilding Co. Ltd of Howdon-on-Tyne in 1928, and went on build 120 ships over forty years with 85 of these being tankers including coastal tankers. A close relationship was formed with Furness,Withy & Co. Ltd with tankers for management by Houlder Brothers, and cargo-liners for their Pacific coast of Canada/U.S.A. service and for the Round the World service of Prince Line. *Pacific Reliance* 6717/27, *Pacific Enterprise* 6722/27, *Pacific Pioneer* 6723/28 and *Pacific Exporter* 6723/28 were open shelter-deckers with two continuous 'tween decks with the lower of these having six refrigerated compartments for the homeward carriage of fruit. They were twin-screw motorships fitted with two 8-cylinder oil engines by J.G. Kincaid & Co. Ltd, Greenock. *Cingalese Prince* 8474/29 and *Siamese Prince* 8456/29 for Prince Line differed from this quartet in having three 'tween decks with eight compartments in each, and their oil engines were built at Hartlepool by Richardsons,Westgarth & Co. Ltd. A passenger tender *Mid Ocean* 730/29 was also built for Furness,Withy & Co. Ltd for service at Hamilton in Bermuda to disembark cruise passengers from New York, and other dry-cargo ships of this time were the cantilever-framed collier *Berwindlea* 5276/29 with topside tanks for J. Esplen of Liverpool and the Pacific trader *Talune* 2742/30 for the Union Steamship Co. Ltd,New Zealand. However tanker construction predominated :-

BENEDICK	6978/28	Bowring, London
CARONI RIVER	7807/28	Houlder Brothers
IRANIA	2186/29	H. Hannevig, Horten
LAUREL	9999/30	Olson & Wright, Stockholm
EL MIRLO	8092/30	Bowring, London
ADELLEN	7984/30	Adellen Shpg. Co. Ltd, London
IMPERIAL TRANSPORT	8022/31	Houlder Brothers
KARABAGH	6427/32	Baltic Trading Co. Ltd, London

However only one coastal tanker and one hopper dredger were completed during 1933, and only the 1500 dwt coastal tanker *Bassethound* 1174/34 during 1934 for the Hadley Shipping Co. Ltd at a cost of £36,000. Deep-sea tanker construction resumed with :-

SAN AMADO	7316/35	Eagle Oil
SAN CONRADO	7982/36	"
SAN CASIMIRO	8046/36	"
SAN CIPRIANO	7966/37	"
ADULA	8040/37	Anglo-Saxon/Shell
RAFAELA	3177/38	Dutch Shell 'mosquito' tanker
SAN DEMETRIO	8211/38	Eagle Oil
KARS	8388/39	Western Oil Shpg. Co. Ltd,London
CEDARDALE	8111/39	Admiralty
DARINA	8113/39	Anglo-Saxon/Shell
DONACILLA	8113/39	"

The relationship with Furness,Withy & Co. Ltd was continued with the dry-cargo *Argentine Transport* 4684/35, *Manchester Port* 5649/35, *Manchester City* 5600/37, *Manchester Progress* 5620/38, *Lynton Grange* 5029/37 and *Scottish Prince* 4917/38, as well as the 100-passenger *Fort Amherst* and *Fort Townshend*, both 3489/36 for their St. John's (NF) to Halifax (NS) to New York service. Five more were completed for Furness during the war as *Welsh Prince* 5148/40, *Javanese Prince* 8875/44, *Manchester Merchant* 7264/40, *Manchester Trader* 7363/41 and *Manchester Shipper* 7881/43. However the bulk of war construction was tankers with thirteen standard tankers of 12000 dwt and two steam coastal tankers for the Admiralty as well as *Empire Bairn* of 850 dwt, one of a class of 23 coastal tankers whose prototype had been *Pass of Balmaha* 758/33 built at the yard during the Depression.

Dry-cargo ships completed during the post-war years included the cargo-liners *Pacific Fortune* 9400/48, *Manchester Regiment* 7638/47 and *Manchester Merchant* 7651/51 for Furness,Withy & Co. Ltd, who also ordered two ore-carriers of 15660 dwt completed as *Sagamore* 10792/57 and *Edenmore* 10792/58. Two general cargo ships were registered under the Medomsley Shipping Co. Ltd by Van Ommeren of Holland as *Langleescot* 7030/47 and *Langleeclyde* 6642/50, and another pair were built for Greek owners as *Merchant Royal* 9722/57 and *Grecian Emblem* 9410/57. Peace-time deep-sea tanker construction had resumed with :-

BRITISH SUCCESS	8200/46	British Tanker Co. Ltd
NEOTHAUMA	8503/46	Anglo-Saoxon/Shell
NERITOPSIS	8231/46	"
LINCOLN ELLSWORTH	2483/48	A/S Laboremus, Oslo
BRITISH CHIVALRY	11217/49	British Tanker Co. Ltd
BRITISH PROGRESS	8573/48	"
BRITISH PRUDENCE	8577/49	"
HAMLET	10259/49	Bruusgaard Kjosterud,Drammen
REGENT LEOPARD	8439/49	Regent Pet. Co. Ltd,London
REGENT CARIBOU	12072/51	"
REGENT SPRINGBOK	12117/51	"
LANCING	12303/50	Melsom & Melsom, Norway
BRITISH PIONEER	8651/51	British Tanker Co. Ltd
HULDRA	2485/50	William Hansens A/S, Bergen
EDDYCLIFF	2173/53	Admiralty
CEARA	11237/52	Petroleo Brasileiro
NORTH KING	12191/52	A. G Pappadakis, Greece
NICOLAS	12395/53	Petroleum Carriers Corp.
HAROLD SLEIGH	8555/52	H.C. Sleigh Ltd.
BORDER KEEP	11321/53	Lowland Tanker Co. Ltd
BORDER MINSTREL	11330/54	"
REGENT ROYAL	10024/54	Regent Pet. Co. Ltd
BRITISH CHANCELLOR	11356/54	British Tanker Co. Ltd
HERTHA	2588/54	William Hansens A/S, Bergen
NAREK	13646/55	Baltic Trading Co. Ltd, London
HERMES	11065/55	Bruusgaard Kjosterud, Drammen
NORTH MONARCH	18210/56	A.G Pappadakis, Greece
NORTH EMPRESS	10904/57	"
NORTH COUNTESS	10962/58	"

NORTH LORD	12139/59	"
ATLANTIC KNIGHT	14839/56	Livanos, Greece
REGENT EAGLE	12384/59	Regent Pet. Co. Ltd, London
PEARLEAF	12353/59	J.I. Jacobs (Admiralty charter)
BRITISH GANNET	10963/59	British Tanker Co. Ltd
TEXACO OSLO	12884/60	Texaco NorwayA/S
HAMILTON SLEIGH	18772/61	H.C. Sleigh Ltd.

The two largest tankers, *North Monarch* and *Hamilton Sleigh*, were 650 feet in length and 27600 dwt and powered by two Rowan - Parsons turbines double reduction geared to a single shaft to give a service speed of 16 knots. The yard then won contracts to build two new sections for the war-built T2 tankers *Texaco London* and *Texaco Bristol* owned by Texas Oil, which also involved moving the navigating bridge aft, with the necessary dry-docking done at the Blythswood repair department at Govan. However by the end of 1961 the outfitting departments at Scotstoun had to be kept busy by the building of caravans and mobile homes, and only one further ship was built, the lighthouse tender *Fingal* of 1342 grt launched on 8th August,1963. The yard was then closed during 1964 and the land purchased by Yarrow to extend their warship yard in 1965.

The Bowring tanker REGENT CARIBOU of 1951.

YARROW & CO. LTD.

Alfred Fernandez Yarrow was born in London in 1842 and served an apprenticeship with marine engineers at Greenwich. He established a yard at Poplar in 1865 to undertake engineering work, and then built 150 steam launches between the years 1868 and 1875. He then graduated to small shallow-draft stern-wheelers and tunnel screw vessels for river service, many of which were shipped in pieces and assembled overseas, and then to torpedo boats and gunboats. He had established a formidable reputation for fast torpedo-boat destroyers for the Royal and overseas navies, but by 1906 had found himself isolated from the cheaper supplies of steel from the north. He then decided to move to the Clyde, a major factor being the depth of water in the Firth of Clyde which produced higher trial speeds of warships than in the shallow waters of the Thames estuary. A site at Scotstoun was chosen and all of his shipyard machinery was shipped north, and four small slipways were constructed and a covered fitting-out quay by the Spring of 1908. Three hundred workers also came north to build ten torpedo-boat destroyers for Brazil, the first being launched as *Amazonas* in July,1908.

The first torpedo boat destroyers built at Scotstoun for the Royal Navy were *Archer* and *Attack*, but in 1911 three prototypes of the modern destroyer design with a raised fo'c'stle and the high steaming speed of 35 knots were ordered. These were completed in 1912 as *Lurcher, Firedrake* and *Oak* and achieved over 35 knots on the Skelmorlie measured mile. Four similar 'L' class had been completed and three more 'M' class were under construction at the start of the Great War. The yard was then geared up for mass production and the workforce increased to 2000 men, and they built the magnificent war total of 29 destroyers, 16 gunboats, the submarine E27, three hospital ships and a floating workshop for the Royal Navy. The shallow-draft gunboats proved especially useful in action against Turkish forces on the Tigris and Euphrates leading to the capture of Baghdad.

One destroyer each was built for the navies of Japan and Italy, but all orders for further warships were cancelled by the Royal Navy at the end of 1918. Three partially completed destroyers were cut up for scrap on the berths, and a fourth afloat was towed south to be fitted out by a Royal dockyard. Yarrows for the first time in fifty years had no naval work in hand for any nation. Sir Alfred Yarrow realised the desperate situation of his yard and turned to merchant orders. One he obtained was for a large turbine-driven yacht and built along the lines of a conventional destroyer, and completed in 1920 for Major Henry Keswick as *Cutty Sark*. Two small cargo ships were completed for A. Krohn of Copenhagen as

Haderslev and *Aabenraa*, both 2088/21, and two coasters for William Robertson Ltd of Glasgow, *Essonite* and *Kyanite*, both 643/21. John Swire & Sons ordered two shallow-draft river steamers for re-erection in China as *Wanhsien* and *Chunshan* built in 1921, while the twin-screw motor-driven *Chwan Tung* was also built for re-erection at Shanghai for a Chinese ferry company in 1921. However when Sir Alfred saw that shipyards were desperately undercutting each other for orders he closed the yard at the end of 1921 and retired.

His son Harold Edgar Yarrow then saw an alternative market for the shipyard in building land boilers, and the yard re-opened later in 1922 with a staff of 24 for their exclusive construction. Harold had also served his apprenticeship as an engineer at Greenwich followed by shipbuilding experience at a French yard at Le Havre, and he was to spend most of his energy in the inter-war years in finding work for the Scotstoun yard. Finally at the end of 1923 a small order was received from the Anglo-Saxon Petroleum Co. Ltd for two shallow-draft river tankers for use on the Yangtze and the shipyard recommenced shipbuilding, completing *Shu Kwang* in 1924 and *Tien Kwang* in 1925. The yard managed to continue shipbuilding with John Swire & Sons ordering five shallow-draft river steamers and built during 1925/26, and similar craft for Argentina and India.

The construction of a Royal Navy destroyer of length 322 feet to be fitted with cruising turbines to give a service speed of 37 knots then began and she was completed as the twin-funnelled *Ambuscade* in 1927. The workforce gradually moved upwards again to 1200 workers, with four river gunboats for the Royal Navy, and three gunboats completed in 1930 for Colombia. However it was an order from Portugal for five destroyers then set the yard on its feet again after ten lean years from 1921. The first two were completely built at Scotstoun as *Vouga* and *Lima* of 1933, with the remainder built at Lisbon but from Yarrow prefabricated sections and with Yarrow also supplying their main machinery, boilers and smaller items. The destroyer leader *Dubrovnik* was completed for Yugoslavia in 1932, and the Yarrow yard was then better off for work than most other Clyde yards with two destroyers under construction for Colombia as *Antioquia* and *Caldas* of 1934. The construction of the second Royal Navy destroyer of the inter-war years then began, and she was completed as *Faulknor* of 1935, and with the build-up of naval strength to match that of Germany five more were built by the yard as *Grenville* (1936), *Isis* (1937), *Ivanhoe* (1937), *Jupiter* (1939) and *Kipling* (1939).

The netlayer and target towing vessel *Protector* was completed for the Royal Navy in 1935, and was used as an Antarctic ice patrol ship for thirty years. Two destroyers were built for the Greek Navy during 1938, *Queen Olga* and *King George I*, and had their armament fitted in Greece. Two overseas yards were also operated at this time by Yarrow, a shipbuilding and repair yard at Esquimalt in British Columbia having been established by Norman Yarrow, second son of Sir Alfred, around 1914; and Yarrow Adriatic Shipyard Ltd at Kraljevica in Yugoslavia. The Canadian yard gave valuable service in two World Wars before being sold to Burrard Drydock Company in 1952, and the Yugoslav yard built destroyers until the Yarrow interest ended in 1939.

The Scotstoun yard built eighteen destroyers during World War II, ten of these being of the 'Hunt' class, and eight 'Black Swan' class sloops of which two were for India, and two river gunboats designed for Chinese service but used elsewhere as they were completed after the fall of Hong Kong, and two steam gunboats. They also built many more geared turbines, reciprocating steam machinery and boilers for warships building in other yards, and part of the Mulberry Harbour for Normandy, and repair and conversion work. The yard was badly damaged in March,1941 by two bombs and a landmine, killing 47 shipyard workers and demolishing the electrical shop, galvanising shop, boiler shop, main office and tracing and cost offices. All the valuable company records were lost, and the engine and boiler shop was out of action for over two weeks, but fortunately the bombs missed the four ships on the berths and the shipyard re-opened after a few days to clear up the rubble. Two 'Weapon' class destroyers were completed after the war as the flotilla leaders *Battleaxe* and *Broadsword*, and orders for two sisters were cancelled.

As had happened after the Great War was repeated again with the nations of the world temporarily no longer wanting warships, and the Scotstoun yard again turned to merchant ship construction to secure its livelihood for the next ten years. It was still a golden era for the yard, nevertheless, with plenty of overtime available at nights and weekends to build a series of shallow-draft vessels for re-erection overseas. A fleet of ten shallow-draft craft, some of them paddle-driven, was built in 1946/47 for service on the Irrawaddy in Burma. Three paddle ferries were completed for the Indian High Commission for service on the Ganges, *Gomati, Yamunu* and *Sarayu*, all 746/50. A second *Ilala* was shipped in 1951 in pieces for re-erection on Lake Nyasa in Africa to replace an earlier craft of the same name built by Yarrow in 1875, and a sister *Nkwazi* was also sent in pieces in 1956. Six ferries were sent to Hong Kong, five stern-wheelers and four with tunnel screws to Burma for service on the Irrawaddy in the 1950s, six stern-wheelers to Sudan for service on the Nile, and two others for service on the Orinoco and Amazon. Three tugs were sent to Nigeria, *Adama* 325/52 for oil-related work and *Gongola* and *Yola* both 204/58 for the United Africa Co. Ltd. Nearer home, the Caledonian Steam

Packet Co. Ltd ordered the motor ferry *Maid of Ashton* 508/53 for service on the Clyde carrying 600 passengers at a speed of 15 knots.

The Admiralty took delivery of two 'Daring' class destroyers in 1953/54, *Decoy* and *Diana*, that had originally been ordered in 1945, and then ordered a much smaller class of cost-effective frigates with their turbines developing only 27% of the power of the 'Daring' class. *Hardy* (1955) was followed by *Keppel* (1956) and *Malcolm* (1957), and four 'Director' class paddle tugs for use in berthing aircraft-carriers, *Director, Dexterous, Forceful* and *Faithful*, all of 473 tons. Larger frigates followed in *Rothesay* (1960) and *Brighton* (1961) and two sisters for the South African Navy *President Kruger* (1962) and *President Pretorius* (1964). The 'Tribal' class destroyer *Ashanti* of 1961 was powered by combined steam turbine and gas turbine boost (COSAG), developed at Scotstoun by Yarrow Admiralty Research Department (Y-ARD), a separate engineering research and consultancy company set-up by Yarrow in 1946. The 'Leander' class frigates *Dido* (1963) and *Naiad* (1965) were followed by the frigate *Mermaid* (1967) originally ordered by Ghana but completed for the Royal Navy, and two seaward defence boats were delivered to Ghana similar to a pair built for the Royal Navy in 1954.

The workforce of the family-owned yard had by now moved up to 2500 workers, with the Chairman Sir Harold Yarrow sadly dying in 1962 at the age of 77 years. Sir Harold had re-opened the yard in 1922 to build land-boilers, which represented with marine boilers one-third of company business for many years afterwards, particularly for overseas power stations. He had a special interest in the Faculty of Engineering at Glasgow University, and was twice Honorary Vice President of the Royal Institution of Naval Architects. He had recently set in motion shipyard upgrading schemes that were completed in 1964 at a cost of £2.75M for prefabrication of 40-ton sections in a new 300 feet long prefabrication shop with new platers shop, sheet iron shop, electricians shop and fitting-out shop. The four old berths were reduced to three, and the yard was expanded in 1965 by the take-over of the adjacent and redundant Blythswood shipyard. Yarrow (Shipbuilders) Ltd was formed in 1966 as a subsidiary of the holding company Yarrow & Co. Ltd, and became briefly a member of Upper Clyde Shipbuilders Ltd in 1968 but withdrew in 1971.

The yard was kept busy with merchant orders in the 1960s for three ferries of 1200 tons for East African Railways in *Victoria, Uhuru* and *Umdja*. Four stern trawlers were then built for Hellyer Brothers of Hull, *Cassio, Orsino* and *Othello* all 1574/66 as well as *Coriolanus* 1105/67, which was later converted into a water quality research ship. Three survey ships were completed in 1965 as *Hecla, Hecate* and *Hydra* and were also to prove useful later in atmospheric research programmes.

The yard was then kept busy by further orders for 'Leander' class frigates *Jupiter* (1969), *Achilles* (1970), *Diomede* (1971), *Apollo* (1972) and *Ariadne* (1972), and *Canterbury* (1971) for New Zealand, *Condell* (1973) and *Lynch* (1974) for Chile. The one-off design frigates *Rahmat* (1971) for Malaysia and *Makut Rajakumain* (1973) for Thailand and S. African survey ship *Protea* (1972) were followed by five gas-turbine powered Type 21 frigates completed between 1975 and 1978 as *Ambuscade, Ardent, Arrow, Alacrity* and *Avenger.* In 1975 the Elderslie dry-docks of the former Barclay,Curle & Co. Ltd shipyard (q.v.) were acquired, and one of these was covered over for out-fitting work with another fitted with sonar pits to ease sonar installation.

The yard with its operating and training companies passed into State ownership on 1st July,1977 although the holding company Yarrow & Co. Ltd stayed outside the national umbrella. Four logistic support vessels for the Iranian Navy were under construction at this time. A covered berth was then built at the west end of the former Barclay,Curle yard to build glass reinforced plastic (GRP) minehunters, and opened in 1979, and completed the 'Brecon' class *Cottesmore* (1983) and *Middleton* (1984) and more recently units of the 'Sandown' class. The yard has played a major role in the construction of the 14-ship Type 22 frigate programme fitted with the horizontally-launched GWS25 Seawolf missile system and built ten of these, and so far has completed six of the Type 23 frigates fitted with the vertically-launched GWS26 Seawolf missile system. These frigates are :-

BROADSWORD	(1979)
BATTLEAXE	(1980)
BRILLIANT	(1981)
BRAZEN	(1982)
BOXER	(1983)
BEAVER	(1984)
BRAVE	(1986)
LONDON	(1987)
CORNWALL	(1988)
CUMBERLAND	(1989)
NORFOLK	(1990)
ARGYLL	(1991)
LANCASTER	(1992)
IRON DUKE	(1993)
MONMOUTH	(1993)
MONTROSE	(1994)

with *Somerset, Grafton* and *Sutherland* under construction. The company was sold back to private owners GEC in 1985, and currently has a good order book .

Main fabrication hall (top) outfitting hall (centre) and G.R.P. construction hall (bottom).
(Author)

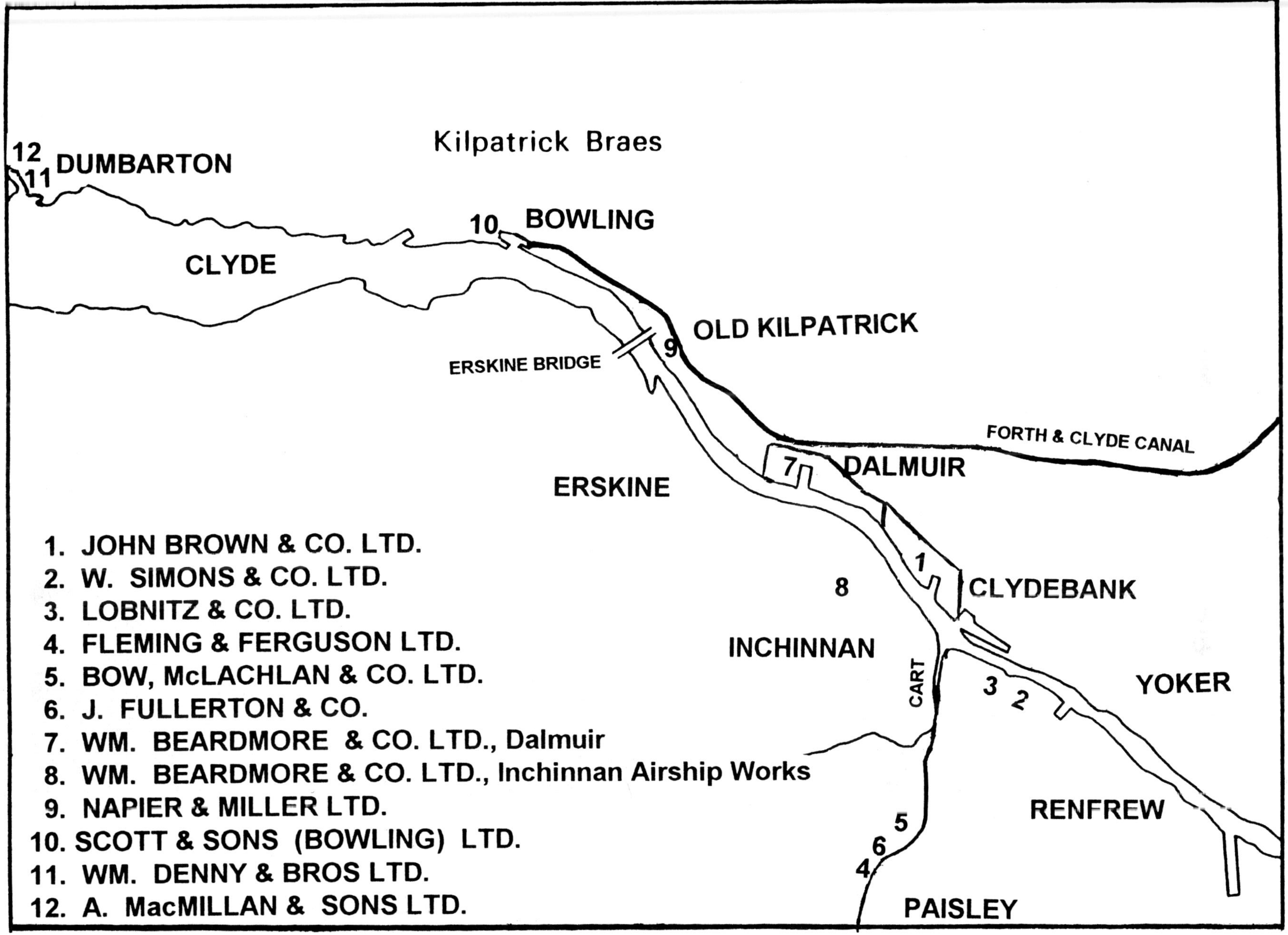

1. JOHN BROWN & CO. LTD.
2. W. SIMONS & CO. LTD.
3. LOBNITZ & CO. LTD.
4. FLEMING & FERGUSON LTD.
5. BOW, McLACHLAN & CO. LTD.
6. J. FULLERTON & CO.
7. WM. BEARDMORE & CO. LTD., Dalmuir
8. WM. BEARDMORE & CO. LTD., Inchinnan Airship Works
9. NAPIER & MILLER LTD.
10. SCOTT & SONS (BOWLING) LTD.
11. WM. DENNY & BROS LTD.
12. A. MacMILLAN & SONS LTD.

JOHN BROWN & CO. LTD

This famous shipyard at Clydebank is best remembered for building the two largest liners in the world, *Queen Mary* and *Queen Elizabeth*, for Cunard. However the policy of the yard from the outset was to build every size of ship, from the smallest Clyde paddle steamers to the largest liners of the day. James Rodger Thomson and his brother George Paul Thomson moved from their existing Clyde Bank yard at Govan to a greenfield site at West Barns farm, Kilbowie due to the Govan site being required by the Clyde Navigation Trust for the building of Prince's Dock. Their father George Thomson and uncle James Thomson had started an engine and boiler making business at Finnieston in 1847 before opening the Govan yard in 1850 and completing 120 ships. The last ship completed at Govan (Y124) was the coaster *Ferret* in 1872 for Burns Line. The Clydebank yard operated at first as J. & G. Thomson, and was taken over in 1899 by Sheffield steel maker John Brown & Co. Ltd.

Construction of the new yard began seven miles down-river from Glasgow bridge at Kilbowie in 1871 and as there was no accomodation for their workers there, they were ferried to and from Glasgow each day by paddle steamer. A new town was then built behind the yard, and the choice of name lay between Kilbowie and Clydebank, and the latter was chosen and thus the town was named after the shipyard. There was ample room to expand the yard, and the largest ocean liners of the day could be launched into the mouth of the river Cart opposite. The six-berth yard with the fitting-out basin to the west went into production in 1872 with the first ship (Y125) launched at the end of the year as the iron *Braemar Castle* of 2182 grt for Thomas Skinner of Glasgow. She was fitted with a compound two-cylinder steam engine by the company engine works at Finnieston and sailed on her trials in February,1873. She was followed by a sister *Cawdor Castle* (Y126) of 2173 grt completed in May,1873, and a further steam powered sister *Fleurs Castle* of 2472 grt in August,1874. Thomas Skinner then took delivery of the sailing ship *Dunottar Castle* of 1750 grt in December,1874 from the yard, followed by the larger steamer *Loudoun Castle* of 2495 grt in 1876. The three-masted barques *Cape of Good Hope* 1399/76, *Cape St. Vincent* 1422/77 and *Cape Breton* 1421/77 for Abram Lyle of Greenock were followed by the last sailing ship from Clydebank in *Albuera* of 1885 with the same dimensions as the Lyle barques.

The Cunarders *Saragossa* 2263/74, *Bothnia* 4535/74 and *Scythia* 4557/75 were built at the new yard and were the latest of some twenty ships so far built by J. & G. Thomson for Cunard, the previous largest from Govan being the record breaker *Russia* 2960/67 and the sisters *Abyssinia* 3376/70 and *Algeria* 3428/70. *Bothnia* and *Scythia* were a step-up in size and had compound steam engines of 3000 ihp built by the company at Finnieston. Cunard then ordered even larger steamers, completed as *Gallia* 4809/79, *Catalonia* 4638/81, *Pavonia* 5588/82 and the twin-funnelled *Servia* 7392/81 and *Aurania* 7269/83, the last pair being the largest vessels ever constructed at the time after the *Great Eastern*. They could carry 480 cabin and 750 steerage passengers as well as cargo, and could cross the Atlantic at 17 knots on a coal consumption of 190 tons/day. Their engines were also constructed at Finnieston, with the engine works then transferred to Clydebank at the end of 1883.

Union Line with services to South Africa from Southampton had taken three large iron three-masted steamers by this time, *Arab* 3170/79, *Trojan* 3555/80 and the twin-funnelled *Moor* 3597/81; and other customers for large iron steamers included Canada Shipping Co. Ltd (later part of Beaver Line service across the Atlantic) with *Lake Winnipeg* 3329/79, *Lake Manitoba* 332280 and *Lake Superior* 4562/84, and Hamburg-Amerika Line with *Hammonia* 3969/82. The latter had dimensions of length 373 feet and beam 45 feet with a three cylinder compound steam engine of 900 horse power ordered from the company works at Finnieston. However before the engine could be fitted the ship had to be righted after listing an alarming forty degrees at her launch !

The paddler *Columba* 602/78 was an early steel-hulled example from the yard for the Western Isles service of D. Hutcheson, which passed in 1879 to David MacBrayne who then ordered *Claymore* 760/81 and *Grenadier* 321/85 from the yard. Cunard had the tender *Skirmisher* 612/84 built for service at Liverpool, and the paddler *Duchess of Edinburgh* 989/80 was built for the South Eastern Railway Company, while Burns Line of Glasgow took three coasters during 1878/79 in *Walrus* , *Rook* and *Mastiff*, with the similar *Dunmore* for the Clyde Shipping Co. Ltd. Other regular customers that spanned the iron/steel changeover period in the early 1880s were Lloyd Brazileiro with their coastal passenger vessels fitted with awning decks for the service from Rio de Janeiro along the Brazilian coast and up the Amazon as far as Para. The iron-hulled *Pernambuco* 1736/75 was followed by the steel-hulled *Manaos* 1719/83, *Maranhao* 1919/87, *Brazil* 2003/90, *San Salvador* 2020/91 and *Olinda* 2020/91. Another ship built by the yard for the same service but this time owned by the Brazilian Government was *Itaipu* 1306/92.

Profile and cut-away drawing of the Blue Riband holders CITY OF NEW YORK and CITY OF PARIS of 1888.

National Line provided the next record breaker from the yard in the brig-rigged twin-funnelled *America* 5528/84, powered by a three cylinder compound engine with which she captured the Blue Riband for a few months after her entry into service. Inman Line ordered the next big Atlantic record breakers in two three-funnelled twin-screw liners built of steel and launched in 1888 as *City of New York* and *City of Paris*, the latter on 23rd October. They were of 10798 grt and were propelled by two triple expansion engines using steam from nine boilers to give a service speed of 20 knots. They were the first twin-screw liners on the Atlantic and captured the Blue Riband shortly after their introduction. They had accomodation for 540 first-class passengers with sumptuous public rooms, 200 second-class and 1000 steerage passengers. The last Atlantic liner fitted with a clipper bow and the last to be triple-expansion powered was the American-owned Red Star Line *Friesland* 6409/89 with accomodation for 328 first and second-class and 600 steerage passengers. The larger liners *Kensington* 8671/94, *Vaderland* 12018/00, *Haverford* 11635/01, *Merion* 11621/01 and *Zeeland* 11905/01 were later completed by the yard for the Red Star Line; with Cunard ordering two completed as *Saxonia* 14281/00 and *Pannonia* 9807/03.

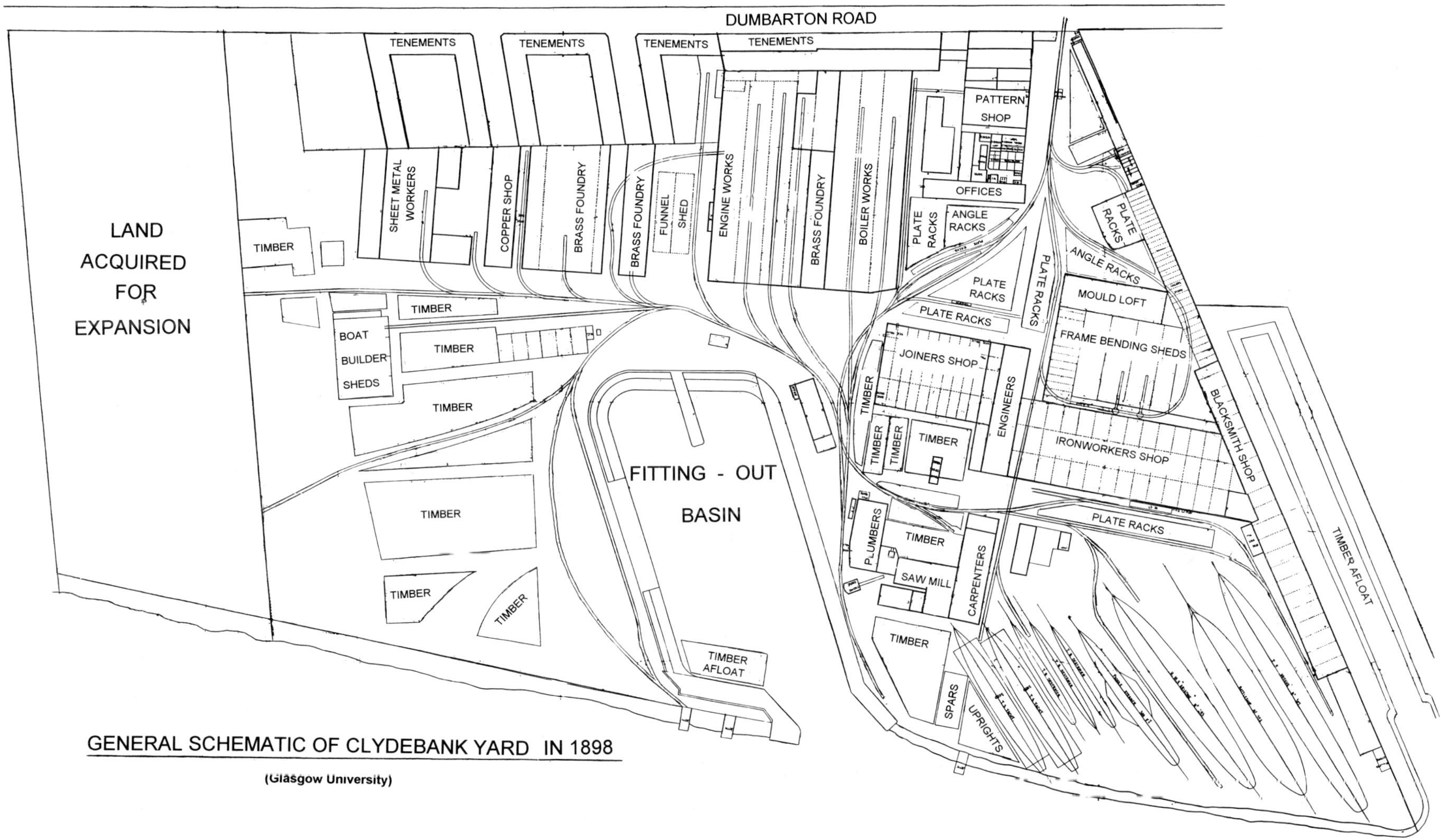

GENERAL SCHEMATIC OF CLYDEBANK YARD IN 1898

(Glasgow University)

The yard began to build a formidable reputation for short-sea packets with eight completed for the Channel Islands service of the London and South Western Railway Company in the 1890s. They were each built in the short time of six months with *Columbia* and *Alma* both 1169/94 the first to be fitted with cabin berths for the night service between Southampton and Le Havre. Paddlers built included *Minerva* 315/93, *Glen Sannox* 610/92, *Glen Rosa* 306/93, *Duchess of Rothesay* 385/95, *Jupiter* 394/96 and *Juno* 592/98 for Clyde service; the Blackpool paddler *Greyhound* 540/95 completed in four months; the Northern Ireland paddlers *Slieve Bearnagh* 383/94 and *Slieve Donard* 341/93; the South Coast paddler *Brighton Queen* 603/97. The steam yacht *Urania* of 650 tons was also completed in the short space of four months at this time.

Royal Mail Line ordered two liners for their Central / South American services completed as *Nile* 5855/93 and *Danube* 5891/93. Two fine twin-screw liners which could double as troop transports were then delivered to the Russian Volunteer Fleet Association as *Kiev* 5566/96 and *Moskva* 7267/98. They were propelled by twin triple-expansion engines, the latter having water-tube boilers and both could carry 1000 troops. The large American yacht *Mayflower* was completed in 1896 and later became the Presidential yacht. However a slump in orders in 1897 forced the Thomson family to sell out to a consortium which renamed the yard as the Clydebank Engineering & Shipbuilding Co. Ltd, and a dozen ships were completed under this title.

In 1899 the yard was taken over by Sheffield steel makers John Brown & Co. Ltd, who were looking for an outlet for steel plate and particularly armoured plate - a speciality of their Atlas works at Sheffield. The Clydebank yard had already acquired a good reputation for building armoured warships and this was to be strengthened by the new owners. The earliest naval vessels built at the yard were two small British gunboats launched in 1877, *Firebrand* and *Firefly*. They were followed by the torpedo gunboat *Scout* of 1885 and sixteen more for the Royal Navy, and many similar vessels for overseas navies including Russia, Spain, and Holland. Several small cruisers followed including the British *Terpsichore, Thetis* and *Tribune* of 1890/91, and the Spanish *Reina Regente* of 1888. Two cruisers were completed for Australian service as *Tauranga* and *Ringarooma*, as well as *Chiyoda* of 1890 for the Japanese Navy. The Royal Navy battleships *Ramillies* and *Jupiter* were completed in October,1893 and May,1897, and were joined by the four-funnelled heavy cruiser *Terrible* launched in May,1895 after the short building time of 14 months on the slipway. The latter was armed with two 9.2" guns and twelve 6" guns when commissioned in 1896, but later returned to the yard in 1902 for an 18 month refit, during which time a further four 6" guns were installed. Further four-funnelled

LUSITANIA arriving at New York at the end of her maiden voyage in September,1907.

cruisers were completed in *Europa* (1899), *Ariadne* (1900), *Sutlej* (1902), *Bacchante* (1903), *Leviathan* (1904) and *Antrim* (1905), as well as the large Japanese battleship *Asahi* of 1899.

A test tank was opened at the yard in 1903 with dimensions of length 400 feet and width 20 feet, and was a sound investment for model trials of liners and warships and later was used to predict the exact finishing position of the large Cunard liners when launched into the mouth of the river Cart. A joint shareholding was taken in 1905 in the Coventry Ordnance Works with the Fairfield yard, in order to secure supllies of naval ordnance. The pre-Dreadnought British battleship *Hindustan* of 1905 was followed by the battlecruiser *Inflexible* of 1908, and the keel was then laid of the Australian battlecruiser *Australia* during 1910. The Parsons steam turbine was widely used to power passenger liners built at the yard, but in 1908 a licence was obtained from Charles G. Curtis of New York to manufacture the simpler, sturdier Curtis turbine, offering advantages to warships with economy at low speed and giving better cruising range. The first Curtis turbine was installed in the destroyer *Brisk* of 1909, followed by the cruisers *Bristol* of 1910 and *Southampton* of 1911, and by the end of the Great War over 250 warships had been fitted with Brown-Curtis turbines including seven capital ships, and during the 1920s they were also fitted to the 'County' class cruisers, of which two were also built at Clydebank.

However the introduction of the direct-drive Parsons turbine to the North Atlantic passenger trade had been made in the twin Allan Line ships *Victorian* from Workman,Clark and *Virginian* from Alexander Stephen in 1904/05. This was reinforced by the Cunarder *Carmania* 19524/05 from the yard, a comparison being made with her quadruple-expansion powered sister *Caronia* 19594/05 also from Clydebank. In *Carmania* three Parsons turbines drove three propellers and came through with flying colours, and Parsons turbines could then be installed with confidence in the record-breaking Cunard sister liners *Lusitania* 31550/07 from Clydebank and *Mauretania* 31938/07 from Swan,Hunter & Wigham Richardson Ltd on the Tyne. *Lusitania* was launched on 7th June,1906 by Lady Inverclyde and ran four days of trials at the beginning of August,1907 and sailed on her maiden voyage from Liverpool on 7th September,1907, two months before the *Mauretania*.

In 1906 the entrance on the west side of the fitting-out basin gained a 150-ton capacity hammer-head crane constructed by Sir William Arrol & Company, and replaced the existing sheerlegs for lifting boilers and engines aboard ship. Vessels were constructed at this time from berths on both sides of the fitting-out basin, termed the East yard and the West yard. The latter had three berths and the sawmill, and had been laid out immediately after the take-over in 1899. New platers and engineers shops were built behind them in the West yard, and the boundary on its west side marked the start of the Beardmore yard at Dalmuir. Two of the three berths in the West yard had been covered over by 1912 and were equipped with overhead gantry cranes.

In 1907 a controlling interest was taken in Belfast shipbuilders Harland & Wolff Ltd, to give further outlets for Sheffield steel plate, with Belfast indirectly gaining the turbine technology it formerly lacked. As a result of this, one of a three-ship order for cargo-liners for Hamburg-Amerika Line was transferred from Belfast to Clydebank and completed as *Preussen* 8046/10. The low-pressure Parsons turbine for the White Star liner *Laurentic*, which had two sets of four-cylinder triple expansion engines exhausting into this turbine and was completed at Belfast in 1909, was also made at Clydebank. The turbines for the Aberdeen Line *Demosthenes* completed at Belfast in 1911 also came from Clydebank.

The New Zealand refrigerated trade had been important to Clydebank throughout this period, using the new Linde refrigerating plant for the Scottish Shire Line managed by Turnbull,Martin & Company and others. A total of eleven refrigerated steamers were built at this time by the yard :-

NAIRNSHIRE	5713/98	Scottish Shire Line
FIFESHIRE	5672/98	"
ESSEX	7130/02	Federal S.N.
DORSET	7060/03	"
SOMERSET	7150/03	"
SUFFOLK	7573/02	"
KAIKOURA	6998/03	New Zealand Shipping Co. Ltd
KAIPARA	7392/03	"
ARGYLLSHIRE	10392/11	Scottish Shire Line
SHROPSHIRE	11911/11	"
WILTSHIRE	10390/12	"

New Zealand liner NIAGARA of 1913 was the first liner to be oil-fired. (W.S.P.L.)

Four views of AQUITANIA of 1914 under construction in the East Yard and in service.

AQUITANIA

Two liners were completed for the Australian trade of Orient Line, *Orsova* 12036/09 and *Orama* 12927/11; while the twin-funnelled *Niagara* 13415/13 for the Union Steamship Co. of New Zealand was the first liner to be oil-fired; and two out of a four-ship order for Russian liners with Clydeside yards were built at Clydebank as *Emperor Nicholas L* 5644/09 and *Emperor Peter the Great* 5556/13. The Pacific Steam Navigation Company had taken delivery of a pair of West Coast South American traders in *Kenuta* 4953/07 and *Lima* 4946/07, while the troopship *Northbrook* had been completed in 1906 for the Indian Government and *Zealandia* 6683/10 was completed for the Australian trades of Huddart,Parker of Melbourne.

The Clydebank yard enhanced its reputation for short-sea packets during this period with further ships for the London & South Western Railway; Midland Railway; Lancashire,Yorkshire & North West Railway; a trio for Fishguard & Rosslare Railway in *St. David* 2529/06, *St. Patrick* 2587/06 and *St. Andrew* 2528/08; and a further trio for the Harwich to Hook of Holland service of the Great Eastern Railway in *Copenhagen* 2570/08, *Munich* 2570/08 and *St. Petersburg* 2548/10. Burns Line continued to build at the yard for their Glasgow to Belfast service with *Partridge* 1523/06 and *Woodcock* 1523/06, and the yard also continued to build Clyde paddle steamers such as the turbine-powered *Atalanta* 480/06 as well as a trio for the Barry Railway Company in *Barry* 497/07, *Devonia* 520/05 and *Gwalia* 562/05, and the more famous Thames paddler *Golden Eagle* 793/10.

In December,1910 Cunard placed an order with the yard for a third larger running partner for *Lusitania* and *Mauretania* with her design under strict Admiralty control. The huge keel and massive frames of the this Transatlantic liner began to take shape during 1912, and she was launched as *Aquitania* on 21st April,1913 with an overall length of 901 feet, breadth 97 feet and depth 64 feet. Her steam turbines had the combined power of 56,000 shp to drive four massive propellers, and she left the fitting-out basin in May,1914 for three days of trials in the Firth of Clyde during which she successfully reached 24 knots. She left Liverpool on her maiden voyage on 30th May with a total passenger capacity of 3230 in three classes of 618/614/1998.

Naval work also started to increase in the years immediately before the Great War, with the battlecruiser *Australia* commissioned in June,1913 and the similar *Tiger* commissioned in October,1914. The battleship *Barham* was laid down in February,1913 and further work was underway at Clydebank on the outbreak of war for Russia, Spain and Turkey. *Barham* was commissioned for war service in October,1915; and was joined by the battlecruiser *Repulse* in August,1916 after the very short building time of 18 months, having been laid down in January,1915 and launched a year later. Two cruisers were also completed by the yard in *Canterbury*

The launch of the battlecruiser HOOD on 22nd August, 1918 at Clydebank
(Glasgow University)

and in commission as the flagship of the fleet.

(1916) and *Ceres* (1917) and 34 destroyers and three 'E' class submarines E35,E36 and E37. The destroyers were completed almost monthly, and the sets of forgings for their machinery were produced at Sheffield at the rate of two/month, with half being distributed amongst other destroyer builders throughout the country. The submarines were launched with their engines installed, but E35 was badly delayed when she slipped off her blocks during launching in 1916. In addition a railway steamer previously ordered by the Great Eastern Railway for Harwich to Hook of Holland service was purchased on the stocks in February,1917 and completed as the seaplane carrier *Pegasus*. She had Brown-Curtis geared turbines powering twin propellers, and had a large hangar aft served by two cranes as well as a forward flight deck and two raked tall funnels. The only merchant ship of note completed during the war by the yard was the Orient liner *Ormonde* 15047/17, and was notable in being the first liner to be fitted with geared turbines.

Naval work still dominated the yard during 1919 with the battlecruiser *Hood*, laid down in September,1916 continuing her fitting-out until March,1920. She had an overall length of 860 feet, breadth of 105 feet and draught of 31 feet and her massive Brown-Curtis geared turbines produced a powerful 144,000 shp and 31 knots. Her armament included eight 15", twelve 5.5", four 4" and nine smaller guns as well as six torpedo tubes. Five standard merchant ships were completed during 1919, the tanker *War Hermit* 5236/19, and the 'A' types *War Thistle* 5211/19 and *War Rider* 5227/19, and 'B' types *Bata* 5328/19 and *Bodnant* 5342/19 for Elder,Dempster with the latter named in honour of Lord Aberconway of Bodnant, Chairman of John Brown & Co. Ltd.

Although John Brown & Co. Ltd ceased to be majority shareholders in Harland & Wolff Ltd in 1918 due to an alteration in the number of shares of the latter, seven ships had already been transferred from Belfast to Clydebank. These were a passenger liner for Union-Castle Line, and five cargo-liners for Elder Dempster and one for Royal Mail Line as the motorship *Lochkatrine* 9419/22, with her oil engine by the Harland & Wolff works at Lancefield. The passenger liner was launched on 9th March,1921 by the Prince of Wales as *Windsor Castle* and was a sister to *Arundel Castle* 19500/21 completed at Belfast. *Windsor Castle* was completed in March,1922 with four funnels and the sisters were the last such liners ever built. The Elder,Dempster cargo-liners were *Ekari* 6711/20, *Calgary* 7275/21, *Calumet* 7268/23, *Cochrane* 7276/23 and *Cariboo* 7275/24, the last four for the West African trade from Canada/U.S.A. The yard then went on to complete more than a dozen large liners over the next decade :-

MONTCALM	16418/22	Canadian Pacific
MONTCLARE	16314/22	"

RANGITATA of 1929 (top) of New Zealand Shipping Co. Ltd
WINDSOR CASTLE of 1922 (centre) of Union-Castle Line
FRANCONIA of 1923 (bottom) of Cunard Line.

FRANCONIA	20175/23	Cunard Line
ALAUNIA	14030/25	"
ORONSAY	20001/25	Orient Line
AVILA	12872/27	Blue Star Line
AVELONA	12858/27	"
DUCHESS OF BEDFORD	20123/28	Canadian Pacific
DUCHESS OF RICHMOND	20325/28	"
DUCHESS OF YORK	20021/29	"
RANGITIKI	16985/29	New Zealand Shipping Co. Ltd
RANGITATA	16969/29	"
RANGITANE	16712/29	"
EMPRESS OF BRITAIN	42348/31	Canadian Pacific

Franconia was one of five sisters Cunard ordered for their New York service, while *Alaunia* belonged to their 'A' class for Canadian service. The *Duchess of Bedford* was launched by Mrs. Baldwin, wife of the Prime Minister, on 24th January,1928 and this Canadian Pacific quartet (the fourth was built by Beardmore as *Duchess of Atholl*) were cabin class twin-screw turbine-driven ships with a service speed of 18 knots. They were notable for high-pressure, high-temperature steam and water-tube boilers, the steam pressure being 350 lb/sq.in. and temperature 686 degrees F, and were among the first liners to be fitted with cupro-nickel condenser tubes.

The importance of Canadian Pacific to Clydebank at this time should not be underestimated as their celebrated *Empress of Britain* represented nearly three years work and they also ordered three smaller ferries from the yard for Canadian service, completed as the three-funnelled *Princess Elaine* 2125/28, *Princess Kathleen* 5875/25 and *Princess Marguerite* 5875/25. *Empress of Britain* was built for a new service from Southampton to the St. Lawrence and her hull was ice-strengthened and had dimensions of length 758 feet and breadth 97 feet, and was designed with two tall masts and three outsize funnels. She had five cargo holds with the first three for general cargo, the fourth for refrigerated cargo and the fifth for passenger baggage, and was launched on 11th June,1930 by the Prince of Wales (later the Duke of Windsor). She was fitted with twelve massive steam turbines and nine water-tube boilers driving four propellers and left the fitting-out basin for trials on 4th April,1931. The Skelmorlie measured mile runs produced speeds in excess of her service speed of 24 knots, and she left Southampton on her maiden voyage on 27th May,1931 capable of carrying 465 first-class, 260 tourist-class and 470 third-class passengers.

The company suffered badly from a shortage of work in 1922 with the shops empty and all of the machines standing idle. Two cable ships were tendered for the Eastern Telegraph Company at cost price to provide work for the nucleus of the best

Launch of EMPRESS OF BRITAIN on 11th June,1930.

Departing for sea trials on 4th April,1931 (centre) and pictured on trials (bottom).

Clydebank workers, and were completed as *Mirror* 1869/23 and *Norseman* 1892/23. The steam-powered engines-amidships tanker *Invergordon* 6921/23 for the British-Mexican Petroleum Co. Ltd was followed by two engines-aft motor tankers, *Lumen* 6483/25 for H.E. Moss,Liverpool and *British Diplomat* 6498/26 for the British Tanker Co. Ltd. The latter pair were the first to be fitted with Sulzer oil engines built at Clydebank. Short-sea packets included *St. Helier* 1949/25 and *St. Julien* 1943/25 for the Great Western Railway, and *Antwerp* 2927/20 and *Bruges* 2929/20 and the three sisters *Vienna* 4326/29, *Prague* 4320/30 and *Amsterdam* 4320/30 for the London & North East Railway service from Harwich to the Hook of Holland. The latter trio had berths for 550 passengers with good public facilities such as smoking lounge and a restaurant served by an all-electric galley.

Admiralty contracts were scarce in the 1920s, with a cruiser which had been launched on 23rd December,1919 and then laid-up for five years finally completing as the three-funnelled *Enterprise* in 1926. She was followed by two 'County' class cruisers completed for the Australian Government as *Canberra* and *Australia* in 1928, their three funnels being raised in height just before they were commissioned. Four destroyers were then completed in 1930 as *Acasta, Achates, Beagle* and *Basilisk*. During 1930/31 negotiations were concluded with Cunard Line for the construction of a giant quadruple-screwed Atlantic liner of length 1019 feet and accomodation for 2200 passengers. The main berth of the East yard was then specially extended and strengthened at a cost of £45900 and a 10-ton hammerhead crane installed, and she was laid down as Y534 on 27th December,1930 and work continued on the hull until construction was stopped a year later when the company overdraft was in excess of bank limits. The East and West yards were closed to all intents and purposes except for apprentices, and a squad of painters employed to continually paint the massive hull of Y534 to prevent corrosion.

In 1933 the Admiralty placed orders for the destroyers *Fortune* and *Foxhound*, and sloop *Halcyon*, minesweeper *Skipjack* and yacht *Enchantress*, which enabled the West yard to be re-opened later that year. The East yard work on the giant liner Y534 resumed on 3rd April,1934 after the Government offered Cunard a repayable loan on condition they merged with the ailing White Star Line. Some four hundred men then worked for over a month to remove 130 tons of rust from her plates, and she was successfully launched as *Queen Mary* on 26th September,1934 by H. M. Queen Mary. Her name had been kept a secret until the last moment before launch, and she was then fitted out by May,1936 and captured the Blue Riband of the Atlantic in August of that year. Her dimensions were impressive with an overall length of 1018 feet, breadth of 118 feet, 80774 grt, with accomodation for 776 cabin, 784 tourist and 579 third class passengers and well furnished public

The magnificent Cunard Line QUEEN MARY pictured just after leaving the Clydebank yard on 24th March,1936 for trials with the yard at the top of the photograph, and also seen in service (below). (Glasgow University)

QUEEN ELIZABETH just before her launch in September,1938 (top); leaving the Clyde in February,1940 (centre) and in service (bottom).

rooms. She had a steam whistle on each of her three funnels, which expelled smoke from her 24 watertube boilers feeding 16 single reduction steam turbines and powering quadruple screws.

The keel of a sister liner for Cunard was on 4th December,1936 laid down on the vacant main berth of the East yard and was launched on 27th September,1938 as *Queen Elizabeth* by H. M. Queen Elizabeth at the time of the Munich crisis. Fitting-out work was still continuing when war was declared, and she left the Clyde in grey war-time paint with some yard workers still aboard on 2nd March,1940 for New York, being converted a year later into a troopship at Sydney(N.S.W.). Her dimensions were equally impressive with an overall length of 1031 feet, breadth of 118 feet, 83673 grt, with accomodation for 823 first-class, 662 cabin, and 798 tourist class passengers in peace-time service. She had only half as many boilers as the *Queen Mary* with a more modern appearance of two funnels, but like her sister huge steam turbines from Clydebank drove quadruple screws. The internal accomodation of both 'Queens' was changed for their war-time service to allow up to 16,000 troops to be carried across the Atlantic in 8,000 bunks on a 'double-shift' sleep system.

Stephen Piggott, an American who had come across the Atlantic to work in the yard with the Curtis turbine in 1909, succeeded Sir Thomas Bell as Managing Director of the yard in 1935. The latter had been with the company for 49 years, and had been manager of the engineering works at Clydebank since the take-over by John Brown & Co. Ltd in 1899. Further Admiralty contracts had been placed in 1934 for a 'Town' class cruiser, which was launched on 10th March,1936 as *Southampton* and commissioned in March,1937; and the submarine depot ship *Maidstone*, which was launched on 21st October,1937 and completed in May,1938; and the destroyer depot ship *Forth* launched in 1938. Four British destroyers *Ilex* (1936), *Icarus* (1937), *Jackal* (1938) and *Javelin* (1939) and two Argentinean destroyers *San Juan* and *San Luis* completed during 1937, in the same year the keel of the battleship *Duke of York* was laid following the end of Treaty limitations. Merchant ship construction consisted of the Port Line cargo-liner *Port Wyndham* 8580/35, three cargo-liners for Federal Steam Navigation as *Essex* 11063/36, *Sussex* 11063/37 and *Suffolk* 11145/39, and the Anglo-American Oil tanker *Comanchee* 6837/36 powered by a Doxford oil engine.

The yard was then turned over to naval construction as had happened during the Great War. The output was enormous, consisting of the battleship *Duke of York* completed in November,1941, the aircraft carrier *Indefatigable* during 1942, the cruisers *Fiji* (1940), *Bermuda* (1940), the monitor *Roberts* (1940), the depot ship *Hecla* (1941) and 28 destroyers, two frigates and eight invasion barges. The battleship *Vanguard* was laid down in October,1941 but was completed too late for

The submarine depot ship MAIDSTONE of 1938 (top), and frigate LOCH FADA of 1944

The battleship VANGUARD passing Greenock for trials in 1946,
QUEEN ELIZABETH is anchored at the Tail of the Bank.

active war service in April,1946. The total warship programme totalled 300,000 displacement tons propelled by machinery built at Clydebank of approximately two million horse power. In addition, repairs and alterations on 116 warships of every type and size had been made, while eleven merchant ships had been converted for war-time needs. The Dalmuir fitting-out basin of the defunct Beardmore yard (q.v.) was used to complete eleven ships during the war. A cargo-liner laid down for Port Line in 1941 was completed as the escort carrier *Nairana*, while a similar hull was completed for the New Zealand Shipping Co. Ltd as *Hororata* 12090/42. Many warship orders were cancelled at the end of the war, and two 'Battle' class destroyers did not complete until the Spring of 1947, with one incomplete cruiser afloat and laid-up indefinitely in the fitting-out basin.

The Royal Fleet Review in 1946 at the Tail of the Bank was a sight to gladden the hearts of all Clydesiders and was recognition of the hard war-time work of the Clydeside shipyards. Another such sight was the Cunarder *Queen Elizabeth* anchored at the Tail of the Bank in 1946, receiving her first Cunard colours and being prepared for Transatlantic service, and she sailed from Southampton on 16th October,1946 on her first commercial voyage. The Clydebank workforce had suffered many casualties in their homes during air-raids on 13th March,1941, which largely missed the yard and the target of the battleship *Duke of York*, but left only seven homes undamaged and further incendiary raids took place in May,1941. Damage to the yard was light and was soon repaired to continue the heavy work oad of the shipyard and engineering works. Apart from the engines built for the Clydebank-built warships, the works produced 48 sets of machinery of 300,000 horse-power for ships being built elsewhere, and also found time to build boilers, bombs and guns of all sizes.

The yard was gradually switched back to merchant construction during 1946 with much shipyard machinery in need of thorough overhaul. The main customers for passenger liners and cargo-liners were Cunard Line, P & O and their subsidiary New Zealand Shipping Co. Ltd, and the Portuguese Cia Colonial de Navegacao. The latter ordered a pair of intermediate passenger liners completed as *Patria* 13196/47 and *Imperio* 13186/48 of similar size to *Media* 13345/47 for Cunard, who had also ordered a cruise liner for delivery in 1948. *Caronia* 34172/48 was the largest post-war liner built in Britain until the *Queen Elizabeth 2* was completed by the yard in 1969, and was given a green hull for long cruises with seasonal use on the Atlantic. She was launched on 30th October,1947 by Princess Elizabeth, her length was 715 feet, breadth 91 feet and depth 70 feet to promenade deck, and she was powered by steam turbines with the high pressure double reduction geared and the others single reduction geared. Her twin propellers drove her at 22 knots and

BUILT AND ENGINED

BY

JOHN BROWN AND CO. LTD.

CLYDEBANK, SCOTLAND.

Company advertisement of 1949 featuring SUSSEX (top), RANGITANE (centre) and CITY OF BIRMINGHAM (bottom).
(John Brown & Co. Ltd)

she entered service in January,1949 with accomodation for 581 first-class and 381 cabin-class passengers. The pre-war Cunard liners *Scythia* and *Samaria* were refitted by the yard, and the company returned to the yard for four liners for their Liverpool to Canada service and completed as *Saxonia* 21637/54, *Ivernia* 21717/55, *Carinthia* 21946/56 and *Sylvania* 21989/57, each propelled by four geared turbines driving twin propellers at 19.5 knots with accomodation for around 900 passengers. The New Zealand Shipping Co. Ltd took delivery of two fine passenger liners for their Antipodes trade in *Rangitane* 21867/49 and *Ruahine* 17851/51, both motorships with accomodation for 416 and 267 passengers respectively; while the owners also took the opportunity to recondition and re-engine the pre-war survivors *Rangitata* and *Rangitiki,* while parent company P & O took delivery of *Arcadia* 29734/54 for their Australian service with accomodation for a total of 1413 passengers.

The most prestigious order completed by the yard in post-war years was the Royal yacht *Britannia*, launched on 16th April,1953 by H.M. The Queen on the same tide as the Greek liner *Olympia* from the Stephen yard, which in courtesy launched her unnamed as Y636 so as not to detract from the glamorous occasion at Clydebank. However the bread-and-butter work of the East and West Yards in post-war years was tankers and cargo-liners, the latter including :-

PORT WELLINGTON	10588/46	Port Line
NORFOLK	11272/47	Federal S.N.
HAPARANGI	11281/47	New Zealand Shipping Co. Ltd
HAURAKI	11272/47	"
HINAKURA	11272/49	"
SUSSEX	11272/49	Federal S.N.
NOTTINGHAM	6689/50	"
CITY OF OXFORD	7593/48	Ellerman Lines
CITY OF BIRMINGHAM	7577/49	"
ADELAIDE STAR	12037/50	Blue Star Line
SINGAPORE	9236/51	P & O
SUNDA	9235/52	"
CLAN MACINTOSH	6454/51	Clan Line
CLAN MACINTYRE	6399/52	"
OTAKI	10923/53	New Zealand Shipping Co. Ltd
ESSEX	10936/54	Federal S.N.
NORTHUMBERLAND	10935/55	"
WHANGAROA	8701/55	New Zealand Shipping Co. Ltd
WHARANUI	8701/56	"
SALMARA	8202/56	P & O
SALSETTE	8202/56	"
OTAIO	13141/58	New Zealand Shipping Co. Ltd
CLAN MACINDOE	8991/59	Clan Line

M.V. "OTAIO"

THE establishment of John Brown & Co. (Clydebank) Limited, covering over 80 acres, contains 6 building berths and is particularly well equipped for the construction of Mail Steamers, Cargo Vessels, Oil Tankers, Channel Steamers and Yachts; Warships of all types, dimensions and horse-power; Reciprocating Machinery, Geared Turbines and Diesel Engines.

JOHN BROWN
& CO. (CLYDEBANK) LTD.
Engineering & Shipbuilding Works
CLYDEBANK, SCOTLAND

Telephone: Clydebank 2020 (10 lines) *Telegrams: "Shipyard" Clydebank*
Registered Office: CARLISLE STREET, SHEFFIELD
London Office: 8 THE SANCTUARY, WESTMINSTER, S.W.1

Company advertisement featuring OTAIO of 1958, and P & O cargo-liner SALSETTE of 1956.

P & O liner ARCADIA of 1954 (top), and Swedish America Line KUNGSHOLM of 1966.

GENERAL SCHEMATIC OF CLYDEBANK YARD IN 1950

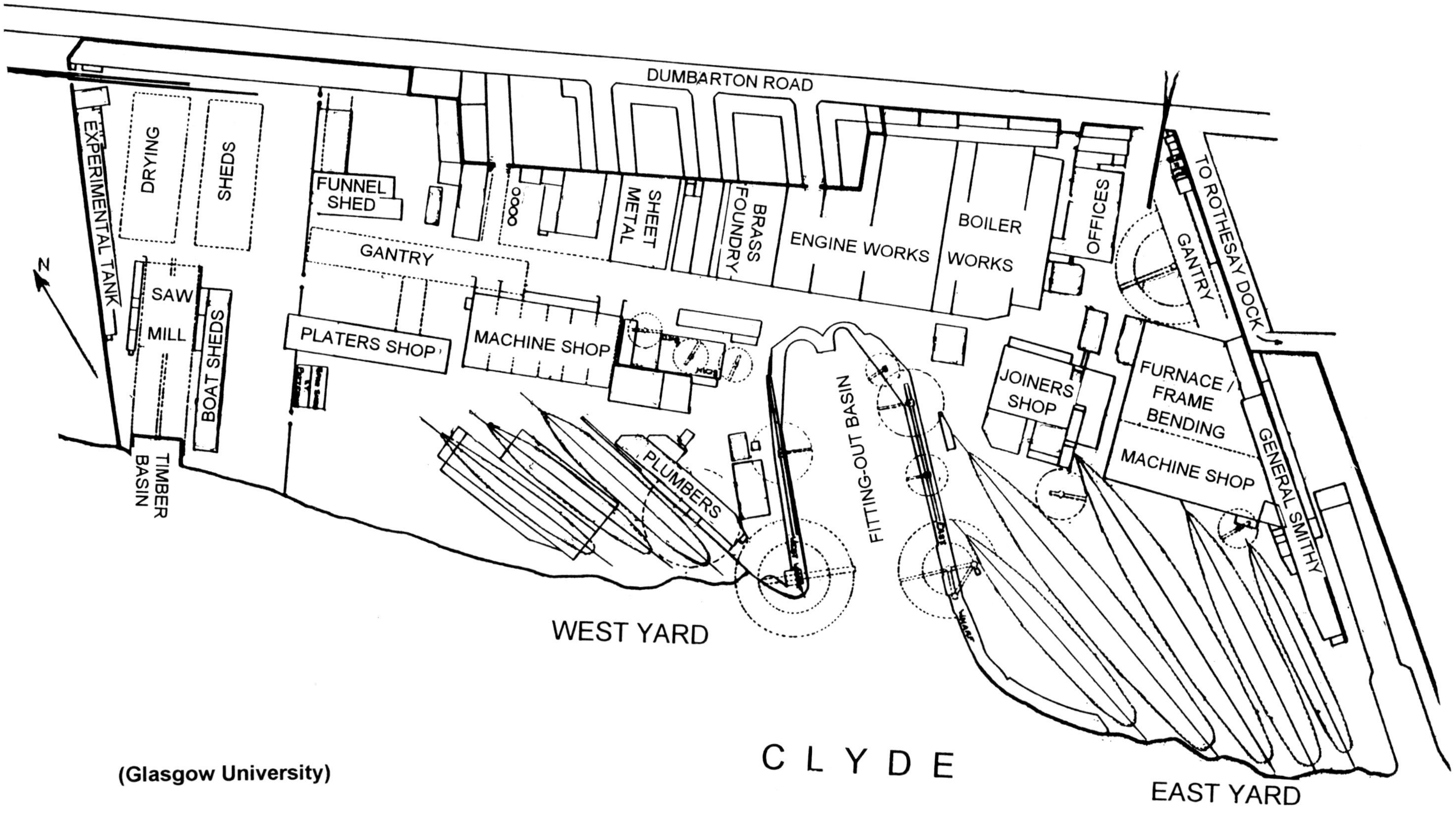

(Glasgow University)

CLAN MACNAIR	9137/62	"
SOMERSET	7602/62	Federal S.N.

and the ever-escalating size of tankers :-

VIKLAND	12802/50	Vestfold Co,Panama (Rasmussen)
VIKFOSS	12812/50	"
OTTAWA	12802/50	Unitas Inc, Panama
KIPAWA	12891/51	"
CLYDEWATER	12703/51	Tidewater Inc., Panama
ALMAK	12618/52	Alva S.S. Co. Ltd,London
ALGOL	12618/52	"
EAST RIVER	12698/54	Tidewater Inc., Panama
STANVAC AUSTRALIA	17297/55	Vacuum-Oil Co. Inc.
ALVEGA	21258/56	Alvega S.S. Co. Ltd
EDGEWATER	12732/57	Tidewater Inc., Panama
SCOTTISH PTARMIGAN	12685/58	Scottish Tanker Co. Ltd
LINCOLN	12780/58	Federal S.N. Co. Ltd
BRITISH SAILOR	20961/53	British Tanker Co. Ltd
BRITISH SOLDIER	21082/54	"
BRITISH INDUSTRY	21083/57	"
BRITISH TRADER	21019/57	"
BRITISH DUCHESS	27585/58	"
BRITISH JUDGE	27124/59	"
BRITISH QUEEN	32187/59	"
DERBY	31791/60	Federal S.N.
KENT	31763/61	"
BRITISH HUSSAR	32341/62	British Tanker Co. Ltd
BRITISH MARINER	43378/63	"
BRITISH CONFIDENCE	37978/65	"

Smaller vessels were built for the Eastern Region of the British Transport commission and included the Harwich to Zeebrugge train ferries *Suffolk Ferry* 3134/47, *Norfolk Ferry* 3157/51 and *Essex Ferry* 3242/57, and the Harwich to Hook of Holland ferries *Arnhem* 5008/47 and *Amsterdam* 5092/50, the latter reviving the name of a ferry built by the yard twenty years earlier. Admiralty contracts included the completion of the laid-up 6" gun cruiser *Tiger* in 1959 with her aft turrets replaced by a hangar, the guided missile cruiser *Hampshire* (1963), and the frigates *Lynx* (1956), *Yarmouth* (1960) and *Aurora* (1963) with *Brahmaputra* (1958) for the Indian Navy. The assault ship *Intrepid* was launched on 25th June,1964 and commissioned in March,1967 with stern launching facilities for four large landing craft and davit handling for four assault craft, and also carried facilities for five helicopters and 111 marines.

The East Yard had four berths in 1960 with two berths in the West Yard, which had better steel fabrication and heavier berth cranage. Under Managing

Three for Cunard Line from Clydebank in CAROLIA of 1948 (top) seen at New York, SAXONIA of 1954 (centre) and QUEEN ELIZABETH 2 of 1969.

Director Dr. John Brown, some important merchant orders were completed in the 1960s at Clydebank including the South African mail liner *Transvaal Castle*, launched by Lady Cayzer, wife of Sir Nicholas Cayzer - Chairman of the British & Commonwealth Shipping Group, in January, 1961. She was of 32697 grt and an innovation on the Cape Town run as for the first time she carried all her 750 passengers in one class, and was later known affectionately as the 'Grand Hotel of the South Atlantic', her maiden voyage being in January,1962. The Ocean Transport & Trading Group (formerly Blue Funnel) took delivery of the white-hulled passenger/cargo *Centaur* 7990/64 for the Singapore to Fremantle service with accomodation for 198 passengers aft and carrying refrigerated cargo, and also the cargo-liner *Glenfinlas* 12094/66. The Swedish-Amerika Line twin-funnelled *Kungsholm* 26678/66 with accomodation for 750 passengers had Gotaverken oil engines specified by her owner, which were brought to Clydebank by sea and on trials gave in excess of her 21 knot service speed. Cunard sent their *Saxonia* and *Ivernia*, completed by the yard in 1954/55, back to the yard for conversion to cruise liners in 1963, and emerged as *Carmania* and *Franconia* in light green hull colours.

In 1966 the engineering works was separated from the shipyard by the creation of John Brown Engineering (Clydebank) Ltd, the shipyard having operated as John Brown & Co (Clydebank) Ltd since 1953. The Geddes Report at this time recommended mergers of shipyards in groups, and the Clydebank, Fairfield, Stephen and Connell yards became Upper Clyde Shipbuilders Ltd in 1968. The East Yard had commenced building jack-up rigs in 1965 with the rectangular platform *North Star* with dimensions 170 feet by 130 feet. This and the next three platforms *Constellation* (1966), *Orion* (1966) and *Gulftide* (1967) were dumb rigs and needed to be towed to their oilfields. However the next two rigs were self-propelled and fitted with ship-like bows and engines to give them a speed of 8 knots. *Offshore Mercury* (1969) and *Oceantide* (1971) had dimensions of 276 feet by 130 feet, and as with the previous rigs were built for American owners.

However the keel of the last liner from Clydebank was laid on 4th July,1965 and launched from the East Yard on 20th September,1967 by H. M. The Queen as *Queen Elizabeth 2*, the sponsor being presented with a speedboat for the Royal yacht after the launch. Her overall length was 963 feet, breadth 105 feet and depth 56 feet, and her three boilers and double reduction geared turbines totalled 110,000 shp and drove her twin propellers at 28.5 knots service speed. Passenger accomodation was provided for 2025 passengers and 900 crew on thirteen decks, and included sumptuous public rooms, three restaurants, 22 lifts and 6000 sq. yards of open deck space. Her smoke-defecting funnel was of new design and her navigational mast doubled as a galley exhaust. She was fitted with two bow stabilisers and two sets of stabilisers and had drive-on facilities for 80 cars. Her turbines proved to be faulty however on a shake-down cruise and she was returned to Clydebank for three months of rectification before she sailed on her maiden voyage from Southampton on 2nd May, 1969.

QUEEN ELIZABETH 2 fitting-out at Clydebank.

The East Yard had only two further ships to build as well as the two self-propelled rigs already mentioned. The Fred Olsen ferry *Blenheim* 12244/70 had accomodation for 1100 passengers and 260 cars on her summer North Sea services, while on her winter Canary Islands service she converted to 400 passengers in cruising cabins. The New Zealand ferry *Arahanga* 3962/72 was built for the Wellington to Picton service across the Cook Strait and had accomodation for 800 passengers and 30 road vehicles and 60 rail wagons with stern-loading. This last pair of ferries were propelled by Crossley-Pielstick diesel engines. The West Yard had better prefabrication facilities for some years and was used for the building of bulk carriers:-

VENNACHAR	18615/65	Harrisons (Clyde) Ltd
CAPE ST. VINCENT	12835/66	Lyle Shipping Co. Ltd, Glasgow
VOLNAY	14779/69	Harrisons (Clyde) Ltd
VANCOUVER FOREST	17659/69	Scotstoun Shipping Co. Ltd
KYOTO FOREST	17660/70	"
VICTORIA CITY	16639/70	Reardon Smith, Cardiff
TEMPLE HALL	13150/71	Lambert Brothers, London

Aerial view of Clydebank yard in the mid - 1970s showing two jack-up rigs under construction (UIE).

The Mexican jack-up rig UXMAL being towed down the Clyde in July, 1981. (UIE).

SAMJOHN GOVERNOR	11487/72	Esperos Shpg. Co SA,Greece
SAMJOHN PIONEER	11487/72	"
VARDA	11895/73	Haverton Shipping Ltd,London
ORLI	11895/73	"
ALISA	11895/73	"

The last five in the above list belonged to the 'Clyde' class of standard bulkers of 19000 dwt, with *Samjohn Pioneer* launched on 25th March,1971 and *Samjohn Governor* on 23rd June,1971 shortly before the collapse of Upper Clyde Shipbuilders Ltd later in 1971. This Greek pair were quickly completed by the reciever and agreement was reached to go ahead with the hull construction of the remaining three for British owners. *Alisa* was the last ship launched at Clydebank on 5th October,1972 but her fitting-out in Rothesay Dock to the East of the yard was delayed due to the limitations of the available workforce, with only one ship being worked on at any one time. A fatal fire with two female cleaners killed in August,1973 further delayed her completion for six weeks, but *Alisa* finally sailed on trials in December,1973 as the last ship built by the famous Clydebank yard.

The Clydebank yard was sold to Marathon Oil of Texas in 1973 for the building of triangular-shaped jack-up oil rigs. These had dimensions of 248 feet by 200 feet by 200 feet and were built in both the East and West Yards across several of the old slipways. The old gantry berths in the West Yard were demolished and new fabrication shops were built parallel to the river. Several rigs were built including *Key Gibraltar* in 1976, and *Key Victoria* in 1977 and a series with *Penrod* names. A conversion of an existing train ferry into a drill ship was completed in 1975 for Reading & Bates of U.S.A., the resultant *Douglas Carver* having a tall drill amidships. However Marathon decided to close the yard, and approval was given in March,1980 for its take-over by the French-owned Union Industrielle et d'Enterprise (UIE), owned by parent company Bouygues Offshore. The triangular rigs *Black Dog* (1980), *Uxmal* (1981), *Chichen Itza* (1981), *Morecambe Flame* (1982), and *Bay Driller* (1982) were completed, the yard having a licence to build these Marathon Le Tourneau rigs as well as offshore fabrications of all types. The last of 21 rigs completed by the yard since 1965 was the 17540 tonne *Mr. Mac* in 1986. The East Yard berths have now been completely demolished and the site levelled except for one hammer-head crane, and the West Yard is currently working on a large offshore module for the Dunbar oilfield for Total Oil.

Views of the fitting-out basin in 1994 showing a large offshore module for the Dunbar oilfield for Total Oil under construction in the West Yard (Author).

WILLIAM BEARDMORE & CO. LTD.

The extensive and impressive Beardmore naval armaments and warship yard at Dalmuir was completed in 1906 to participate in the many expected orders for British Dreadnought battleships and smaller warships. However the reality was far from the ambitions, and only three battleships had been completed by the yard by the outbreak of the Great War, with three times as many battleships completed by other Clyde yards alone, and many more by private yards and Royal Dockyards throughout the country. However, the yard and associated armaments works was put to very good use during the war, but following the absence of any large naval orders during the 1920s was reduced by 1930 to building tugs, yachts, sludge carriers and lighthouse tenders. The yard closed later that year after only 24 years of operation.

Dalmuir works and yard was the brainchild of William Beardmore (1856 - 1936), whose father had become a partner in the Parkhead forge in the east end of Glasgow in 1861. William jnr. was responsible for the introduction of steelmaking into the forge in 1881, and was in charge of a profitable business by 1900 when he purchased the Govan East yard. Some thirteen ships were built at Govan while his ambitious plans began to take shape on a greenfield site at Dalmuir, financed by an influx of Vickers capital in William Beardmore & Co. Ltd, a limited company set-up in 1902 with Vickers holding 50% of the ordinary shares but taking two of the five seats on Beardmore Board. Vickers and Armstrong were the leading armaments suppliers of the time, and viewed the plans of Beardmore with natural suspicion, the two Vickers directors however were able to steer the general Beardmore direction in return for their investment.

The yard was planned with six berths of which two were one thousand feet long, and one of these was equipped with a high overhead gantry of 750 feet in length, 115 feet wide and 133 feet high and built by Sir William Arrol & Co. Ltd during 1905/06. The four 5-ton side cranes of the gantry were designed for light lifts, and the overhead gantry cranes of 20-ton capacity were either used by themselves or together for heavier loads. The yard was adjacent to and west of the Clydebank yard of John Brown & Co. Ltd, but unfortunately the site also included the Clyde Navigation Trust workshops at Dalmuir. The yard engine and boiler works were to be built to the west of these workshops and although the boiler works was in operation during 1906 the engine works was not finished by that date. The Govan shipyard machinery and workforce were transferred to Dalmuir in May, 1905 and the first vessel constructed was the private yacht *Zaza* for William Beardmore himself, launched on 5th July,1905 and completed in September. The full cost of the Dalmuir yard including engine and boiler works, fitting-out basin, hammerhead crane and gantry, and all shipyard shops and new fittings was £1M with further sums later for turbine making machinery - a huge sum in today's equivalent money !

The keel of the first battleship had also been laid down in May, 1905 and she was launched on 23rd June, 1906 as *Agamemnon* by the Countess of Aberdeen, at a cost of £1.615M with engines to be supplied by Hawthorn, Leslie on Tyneside. The first commercial orders were won in March,1906 from the Pacific Steam Navigation Company for four passenger/cargo-liners for their South American service and powered by triple expansion engines and completed as *Quillota* 3673/07, *Quilpue* 3669/07, *Huanchaco* 4524/07 and *Junin* 4536/07. Heavy yard lay-offs were averted in March,1907 due to the same company placing an order for a larger liner *Orcoma* of 11533 grt. However the completion of the battleship *Agamemnon* had been delayed by the non-availabilty of her 12" guns until the summer of 1908, and *Orcoma* also left the yard in August of that year leaving the yard without work until the end of the year. The New Year brought work on the construction of the cruiser *Gloucester*, launched in October of that year, and was the first warship to be fitted with a complete set of engines and boilers from the Dalmuir works. Two small orders were also won, one for the lighthouse tender *Pharos* 921/09 and the other for the sludge carrier *Shieldhall* 1375/10.

The new engine works helped the yard to be more successful from 1910 in securing naval orders including the battleships *Conqueror* (1912), *Benbow* (1914), cruisers *Falmouth* (1911), *Dublin* (1913) and destroyers *Goshawk* (1912), *Llewellyn* (1914) and *Lennox* (1914). Further commercial orders were also obtained for coastal liners for the Adelaide Steamship Co. Ltd, completed as *Warilda* 7785/12, *Wandilla* 7785/12 and *Willochra* 7784/13 powered by quadruple expansion steam engines. These single-funnelled Australian liners had long bridge decks with extensive accomodation and awning decks for tropical service but were built at a huge financial loss by the yard. The twin-funnelled turbine-powered *Alsatian* 18485/13 was completed for the local Allan Line, which was at the time owned by Canadian Pacific and was renamed *Empress of France* in 1919, with Canadian Pacific returning to the yard for a larger liner after the war.

The Great War saw the Dalmuir yard contribute greatly to the British victory with extensive output including the battleship *Ramillies* (1917), aircraft carrier *Argus* (1918), cruisers *Galatea* (1915), *Inconstant* (1915) and *Royalist* (1915), and 15 destroyers, two sloops, nine submarines, four small hospital ships, and twenty 'X' craft powered lighters as well as dumb lighters. However many orders for destroyers and submarines were cancelled at the end of the war, but the incomplete cruiser *Raleigh* was allowed to continue and was completed during 1921. Some of the destroyers had been built three to a berth on the larger berths, and the submarines had been built on the slipways of the former Clyde Navigation Trust workshops. The Dalmuir shipyard workforce rose to in excess of 10,000 workers with many more working on armaments work e.g. howitzers, guns, mines, tanks, fuses and aircraft, with a special airship factory also constructed on the south side of the river at Inchinnan, now Renfrew Airport. A possible use for the airship in Transatlantic flights led to the formation of Beardmore Aero Engines Ltd after the war, however the company was liquidated in 1921 as flights took almost as long as by ship !

The almost total absence of naval orders in the 1920s for which the Dalmuir works had been built, with only the cruiser *Shropshire* (1929) and submarines *Olympus* (1929) and *Orpheus* (1929) completed, meant that the yard had to be turned to merchant construction. The long berths were particular suitable for passenger liner construction and the following were built :-

CAMERONIA	16280/21	Anchor Line, Glasgow
LARGS BAY	13851/21	Commonwealth Govt. Line
ESPERANCE BAY	13851/22	"
TYRRHENIA	16243/22	Cunard Line
CONTE ROSSO	18017/22	Lloyd Sabaudo, Genoa
CONTE VERDE	18017/23	"
CONTE BIANCAMANO	24416/24	"
DUCHESS OF ATHOLL	20119/28	Canadian Pacific Line
MANUNDA	9115/29	Adelaide S.S. Co. Ltd
ARCOONA	4212/24	"
ALLARA	3279/24	"
ULOOLOO	3237/24	"
ITAPE	4978/27	Cia Nacional de Nav Costiera,
ITAQUICE	4969/28	Brazil
ITANAGE	4966/28	"

All of the large liners were turbine-powered, with *Manunda* supplied with a H & W built oil engine and the smaller Australian passenger ships fitted with triple expansion machinery, and the Brazilian ships were fitted with Italian-design Tosi oil engines for which the Dalmuir engine works took out a licence. A new four-berth East yard was laid out for the construction of tankers and the following were built :-

BRITISH TRADER	4214/21	British Tanker Co. Ltd
BRITISH MERCHANT	6994/22	"
BRITISH ENTERPRISE	4204/22	"
BRITISH INDUSTRY	4121/22	"
BRITISH COMMERCE	4205/22	"

CARLOTA	2696/24	Anglo-Saxon/Shell
CASSANDRA	2701/24	"
CHEPITA	2702/25	"
CONCHITA	2702/24	"

In addition, *Setter* 1217/20 was built for Burns Line service to Belfast, and fruit ships *Pinzon* 1367/22 and *Pizarro* 1367/23 for MacAndrews & Co and fitted with Tosi oil engines, Latvian ice-breaker *Krisjanis Valdemars* 2800/25, railway ferries *Rye* and *Hebble* both 1040/24, and three sludge carriers, two tugs and two yachts. The last ships built were the Glasgow tramps *Dalhanna* and *Daldorch*, both 5571/30 for John M. Campbell & Son, and the lighthouse tender *Pole Star* of 1275 grt launched on 4th November,1930 and completed before the end of the year.

The Dalmuir yard was one of the first to be purchased by National Shipbuilders Security Ltd in 1931, with Sir James Lithgow assuming responsibility for its redevelopment between 1932 and 1949. Engine production ceased in 1934 as a result of further rationalisation by N.S.S. Ltd. The great Dalmuir works was reduced to a trading estate during the 1930s with the fitting-out basin used by W. Arnott Young to break-up ships including ironically the Dalmuir-built *Empress of France* in 1934/35. The fitting-out basin was used during the war by John Brown & Co. Ltd, and the engine and boiler works and former Clyde Navigation Trust works became a Royal Ordnance Factory. All commercial activity had ceased by 1970 and the fitting-out basin was filled in by 1990 with eight-storey housing development now occupying this historic site.

One of the last ships from Dalmuir, the Australian passenger liner MANUNDA of 1929, which was notable as being the first large motorship in Australian coastal service.

NAPIER & MILLER LTD.

This yard at Old Kilpatrick built some 120 ships before its demise in 1930 at the beginning of the Depression. Henry Napier, the grandson of Robert Napier, and George McEwan Miller formed a limited liability company in 1898 with the above name to operate the Yoker yard adjacent and to the east of the famous Clydebank yard. This had previously been run by Henry Napier in partnership with David Bell and J. Shanks as Napier,Shanks & Bell since 1877 and had built 84 ships to 1898, and local customers had included the Allan Line; Gow & Harrison; Raeburn & Verel. The last ship built at Yoker was *English Monarch* 4947/05 for Raeburn & Verel.

The company was forced to move down-river to a new greenfield site at Old Kilpatrick in 1906 due to their land at Yoker being required for the construction of the new Rothesay Dock by the Clyde Navigation Trust. A site adjacent to Erskine ferry and Old Kilpatrick Goods Station was chosen for easy delivery of steel and timber and other materials. The five-berth yard was also situated between the Forth & Clyde Canal and the river Clyde, and had a well-planned layout for steel flow and plenty of room to the east for expansion. The contractor appointed was James Goldie & Son and work was sufficiently advanced to lay the first keel during 1906 which was completed as *Irish Monarch* 4296/06 for Raeburn & Verel. More steam tramps were then completed at the new yard including ten for Hugh Hogarth of Ardrossan e.g. *Baron Minto* 4357/08, *Baron Napier* 4943/09 and *Baron Polwarth* 4913/11; seven for Raeburn & Verel of Glasgow e.g. *Norman Monarch* 4997/09, *Saxon Monarch* 4828/12, *British Monarch* 5749/13 and *Scottish Monarch* 5658/13; two for William Burrell in *Strathblane* 4358/07 and *Strathendrick* 4379/07; and *Belle of Scotland* 5007/07 for Belle of Scotland Shipping Co. Ltd. The last two barques built in Britain for home ownership were completed by the yard as *Sunlight* and *Rendova* both 1433/07 for Lever Brothers for the carriage of coconut oil from Rendova Island in the Pacific to Port Sunlight on the Mersey. Two tankers were completed for the Anglo-American Oil Co. Ltd as *Tamarac* 5263/08 and *Cadillac* 5251/08, as well as the ice-breaker *Bruce* 1553/11 for Reid (Newfoundland) Ltd and the Welsh auxiliary schooner *Y Draig Goch* 952/12 for Godfrey Williams.

Output during the Great War included sloops, minesweepers and aircraft, as well as merchant ships such as a tramp laid down to the order of Raeburn & Verel but completed instead for Warren Line of Liverpool as *Rhode Island* 5655/18, and the ice-breaker *Iceland* 2568/15. Standard ships were also built, including three 'A' types *Taransay* 5241/19, *Knockfierda* 5231/19 and the modified *Lusiada* 6445/20 for Blue Star Line, as well as the 'AO' type tanker *War Persian*.

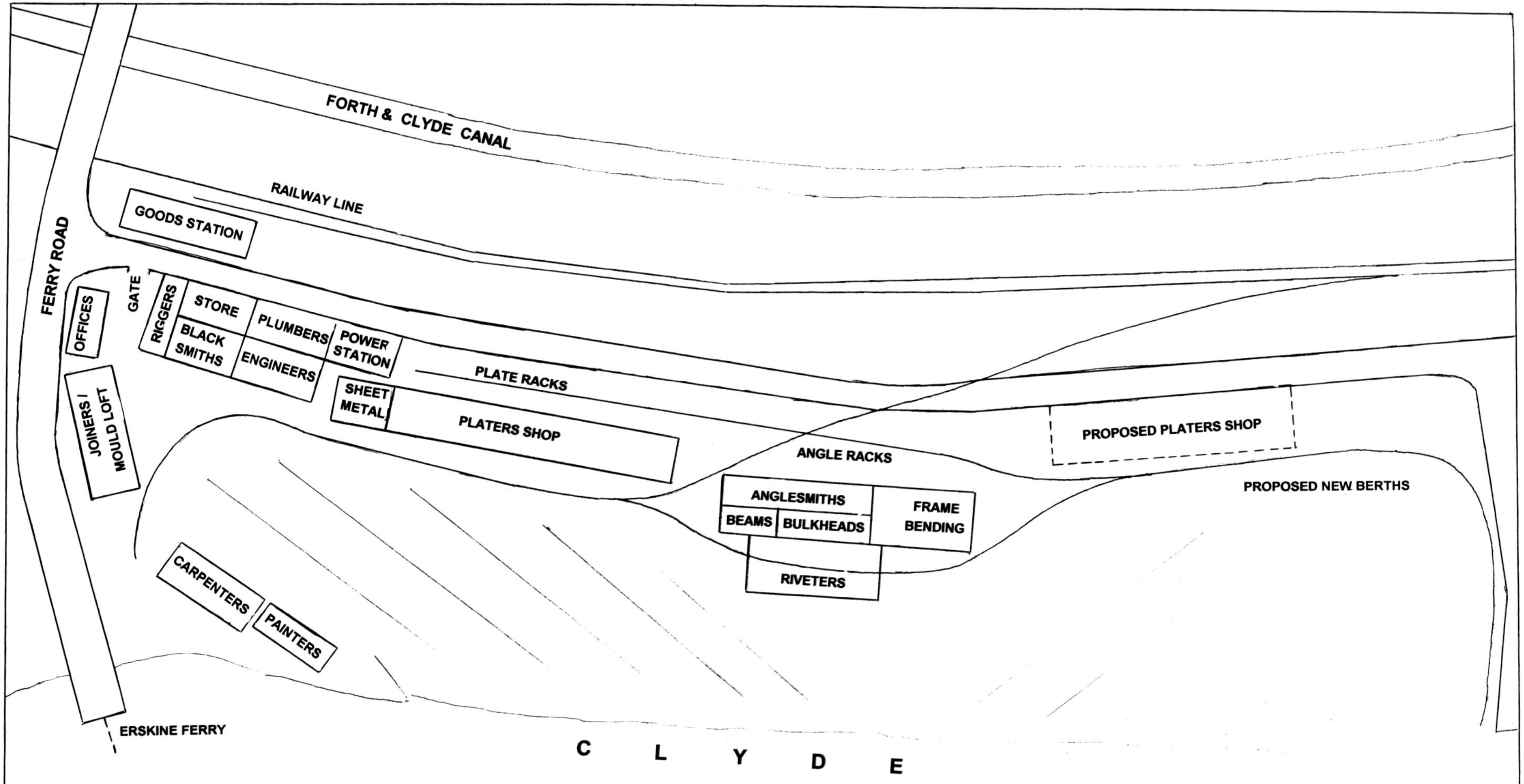

(Author)

NAPIER & MILLER LTD. OLD KILPATRICK SHIPBUILDING YARD

The yard then started work on a four-ship order for Norwegian-Amerika Line, with *Kristianiafjord* 6759/21 completed first with some passenger accomodation and powered by three steam turbines with twin propellers. Three identical single-screw triple-expansion powered cargo ships followed in *Trondhjemsfjord, Tanafjord* and *Skiensfjord*, all of 5922 grt. Several Great Lakes traders were built at the yard for American and Canadian owners e.g. *Charles R. Huntley* 1760/26, *James Stewart* 1760/26, *John B. Richards* 1743/25, *Norman B. McPherson* 1743/25 as well as the following ships :-

BRITISH MONARCH	5661/23	Raeburn & Verel, Glasgow
BARON GLENCONNER	3001/23	H. Hogarth, Ardrossan
BARON MURRAY	3103/24	"
FRAMLINGTON COURT	4888/24	Court Line, London
BLAIRGOWRIE	3259/24	Clydesdale Navigation Co. Ltd
BLAIRATHOLL	3319/25	"
BLAIRESK	3300/25	"
BLAIRDEVON	3282/25	"
BARON GRAHAM	3242/25	H. Hogarth, Ardrossan
WAIPATA	2826/26	Union S.S. Co. Ltd,New Zealand
IMPERIAL MONARCH	5831/26	Raeburn & Verel, Glasgow
BARON KINNAIRD	3355/27	H. Hogarth, Ardrossan
KENSINGTON COURT	4863/27	Court Line, London
BRADDOVEY	3359/27	Reardon Smith, Cardiff
BRADESK	3353/27	"
CALEDONIAN MONARCH	5851/28	Raeburn & Verel, Glasgow
WEST LYNN	4702/28	Reardon Smith, Cardiff
ANTIGONE	4545/28	New Egypt & Levant S.S.Co. Ltd
ANTIOPE	4545/30	"
BARON POLWARTH	3661/29	H. Hogarth, Ardrossan
JUAN DE ASTIGARRAGA	3564/29	Hijos de Astigarraga, Spain
EASTERN PRINCE	10926/29	Prince Line
WESTERN PRINCE	10926/29	"
MORON	4128/30	Cie de Nav Orbigny, La Rochelle
PAVON	4128/30	"
PENERF	2151/30	Cie Nantaise de Nav.Vap,Nantes

West Lynn and the Prince Line pair for the service between New York and South America were the only motorships built by the yard, and *West Lynn* was fitted with a B & W 6-cylinder oil engine by J. G. Kincaid & Co. Ltd and was initially employed in the homeward trade from British Columbia. The Prince Line pair were fitted with two sets of B & W oil engines by Kincaid and were twin-screw to give a service speed of 16.5 knots. They were the largest vessels built at the yard, and had luxurious accomodation for 101 first-class passengers on their New York to Brazil and Argentina service terminating at La Plata. They were good-looking ships with long, extended superstructures with three holds forward and three holds aft of the engine room. They were part-refrigerated and carried cargo gear on four masts and two pairs of derricks.

An interesting pair of double-ended steam ferries for Sydney Harbour had been completed in 1928 as *Dee Why* and *Curl Curl* , and were twin-screw vessels with two sets of four-cylinder triple-expansion steam engines. Two vehicle ferries for a service across the St. Lawrence river were completed in 1930 as *Cite de Levis* and *Cite de Quebec*, both 1259/30, for Levis Ferry Ltd. The last ship completed at the yard was *Penerf* in 1930 for French owners. A proposed extension of four berths and a second platers shop at the eastern side of the yard featuring travelling cranes on concrete piers was never built. The Old Kilpatrick yard was the first yard to be purchased by National Shipbuilders Security Ltd in 1930, and the contents were sold off during 1931 and the yard demolished.

Largest ships built at Old Kilpatrick were the Prince Line sisters WESTERN PRINCE and EASTERN PRINCE of 1929. (A. Duncan)

SCOTT & SONS (BOWLING) LTD.

This four-berth yard on the west side of the harbour at Bowling, where the Forth & Clyde Canal meets the Clyde, was founded in the 1850s by the merging of the two small Littlemill and Bay yards of Scott and Macgill as Scott & Macgill. The title was later changed to Scott & Co., and Scott & Sons and built some 450 coasters, tugs, barges, steam yachts and Clyde puffers. *Marmion* 324/93 was a typical example for service from Nobel's explosive wharf at Ardeer near Irvine, and the David Macbrayne passenger steamers *Lapwing* 211/03, *Clydesdale* 394/05 and *Lochinvar* 216/08 for Western Isles service. The main customers in the inter-war years were the Glasgow coaster fleets of J. & A. Gardner and J. G. Stewart, the former taking a dozen coasters e.g. *Saint Bedan* 452/37, and the latter six coasters e.g. *Yewpark* 827/30. *Minard* 241/25 and *Ardyne* 242/28 of Clyde Cargo Steamers Ltd served outlying Clyde ports with cargo.

The Clyde puffers *Anzac* and *Lascar* were launched in August,1939 at the yard and became the prototype for the 'VIC' war-time coasters built by several yards throughout the country. Many tugs were built for Steel & Bennie Ltd for service on the Clyde, and *Warrior* 280/35 was used as the prototype for the Warrior class of 'Empire' tugs, of which thirteen were built during the war at Bowling, as well as five 'Empire' coasters. Post-war newbuildings included six tugs for Tees Towing Co. Ltd e.g. *Ingleby Cross* 132/55, and *Chieftain* 205/68 and *Flying Scout* 290/69 for the local tug fleets, and the coasters *Lochbroom* 325/46 for David Macbrayne Ltd; *Saint Ronan* 432/66, *Saint William* 781/67 and *Saint Bedan* 1251/72 for J. & A. Gardner Ltd; and *Storm* 931/61 for the Canterbury Steam Shipping Co. Ltd,New Zealand and *Fendyke* and *Westondyke* both 696/71 for the Klondyke Shipping Co. Ltd. Five Mexican fishery protection ships were built in the mid-1970s, as well as three stern trawlers for George Craig & Sons as *Grampian Monarch, Grampian Glen* and *Grampian Hill*, and the largest ships from the yard - the fish factory trawler *Norse* 1448/75 and the Cawood collier *Pinewood* 1599/78. The yard became a limited liability company as Scott & Sons(Bowling) Ltd in 1958, and was taken over by Scotts of Greenock in 1965, and became a member of British Shipbuilders in 1977. The last two tugs launched from the yard in 1979 were *Carron* and *Lagan* for Firth of Forth service, and the yard was then placed on a 'care and maintenance basis'.

WILLIAM DENNY & BROS. LTD.

This prolific shipyard produced all manner of ships and river craft, and their rise into illustrious shipbuilding history began when William Denny built the first steamer to ply the Thames in 1814, *Margery*. His three sons William, Alexander and Peter began work as Denny Brothers in 1844 with the first ship being the Clyde paddle steamer *Lochlomond*. The partnership was reconstituted in 1849 as William Denny & Brothers by William, Peter and James Denny, and they moved from the Wood Yard into a new Leven shipyard in the shadow of Dumbarton Rock on the east bank of the Leven on land purchased in 1864 by Peter Denny. The third William Denny (1847 - 1887) entered the yard at this same time and his brilliance, dynamism and enterprise was responsible for world-beating advances such as the first ocean-going steel ships, design testing in his own privately-owned test tank, and precise evaluation of trials data. Peter Denny employed Richard Ramage as yard manager from 1870 until May,1877 when Ramage left to set-up his own yard as Ramage & Ferguson at Leith. Peter enlarged and modernised the Leven yard from 19 to 42 acres in 1881 with nine berths and a fitting-out basin on the south side below Dumbarton Rock.

In 1875 William Denny sent some plans of a ship to William Froude at the Admiralty tank in Torquay for test evaluation. The predicted speeds of the results made a tremendous impact on Denny with visions of the commercial advantages it gave of designing fast craft of all types in his own privately-owned test tank. This tank was completed in 1883, and repaid its investment from the testing of a hull form for a cross-Channel steamer for the Belgian Government in 1888. This contract had draconian penalty clauses for late delivery, and also on speed with a £500 penalty for every tenth of a knot below the loaded speed of 20.5 knots on four continuous runs between the Cloch and Cumbrae lighthouses. Two designs were tested in the tank before predicted contract speeds were obtained and to give sufficient confidence for the yard to build *Princesse Henriette* 1101/88 and avoid penalty clauses. The hopes of the yard were fully justified when the steamer obtained 21.09 knots on trials, and an order was then obtained with similar penalty clauses for a sister for the Belgian Government, *Leopold II* 1632/92. The test tank was kept going on other contracts after the Denny shipyard closure in 1963, and was taken over by the Scottish Maritime Museum in 1984.

The Leven yard built a mixture of iron steamers from the Transatlantic liner *Parthia* 3431/70 for Cunard, and *Indus* 3478/71 for the eastern trades of P & O to humble river craft. The first ocean-going steel steamers in the world were then completed as *Rotomahana* 1727/79 and *Te Anau* 1652/79 for the Union Steamship Co. Ltd, New Zealand; and *Buenos Ayrean* 4005/79 for the local Allan Line; and *Ravenna* 3382/80 for P & O. The best customer of the yard was William Mackinnon and his British India Line and subsidiaries with 84 ships completed starting with *Orissa* 359/63 and ending with *Ordia* 5449/50 with many ships built as joint speculations; James Mills and his Union Steamship Co. Ltd, New Zealand with 45 ships starting with the sisters *Hawea* and *Taupo*, both 720/75 and ending with *Tofua* 5299/51; and the British & Burmese Steam Navigation Co. Ltd of Patrick Henderson of Glasgow with 44 ocean-going ships built starting with *Tenasserim* 1840/71 and ending with *Kentung* 5554/54. Close links were forged with this latter company with members of the Denny family on the Henderson Board of directors and only the very occasional order ever going to other Clyde yards. This virtual monopoly also extended to the huge shallow-draft river craft fleet of their two subsidiaries, the Irrawaddy flotilla in the Burmese oilfields, and the much smaller Platense flotilla in the grain trades around the Plate delta and rivers. The tragic suicide of William Denny occurred in the Plate area in 1887 after many difficulties and debts over this flotilla. The yard later built three topsail schooner river barges for Plate service as *Europa, Asia* and *Africa* all 835/06.

A large steel steamer was laid down for British India Line and launched on 25th May,1889 and immediately sold to Cia Transatlantica of Spain for completion as *Montevideo* 5096/89. She followed other large steel steamers from Dumbarton for the same company in *Antonio Lopez* 3460/81, *Cataluna* and *Ciudad de Santander* both 3488/83, *Buenos Aires* 5195/87, and the sisters *Alfonso XIII* and *Reina Maria Cristina* both 4381/88. The Union Steamship Co. Ltd then ordered a record-breaking mail steamer for the South African run and completed as the twin-screw *Scot* 6844/91 powered by two sets of triple expansion engines to give a service speed of 18.5 knots and accomodation for 425 passengers. The large liner *Southwark* 10505/93 followed for American Line, and then the first twin-screw liner for the local Allan Line in *Bavarian* 10376/99 powered by two sets of triple expansion engines to give a service speed of 17.25 knots.

However it was another type of ship for which Denny's ultimately became famous - the cross-Channel steamer - and they were generally accepted as the leading builder of these ships from the turn of the century until the demise of the yard in 1963. Prior to the formation of the Southern Railway Company in 1923, there were several competing railway companies operating across the Channel to France and the Channel Islands, as well as others operating across the Irish Sea to Eire and Northern Ireland. All of these companies used Denny-built steam packets, and some of the larger packets on the English Channel before the Great War were

Sussex 1117/96, *Brighton* 1129/03, *The Queen* 1676/03, *Onward* 1671/05, *Invicta* 1680/05, *Victoria Empress* 1689/07, the turbine-powered *Riviera* and *Engadine* both 1675/11, *Paris* 1774/13 and *Biarritz* 2495/14. Similar craft operating on services to Northern Ireland and Eire from Denny included *Princess Victoria* 1096/90, *Princess May* 1123/92, *Duke of York* 1531/94, *Connemara* 1066/96, *Cambria* 1842/97, *Galtee More* 1112/98, the turbine-powered *Princess Maud* 1746/04 and *Princess Victoria* 1687/12, *Londonderry* 2086/04 and the sisters *Duke of Argyll* and *Duke of Cumberland*, both 2052/09. The three-funnelled large turbine ferries *Princess Margaret* and *Princess Irene*, both 5934/14 were built for the Vancouver - Victoria - Seattle service of Canadian Pacific. Japanese Railways ordered two turbine ferries for their Honshu to Hokkaido route as *Hirafu Maru* and *Tamura Maru*, both 1484/07 and they were the first turbine steamers under the Japanese flag.

The introduction of the Parsons steam turbine to the Clyde excursion fleets came in June,1901 with the Denny-built two-funnelled *King Edward* 551/01 to the order of Capt. Williamson and his Turbine Steamer Syndicate. She was originally designed with five propellers on three shafts, the outer shafts each having two propellers and obtained 20.84 knots on trials with this arrangement. However in 1905 she and her sister *Queen Alexandra* 665/02 were altered to three propellers on three shafts and improved speeds were then obtained. After *Queen Alexandra* was destroyed by fire at Greenock in 1911 the yard built a turbine replacement of the same name in 1912. She also had two funnels, but was later given a third funnel during a refit by Lamont in 1946 as *Saint Columba*. Another early Denny-built turbine-powered Clyde steamer was the *Duchess of Argyll* 593/06.

Ten large refrigerated steamers were built in the first decade of the century for the New Zealand Shipping Co. Ltd, and culminated in a trio of the largest vessels ever built at Dumbarton in *Ruahine* 10758/09, *Rotorua* 11130/10 and *Remuera* 11276/11. The large Spanish liner *Infanta Isabel de Borbon* 10348/12 was completed for Cia Transatlantica of Barcelona, and the twin-funnelled *Indarra* 9735/12 was built for the Australian coastal service of the Australasian United S.N. Co. Ltd. The yard also won half of a four-ship order placed with Clyde yards for Russian liners in *Empress Ekaterina II* 5151/13 and *Emperor Alexander III* 5153/13 with Clydebank building the other pair, and they carried 435 passengers on a service between Odessa and Egypt. The emigrant ship *Hororata* 9461/14 was launched on 23rd December,1913 as the longest vessel yet built at Dumbarton at 510 feet, and was completed for the New Zealand Shipping Co. Ltd capable of carrying 1066 emigrants in portable accomodation.

A member of the Denny family relinquished his seat in Parliament in 1905 in order that the yard could tender for Admiralty contracts. They were successful with two fast torpedo boats completed in 1907/08, followed by the destroyers *Maori* (1909), *Pincher* (1910), *Defender* (1911), *Druid* (1911), *Badger* (1912), *Beaver* (1912), *Ardent* (1913), *Loyal* (1913) and *Legion* (1914) as well as the Australian destoyer *Yarra* (1910). The yard was switched over to naval construction shortly after the outbreak of war and completed 28 destroyers, five submarines and two river hospital ships during the war, as well as *Burma* 7564/14 for P. Henderson and the packets *Lorina* 1457/18 and *Maid of Orleans* 2384/18, as well as 150 fighter aircraft. Four large ferries were built just after the war for the Holyhead route as *Anglia* 3460/19, *Hibernia* 3467/20, *Cambria* 3445/20 and *Scotia* 3441/20.

In 1918 both the Leven yard and the engine works higher up the Leven were combined in a single limited liability company, William Denny & Brothers Ltd with James Denny as the first chairman. One of his daughters married a member of the other great Dumbarton shipbuilding family, MacMillans. Engines were brought down by barge to the fitting-out basin for installation in ships, except when bought in from other suppliers as in the case of the first oil engine installed in a large Denny-built ship. *Hauraki* of 1921 had two 4SCSA eight-cylinder diesels manufactured by the North British Diesel Engine Works Ltd at Scotstoun, and was one of the following cargo-liner products of the yard during the lean 1920s :-

AMARAPOORA	8084/20	P. Henderson, Glasgow
PEGU	8084/21	"
HAURAKI	7113/21	Union S.S. Co. Ltd
CHILKA	4360/21	British India Line
NAGASAKI MARU	5306/22	Nippon Yusen Kaisha
SHANGHAI MARU	5293/22	"
KEMMENDINE	7837/24	P. Henderson, Glasgow
SAGAING	7994/25	"
YOMAH	5047/26	Speculation
BEAVERBURN	9876/27	Canadian Pacific Line
YOMA	8230/28	P. Henderson, Glasgow
AUSTRALIND	5020/29	Australind S.S. Co. Ltd
ARMADALE	5066/29	"
ARDENVOHR	5237/31	"

Yomah was built as a speculation with an empty order book, and was managed by Henderson Line on her maiden voyage to Australia and New Zealand via the Panama Canal. She was then sold to Henderson and then on to the Australind Steamship Co. Ltd (Trinder,Anderson) and renamed *Ashburton*. The new owners were so impressed with her that they placed orders for three more similar ships ! Lord Pirrie of Harland & Wolff Ltd, Belfast had reserved berth no. 8 in March,1920 for a period of five years, with the first ship to be an oil tanker from the supplied parts of a war-time standard ship. Construction was suspended in the bad freight slump later in 1920 and the hull lay idle until April,1923 when Andrew Weir and his British - Mexican Petroleum Co. Ltd took over the contract, and she was launched on 30th September,1924 as the engines-amidships *Inverglass* of 6901 grt and completed in November,1924. She carried crude oil in six cylindrical tanks on the centreline, with light oil in the outside smaller tanks fitted around these. Tankers Ltd of Glasgow had in the previous year taken delivery of the engines-aft tanker *Scottish Borderer* 6996/23 of 9820 dwt.

The formation of the Southern Railway Company in 1923 led to orders for the yard for Isle of Wight double-ended ferries and the following cross-Channel packets:-

DINARD	2291/24	ISLE OF JERSEY	2143/29
ST. BRIAC	2291/24	ISLE OF GUERNSEY	2143/29
ISLE OF THANET	2664/25	ISLE OF SARK	2211/31
ISLE OF KENT	2664/25	BRIGHTON	2391/32
WORTHING	2288/28	BRITANNY	1445/33
CANTERBURY	2912/28		

Dinard was the first oil-fuelled cross - Channel steamer, and packets built for service across the Irish Sea included *Duke of Lancaster* 3608/27, *Duke of Argyll* 3604/27 and *Duke of Rothesay* 3606/28 for the Heysham to Belfast route; and *Princess Margaret* 2523/31 and *Princess Maud* 2886/33 were built for the Larne to Stranraer route; and *Slieve Bloom* 1297/30, *Slieve More* 1397/32 and *Slieve Bearnagh* 1450/36 for the Holyhead to Dublin route. The large turbine-ferry *Princess Helene* 4055/30 was completed for Canadian Pacific for their Bay of Fundy service. The luxury three-masted schooner yacht *Sunbeam II* 505/29 for Sir Walter Runciman was an interesting diversion from the austerity merchant orders of the 1920s.

The yard survived the Depression on the above orders and those for Clyde excursion steamers including the turbine-powered twin-funnelled *King George V* 789/26 and her sister *Queen Mary* 870/33; *Glen Sannox* 664/25; *Duchess of Montrose* 806/30; *Caledonia* 624/34; and the diesel-electric *Lochfyne* 748/31 and *Lochnevis* 568/34. Thames excursion ships were then built including the motorships *Queen of the Channel* 1162/35, *Royal Sovereign* 1527/37 and *Royal Daffodil* 2060/39 together with *Sandown* 684/34 for Isle of Wight service. The Admiralty then began building up its strength with the destroyers *Echo* (1934), *Eclipse* (1934), *Hasty* (1936), *Havock* (1936), *Ashanti* (1937), *Bedouin* (1937), *Jaguar* (1939) and *Kandahar* (1939); the sloops *Stork* (1936) and *Auckland* (1938) and the coastal minelayer *Plover* (1937). Merchant orders then began to reappear at the end of the

Depression with *Anselm* 5954/35 for Booth Line; *City of Agra* 6361/36 for Ellerman Lines; and *Prome* 7043/37, *Salween* 7063/38, *Katha* and *Kindat* both 4357/38 for Henderson Line.

The last ship delivered before the outbreak of war was the stern-loading drive-on car ferry *Princess Victoria* 2197/39 which was only in service on the Stranraer/Larne route for two months before being recalled to the yard for fitting-out as an auxiliary minelayer. The yard built a mixture of warships and merchant ships during World War II, with twelve destroyers including two for Holland and two for Turkey, twelve sloops including two for India, two minesweepers, two steam gunboats and a large tank transport ferry. Six cargo-liners were built to private order and one cross-Channel packet and four paddle steamers for India, while for Government order two standard tramps and two merchant aircraft carriers *Empire MacAndrew* 7952/43 and *Empire MacDermott* 7952/44 and the aircraft transport ship *Engadine* 9909/41 were completed. *Engadine* had been laid down for Clan Line, and the design of the merchant aircraft carriers was changed from that of a standard grain-carrying tramp, and as a consequence the pair spent 18 months in the fitting-out basin.

The production of shallow-draft river craft was not resumed in peace-time, and the number of berths was reduced to five with the largest to 540 feet continuing to build deep-sea merchant ships, with the others building a mixture of short-sea ferries, excursion craft, three Scottish fishery protection cruisers and one frigate *Jaguar* (1957). The deep-sea ships were :-

ASHBURTON	5005/46	Australind S.S. Co. Ltd
ORMARA	5417/47	British India Line
CITY OF KARACHI	7320/52	Ellerman Lines
CITY OF WINCHESTER	10594/52	"
EASTERN QUEEN	8644/50	Indo-China S.N. Co. Ltd
OLINDA	5424/50	British India Line
ORDIA	5424/50	"
YOMA	5809/48	P. Henderson
MARTABAN	5740/50	"
TOFUA	5299/51	Union S.S. Co. Ltd,New Zealand
GEORGE	9143/53	A.G. Pappadakis, Greece
NICKY	9151/53	"
KENTUNG	5558/54	P. Henderson
MARKLAND	6037/53	Vinland Shipping Co. Ltd
COTOPAXI	8559/53	Pacific Steam Nav. Co. Ltd
MARGARET BOWATER	6581/54	Bowater Steamship Co. Ltd
SARAH BOWATER	6581/55	"
EASTERN ARGOSY	6907/55	Indo-China S.N. Co. Ltd
VALLETTA	9367/56	O. Ditlev - Simonsen
KOOLAMA	3777/57	Govt of Western Australia

KEMMENDINE of 1924 for P. Henderson (Scottish Maritime Museum).
Turbine-driven CAPE SABLE of 1960 for the Lyle Shipping Co. Ltd (L. Dunn).

NICOLAS BOWATER	7136/58	Bowater Steamship Co. Ltd
GLADYS BOWATER	4045/58	"
PHYLLIS BOWATER	4083/59	"
CAPE SABLE	10660/60	Lyle Shipping Co. Ltd,Glasgow
CAPE WRATH	10905/60	"
CITY OF ST. ALBANS	6980/60	Ellerman Lines
CITY OF LICHFIELD	7021/61	"
CITY OF GLOUCESTER	6918/63	"

The majority of the above ships were turbine-powered including three out of the five Bowater newsprint carriers, and the general cargo ships *George, Nicky, Cape Sable* and *Cape Wrath*. However the other newsprint carrier *Markland* had the more unusual two sets of compound reciprocating Frederiksstad engines by Rankin & Blackmore Ltd, for her normal service from Newfoundland to east Coast ports of America. The nationalisation of the railway companies into British Rail produced plenty of orders for ten large ferries for the following routes around the British coast :-

PRINCESS VICTORIA	2649/47	Stranraer - Larne
FALAISE	3710/47	Southampton - St. Malo
WINCHESTER(cargo)	1149/47	Southampton - Channel Isles
MAID OF ORLEANS	3777/49	Folkestone - Boulogne
BRIGHTON	2875/50	Newhaven - Dieppe
NORMANNIA	3543/52	Southampton - Havre
LORD WARDEN	3333/52	Dover - Boulogne
DUKE OF ROTHESAY	4780/56	Heysham - Belfast
MAID OF KENT	4413/59	Dover - Boulogne
CALEDONIAN PRINCESS	3630/61	Stranraer - Larne

as well as for three Isle of Wight ferries in *Southsea* and *Brading*, both 837/48 and *Shanklin* 833/51. *Falaise* was the first ferry to be delivered with Denny - Brown stabilisers fitted, the first set having been fitted in 1934 into the Channel Islands ferry *Isle of Sark* of 1931. The private British & Irish Line took the motor passenger ferry *Inisfallen* 3706/48 for their Fishguard to Cork service, and Burns Line took two cargo ships in *Lairds Moor* 989/48 and *Lairds Ben* 995/49. David Macbrayne Ltd took the small ferries *Loch Seaforth* 1090/47 and *Claymore* 1024/55 for Western Scotland services; and *Royal Sovereign* 1851/48 and *Queen of the Channel* 1472/49 were completed for the Thames excursion services of the General Steam Navigation Company. The Mersey ferry *Royal Iris* 1234/50 was followed by two small ferries for Denny's own account in *Mary Queen of Scots* 230/50 and *Sir William Wallace* 277/55 for the Queensferry service on the Firth of Forth, owned and operated by Denny since 1934 with two other yard-built similar paddle ferries. Two Bosphorus ferries *Fenerbahce* and *Dolmabahce*, both 994/52 were followed by the

The launch of CALEDONIAN PRINCESS on 5th April,1961 (W. Ralston & Co. Ltd).

The turbine-propelled DUKE OF ROTHESAY was built by Denny in 1956 for the Heysham to Belfast service, pictured is her Belfast-built sister DUKE OF LANCASTER.

Cross-Channel ferry INVICTA of 1940 did not enter commercial service until 1947.

MAID OF ORLEANS of 1948

PRINCESS VICTORIA on launch day in August,1946 with the Dumbarton whiskey distillery in the background. (Glasgow University).

launch of the first of a new class of general purpose Clyde ferries on 22nd September,1953 as *Arran*. She could carry up to 34 cars and 650 passengers and was powered by British Polar diesels to give a service speed of 16 knots.

Two of the new breed of roll-on/roll-off ferries were completed for the Preston to Larne service of the Atlantic Steam Navigation Co. Ltd in *Bardic Ferry* 2550/57 and *Ionic Ferry* 2548/58 capable of carrying 55 cars and lorries through her stern doors and 200 passengers, and they had twin Sulzer diesels to give a service speed of 14 knots. The stern-loading diesel-electric car and train ferry *Aramoana* 4160/62 for the Wellington to Picton service of New Zealand Railways was launched on 24th November,1961, and left Dumbarton in June,1962 for the Antipodes.

The yard had been modernised in 1959 for partial prefabrication but could not compete for the bulk carrier orders that were necessary for survival in the early 1960s. The last deep-sea merchant ship *City of Gloucester* left the yard in March,1963, with the only ship on the stocks being a 15000 dwt engines-aft general cargo ship laid down as a speculation at the end of 1962. The cash-flow of the company had been weakened by a £0.5M venture into hovercraft, and the company was forced into liquidation in September,1963. The hull on the stocks was then sold and launched on 27th February,1964 and towed to the Linthouse yard of Alexander Stephen & Sons Ltd to be completed as their Y685, and began trading for Hall Brothers of Newcastle as *Melbrook*. It is interesting to note that the engine-builder for this ship also went into liquidation during its construction, and the 6-cylinder Sulzer oil engine of 9600 bhp was finally completed at the Newcastle factory of Hawthorn,Leslie (Engineers) Ltd.

The Denny family had lost majority control of the yard in post-war years, with Edward L. Denny as Chairman of the company from 1953 to 1961, having replaced Sir Maurice Denny who had held the position since 1922 and who died in 1955. The historic Denny yard was later demolished with the fitting-out basin used by a sawmill company. One of the ill-fated D2 Denny passenger hovercraft was used in 1968 for a service across Morecambe Bay from Barrow to Fleetwood.

A. MacMILLAN & SON LTD.

Archibald MacMillan and his son John began shipbuilding at Dumbarton in 1834 on the western bank of the Leven, but moved to the eastern bank in 1838 to a yard which had been previously rented by James MacAlister and more importantly possessed a slipway allowing repair work as well. Archibald died in 1854, and his son John extended the yard in area to the north by the purchase of the Church yard in 1867, and his grandsons Robert and John were taken into partnership in 1868. The yard began building small wooden barques in the 1860s for Donaldson Line e.g. *Mary Falconer, Parama, La Plata* and *Colorado* with the slipways launching up-river. The yard built many sugar traders for the 'Diamond K' fleet of John Kerr of Greenock with the last ship being the composite *Trinidad* of 1868. Some larger examples of iron sailing ships from the yard were *Pleiades* , which later served in the Shaw,Savill fleet; the fast composite schooner *Eastern Isles* for the Far East services of Gow of Glasgow; *Dunbritton* for J.H. Watt & Sons,Glasgow; *Coriolanus* for Patten & Co., London; *Maraval* for Bruusgaard Kjosterud of Drammen; with *Macbeth, Macduff, Macmillan*, and *Macleod* as speculations by the yard.

The first steel steamer was the two-decked *Lydian Monarch* 2113/81 for the London to New York emigrant trade of William Patton, followed by *Clan Buchanan* 2933/82 and *Clan Drummond* 2922/82 for The Clan Line Steamers Ltd. Steel sailing ship customers included W.H. Price of London with *Imberhorne* 2042/82; Andrew Weir with *Fernbank* and *Oakbank*, both 1429/92; G. Milne of Aberdeen with *Invercauld, Inveresk, Invergarry, Invercoe* and *Inversnaid*; R. Smith of Liverpool with *Conway* 1900/96, with the last sailing ships from the yard being *S. Celeste* 1946/02 and *S. Margarita* 1929/02 for P. Samengo, Castellamare; *Ama Begonakoa* 2516/02 for Sota y Aznar, Bilbao; *Alsterberg* 3239/02 for A.G. Alster, Hamburg; and *Urania* 3283/02 for B. Wencke, Hamburg; and *Gostwyck* 1827/04.

John MacMillan snr. retired in 1885 and John Steele of the well-known Clydeside shipbuilding family was appointed yard manager. Unfortunately John MacMillan jnr. died at an early age in 1889 and his father was forced to return to the business. Archibald Macmillan & Son Ltd was registered on 1st March,1890 with Robert Macmillan as Managing Director for whom the steamer *Vortigern* 3026/92 was built on his own account. Orders from liner customers for steamers were then secured from Saint Line of Liverpool; R.P. Houston; Elder,Dempster; Clan Line; Bucknall Line; Fraissinet of France; Irish Shipowners Co. Ltd (T. Dixon); Lancashire Shipping Co. Ltd (J. Chambers) and Barber & Co.,Liverpool. A serious fire occurred at the yard in 1901 which destroyed several buildings with *Clan Macmillan* 4525/01, still on the stocks, having a narrow escape. In 1908 the yard had four berths capable of building vessels up to 450 feet, and during the next year four tramps were built for the local William Burrell. In 1911 Robert Macmillan died and was succeeded by his eldest son William Macleod Macmillan, who soon formed an association with Lamport & Holt Ltd.

The yard built a number of 'Flower' class sloops, twin-screw and paddle minesweepers and small fleet oilers for the Admiralty during the Great War. Unfortunately William M. MacMillan, grandson of the founder, was killed in France during the war while serving with the Argyll & Sutherland Highlanders, and was succeeded by James Macmillan. The yard also built during the war for the Shipping Controller with four 'A' and 'B' type tramps, one 'AO' type tanker and the standard coaster *War Clyde* 1420/18. The tanker *Tamarac* 5042/16 was completed for the Anglo-American Oil Co. Ltd, and tramps completed included *Honiton* 4914/15, *Chulmleigh* 4911/16 and *Buckleigh* 4920/17 for William J. Tatem; and cargo-liners *Memling* 7307/15, *Swinburne* 4665/17 and *Sheridan* 4665/17 for Lamport & Holt Ltd. The latter company purchased the yard during 1918 and it was subsequently managed by Harland & Wolff Ltd with Lord Pirrie as Chairman. The yard was modernised at great expense with the town gas works demolished to make extra space, and the following ships were then completed :-

BRONTE	5331/19	Lamport & Holt Ltd
BROWNING	5332/19	"
BRUYERE	5335/19	"
LAPLACE	7327/19	"
LEIGHTON	7412/21	"
LINNELL	7424/21	"
LASSELL	7417/22	"
ARABY	4936/23	Royal Mail Line
GASCONY	4716/25	"
BRITANNY	4772/28	"
ELMWORTH	4963/24	R. S. Dalgleish Ltd, Newcastle
OAKWORTH	4963/25	"
CEDARTON	899/24	Matthews S.S. Co. Ltd
OAKTON	1727/23	"
BIRCHTON	1732/24	"
KAVAK	2743/29	Moss S.S. Co. Ltd, Liverpool
KANA	2743/29	"
DUNKWA	3789/27	Elder, Dempster
DIXCOVE	3789/27	"
DARU	3838/27	"
DAGOMBA	3845/28	"
DAVID LIVINGSTONE	4091/30	"
MARY SLESSOR	4026/30	"

Leighton, Linnell, Lassell, Elmworth, Oakworth and the Royal Mail and Elder, Dempster ships were all motorships. *Mary Slessor* was delivered last in March,1930, with the profit margin of each of these motorships having been very poor. A final barge of 900 tons was launched in March,1930 for the Argentine fleet of Mihanovich, and the yard then closed in April,1930. The yard was acquired by National Shipbuilders Security Ltd in April,1932 and demolished in 1937 to make way for other business uses.

LEIGHTON was built at Dumbarton in 1921 for Lamport & Holt Ltd, owners of the MacMillan yard at that time. (W.S.P.L.)

SIMONS - LOBNITZ LTD.

The two greatest dredger building yards in the world were neighbours at Renfrew, and finally merged under the above title in 1959. William Simons had previous shipbuilding experience at Greenock and in Canada before he purchased the East yard of J. W. Hoby & Company in Renfrew in 1860. The nearby iron foundry of Fox, Henderson & Company was purchased at the same time, and their title of London Works was used thereafter for the shipyard as well. The yard was then run by William Simons jnr. and his brother Walter Simons and Andrew Brown, the latter a marine engineer with experience at the Pointhouse yard of Inglis, where he had designed the engines of the paddle tug *Clyde* of 1851. These were removed when the tug was taken out of service in 1912 and mounted on the Renfrew shore. Brown became renowned as a designer of dredging equipment, with the Clyde Trust placing their first order with the yard for two self-propelled hoppers for which Andrew Brown created an entirely new design with hinged underwater compartments to release the spoil at the mouth of Loch Long. They were delivered in 1862 and were the first in a very long association with the Clyde Navigation Trust that included the twin-screw *Clyde* 337/82, and twin-screw dredger *Craigiehall* 693/03.

Andrew Brown became in 1886 the controlling partner of **William Simons & Company**, having built small steamers for a wide range of liner customers with six steamers for British India Line e.g. *Chaldea* 1434/72, and others for Nav. Gen. Italiana, Palermo e.g. *Principe Amadeo* 1214/64 and for the City of Cork Steam Packet Co. Ltd e.g. *Lee* 1195/80, and for the Clyde Shipping Co. Ltd e.g. *Aranmore* 838/81. The double-ended Clyde ferry *Finnieston* 236/90 had a new type of raised deck which could be moved to suit the tide during her crossings from Finnieston to Mavisbank. The yard then built the twin-screw sewage disposal hopper *Salford* in 1895, the first of its kind in the world, with many other examples being built at the seven-berth Simons yard e.g. *Dalmarnock* 1371/25 for Glasgow Corporation.

Bucket and suction dredgers were then built for harbours around the country, on the Thames, Mersey, Bristol, Preston, Tyne and Tees, and with many for overseas customers particularly for sand pump dredgers for South Africa including *Agnes* 1891/03, *Nautilus* 2034/03, *Cetus* 2414/05, *Labrus* 2097/11 and the very large twin-screw dredger *Rietbok* 4538/30, the largest in the world at that date. Many drag and cutter suction dredgers were supplied to the main harbours of India at Calcutta, Chittagong and Vizagapatnam with two of the largest being *Vizagapatnam* 2275/26 and *Patunga* 2444/28. The U.S. Government ordered the

A good view of the Lobnitz and Simons yards at the turn of the century. (Glasgow University)

Aerial view of the Lobnitz and Simons yards, the Renfrew to Yoker ferry is in mid-river (top). (Glasgow University)

bucket hopper dredger *Corozal* 1925/11 to complete the digging of the Panama Canal particularly at the Culebra Cut, and the Nigerian Government the sand pump dredgers *Sand Grouse* 2061/09 and *Lady Bourdillon* 3944/44. The Anglo-Persian Oil Co. Ltd ordered the dredger *Tigon* 2223/24 to keep open the Shatt-el-Arab waterway around the Abadan oil refinery, and the twin-screw dredger *Baghdad* 2790/39 was completed to work in the same estuary for the Government of Iraq.

The Simons yard had built sloops, minesweepers, tugs and shallow-draft craft for the Admiralty during the Great War, and this was repeated during the subsequent war, to be followed by the deep-diving ship *Reclaim* (1950). War-time hoppers and dredgers included one large twin-screw dredger completed as *Empire Forager* 2588/46, which was sold to Argentina in 1947, and she was joined by two larger twin-screw dredgers in 1949 from the yard. Post-war dredgers included *Jalengi* 4300/49 for service in India; *Ibadan* 2879/50 and *Oyo* 3944/50 for service in Africa.

The other major dredger builder at Renfrew was the West yard of **Lobnitz & Co. Ltd**, a company formed by a Danish immigrant Henry C. Lobnitz from Fredericia, who had worked with John Scott Russell on the construction of the *Great Eastern* on the Thames. He joined the Renfrew yard of James Henderson in 1857 and by his retirement in 1894 was the owner of the yard. The Danish connections of Lobnitz resulted in many small ships being built for Danish owners, with 25 for DFDS between 1876 and 1900, the largest being *L. P. Holmblad* 2141/93, *Nicolai II* 2567/95, *Alexandra* 2567/95 and *Xenia* 2455/95. He strengthened the management team in 1890 by the appointment of his son Frederick and William A. Young, who had recently left the Leith yard of Hawthorn & Company. Lobnitz & Company became of limited liability in 1895, the year before the death of Henry C. Lobnitz at the age of 65 years. William Young was then appointed Chairman, and the cable ship *Okinawa Maru* 2221/96 was then built for the Japanese Government, followed by the mini-liners *Hakuai Maru* 2636/98 and *Kosai Maru* 2635/99 for Nippon Yusen Kaisha.

The Lobnitz yard built the dredging fleet of Weetman Pearson, the civil engineer who discovered oil in the Tehuantepec region of Mexico after the drainage of marshlands and construction of Vera Cruz harbour in 1893. Several dredgers were then built at the yard and sent to Mexico e.g. *Pearson* 1242/07, as well as other craft for Mexican service e.g. the lighthouse tender *Melchor Ocampo* 439/00 and the coastal steamer *Beryl* 227/06. Many rock breakers and dredgers were then supplied to the U.S. Government for the building of the Panama Canal between 1904 and 1914, and the Lobnitz yard from this point of time became committed to dredger and rock breaking/cutting craft for home and overseas customers e.g. *Lord Joicey* 1204/06 for service at Hull, *Rosslyn* 902/12 for service on the Clyde, *Margerison* 1145/14 for service at Preston, and *Sir Thomas Price* 1474/25 for service at East London in South Africa.

Many small gunboats and warships were completed for the Admiralty during the Great War, with Frederick Lobnitz offering his services to the Government and joining the Ministry of Munitions in May,1915 and serving under William Weir (later Lord Weir) as Director, and took over that post at the end of 1916. Frederick Lobnitz was knighted in 1920 and took over at the same time as Chairman of the company from William Young, continuing until his death in December,1932 when he was succeeded by his son H. Pearson Lobnitz, his middle name showing the relation by marriage with the Pearson family, who had continued to have dredgers built at the yard. During the subsequent war the five-berth yard with fitting-out basin at the west end came under naval control, and built boom defence vessels, minesweepers, landing craft, dredgers, store ships as well as sections and the piers for the Mulberry Harbour. This war-time port at Arromanches was only made possible by the adaptation of the 'spuds' of Lobnitz-built dredgers. One dredger was also completed during the war as *Empire Clydesdale* 1747/44, having been laid down for the Mexican Government, and then four small Admiralty steam tankers as *Birchol, Oakol, Rowanol* and *Teakol*, all 1440/46.

After the return to peace-time Lobnitz constructed large suction dredgers e.g. the Mexican *Campeche* 1833/49, and *Haffar* 1180/49, and four dredgers for Preston harbour *Astland* and *Ribble,* both 1287/49, and *Calder* and *Savick* both 618/49, and small grab dredgers such as *Wilton* 208/55 for the Tees and the Finnish dipper dredger *Pera* 293/57, as well as sludge carriers such as the local steam-powered *Shieldhall* 1792/55 and now preserved at Southampton.

The Simons yard was taken over by the Weir Group in 1957, which also purchased the adjacent yard of Lobnitz in 1959 creating a single company, **Simons-Lobnitz Ltd**. A very large suction dredger was then built for Calcutta Port Commission as *Churni* 4582/61, as well as the Tees suction dreger *Heortnesse* 604/59 and the diesel-electric firefloat/tug *Cardon* 324/59 for Shell Venezuela. However financial reasons forced the announcement of closure in 1963, and the goodwill of both the Simons and Lobnitz names were sold to Alexander Stephen & Sons Ltd (q.v.), who continued to build dredgers. A hopper barge for Calcutta Port Commissioners was the last to leave Renfrew in the Spring of 1964, when the yards were closed.

Andrew Brown - designed steam engine of paddle tug CLYDE of 1851 mounted on the Renfrew shore (Author); and Clyde steam sludge carrier SHIELDHALL completed by Lobnitz in 1955.

FLEMING & FERGUSON LTD.

The narrow Cart river joins the Clyde opposite the famous Clydebank yard of John Brown & Co. Ltd, and here over the years a steady stream of new small craft emerged from five Paisley yards. However, only three of these yards have built ships over the last hundred years, with the yard of greatest longevity being the Phoenix yard of Fleming & Ferguson Ltd. Members of both founding families took over the four-berth yard of H. McIntyre & Company in 1885 to build dredgers, hoppers and lighters for British ports and harbours. They had a healthy export trade in 'knock-down' dredgers and estuary craft for re-erection overseas amounting to nearly half of the production. Home customers included Clyde Navigation Trust with the dredger *Cairndhu* 698/92, and the ports of Mersey, Manchester, London, Tyne, Tees, Hartlepool and Irvine, as well as private dredging contractors such as James Dredging Co. Ltd and Westminster Dredging Co. Ltd. The Ferguson brothers left the partnership in 1903 to take over the Newark yard (q.v.) at Port Glasgow, leaving W. Y. Fleming in control, and evidently thought that by withdrawing their interest, the original company of Fleming & Ferguson would be forced to close down. However this was not the case and Fleming & Ferguson remained in business, and the yard and its engine works had gained a world-wide reputation for quality small ships and steam reciprocating machinery.

Large steam-powered suction and grab dredgers left the Phoenix yard for many distant harbours, particularly in New Zealand, with *Eileen Ward* 1023/09 for Wellington, *Paritutu* 564/10 for New Plymouth, *Kaione* 830/18 for Wanganui, and *Otakou* 1933/29 for Otago harbour at Dunedin. The floating cranes *Rapaki* and *Hikitia* , both 746/26, were despatched for service at Lyttelton and Wellington respectively, and the tug *Te Awhina* 220/08 to Auckland. Dredgers were also built in quantity for the Indian sub-continent, with *Sir William Matthews* 1375/21 for Colombo, *Thomas Coad* 852/27 and *Thomas Downie* 853/29 for Karachi, and *Tuticorin* 773/31 for the port of the same name. The Roumanian bucket dredger *Sulina* 1201/23 was built for service at the mouth of the Danube for the port of the same name, and other dredgers were sent to Nigeria, Canada, Argentina and many other countries. Non-propelled dredgers, buoy-lifters and land reclamation pump craft were sent out in 'kit-form' for re-erection overseas, with tugs, pilot cutters and other small craft being shipped overseas on the decks of cargo ships.

Small warships, standard coasters, dredgers, self-propelled cranes and other harbour craft were built at the Phoenix yard during two world wars. The Canadian Government, which previously had the cable layer *Lady Laurier* 1051/02 built at the yard, became good customers for Newfoundland coastal passenger ships with *Baccalieu* and *Burgeo*, both 1421/40 and accomodation for over one hundred passengers, *Cabot Strait* 2045/47 with accomodation for 150 passengers, and *Springdale* and *Bar Haven*, both 1138/48 and with accomodation for 50 passengers. Two large twin-screw salvage tugs were built for the South African Government in 1950, as well as whalers for service from the Falkland Islands, for which Crown Agents also placed an order for a diesel-electric survey ship for delivery in 1956. The well-decked *John Biscoe* 1584/56 replaced a converted wooden minesweeper of the same name, and was ice-strengthened with an ice-knife bow and heavy fins to protect the propeller and rudder. She had a crew of 34 with accomodation for 34 scientists, and spent each of the next thirty years voyaging to the South Atlantic for the benefit of Antarctic research.

The Phoenix yard also built the lighthouse tender *Relume* 1516/52 for the Middle East Navigational Aids Service, the motorship *Pyidawnyunt* 2217/55 for the Burma Five Star Line, the coaster *Soutra* 1334/58 for Christian Salvesen of Leith and the tug *Aucklander* 454/58 for service at Auckland. Some of the last ships from Fleming & Ferguson Ltd were the Thames dredger *Long Reach* 1972/61, the Calcutta dredger *Ajoy* 1068/61 and the Hull dredger *Clee Ness* 1436/62. The American Marine & Machinery Co. Inc. took over the Phoenix yard in 1964, and built a dozen small craft before the yard finally closed in 1969, with the last ship being the 400 ton cutter suction dredger *Bled* for Yugoslavia.

BOW, McLACHLAN & CO. LTD.

The Thistle shipyard of J. McArthur & Company was taken over in 1900 by William Bow and John McLachlan, previously makers of light marine engines and steering gear, with Bow,Maclachlan & Co. becoming of limited liability at the same time. A reputation was soon established for building tugs with two each for Steel & Bennie Ltd and the Clyde Shipping Co. Ltd for Clyde service. Ships were built for overseas service, particularly British Columbia e.g. *Camosun* 1369/05 and *Princess Mary* 2155/10, the latter for Canadian Pacific who had her rebuilt in 1914 by the Esquimalt yard of Yarrows Ltd., and the powerful deep-sea steam salvage tug *Salvage King* 1164/25 for the Straits Towing Company of Vancouver and which took part in many ocean rescues until she caught fire and sank in Victoria harbour in October,1953.

The American twin-screw coastal tanker *J. Oswald Boyd* 1806/13 was supplied with two sets of compound steam engines for service with the Gotham Marine Corporation of New York. Small warships were built during the Great War, followed by four coasters for the General Steam Navigation Co. Ltd, *Lapwing* 1449/20, *Auk* 1445/21, *Gannet* 1443/21 and *Teal* 1444/21. The Greek coaster *Maria Kyriakides* 1556/21 was followed by the similar *Balmaha* 1428/24 for the Shield Steamship Co. Ltd of Grangemouth, and two for the Bombay Steam Navigation Co. Ltd in *Kalavati* 1185/28 and *Dayavati* 1188/29. The Shell Australian coastal tanker *Phasianella* 866/29 was followed by another for Finnish service as *Helena* 215/30, and the last ships built at the Thistle yard were six naval tugs for Chile during 1930/32 e.g. *Galvarino* 361/31, and the paddle tug *John H. Amos* 202/31 for Tees Conservancy Commissioners, which is still in existence today at Chatham. The company went into liquidation in 1932 and the yard was closed, re-opening only during World War II to build landing craft.

JOHN FULLERTON & COMPANY

The Merksworth yard was taken over by John Fullerton in 1866, and his yard launched the small steam coaster *Kyles* of 122 grt on 12th March,1872 for Stuart Manford of Glasgow. Anyone witnessing the launch would never have thought that this little coaster would still be in existence over 120 years later, and she is currently moored on the river Irvine near the defunct Ayrshire Dockyard Ltd (q.v.) as a static exhibit of the Scottish Maritime Museum. The iron screw steamer *Earl of Zetland* 253/77 was built for the North of Scotland, Orkney & Shetland Steam Navigation Co. Ltd and also had a very long career of 73 years before being broken up. The iron Clyde paddler *Minard Castle* 223/82 was built for service between Glasgow and Loch Fyne, and iron was being used as late as 1894 for part of the hull of *Mourne* 221/94 for Coppack Brothers, steel being used for the rest of the hull.

The founder died in 1905 and the yard was then run by his youngest son James, building mostly small coasters, tugs and trawlers. Standard war-built coasters were followed by the well-decked passenger/cargo steamer *Oorama* 1051/21 for the Adelaide Steamship Co. Ltd, the Newry coasters *Palm* and *Poplar*, both 344/27, and six coasters for R. Hughes & Company of Liverpool in *Haig Rose* 1117/20, *Jellicoe Rose* 1118/20, *Dorrien Rose* 1039/22, *Foch Rose* 1135/22, *Louise Rose* 1596/24 and *Fullerton Rose* 1596/25. James Fullerton died in 1925 and the last coaster was launched as *Greta Force* of 914 grt in 1928 for the Kennaugh coaster fleet, and the yard was then closed and demolished.

The Fullerton - built coaster KYLES pictured as a static exhibit at the Scottish Maritime Museum (M.F. Haddon). She served as a coaster between 1872 - 1921 and sand dredger between 1921 - 1942, coaster between 1945 - 1960 and tanker between 1960 - 1984, when acquired by the Scottish Maritime Museum.

The Antarctic research ship JOHN BISCOE was built by Fleming & Ferguson Ltd in 1956.

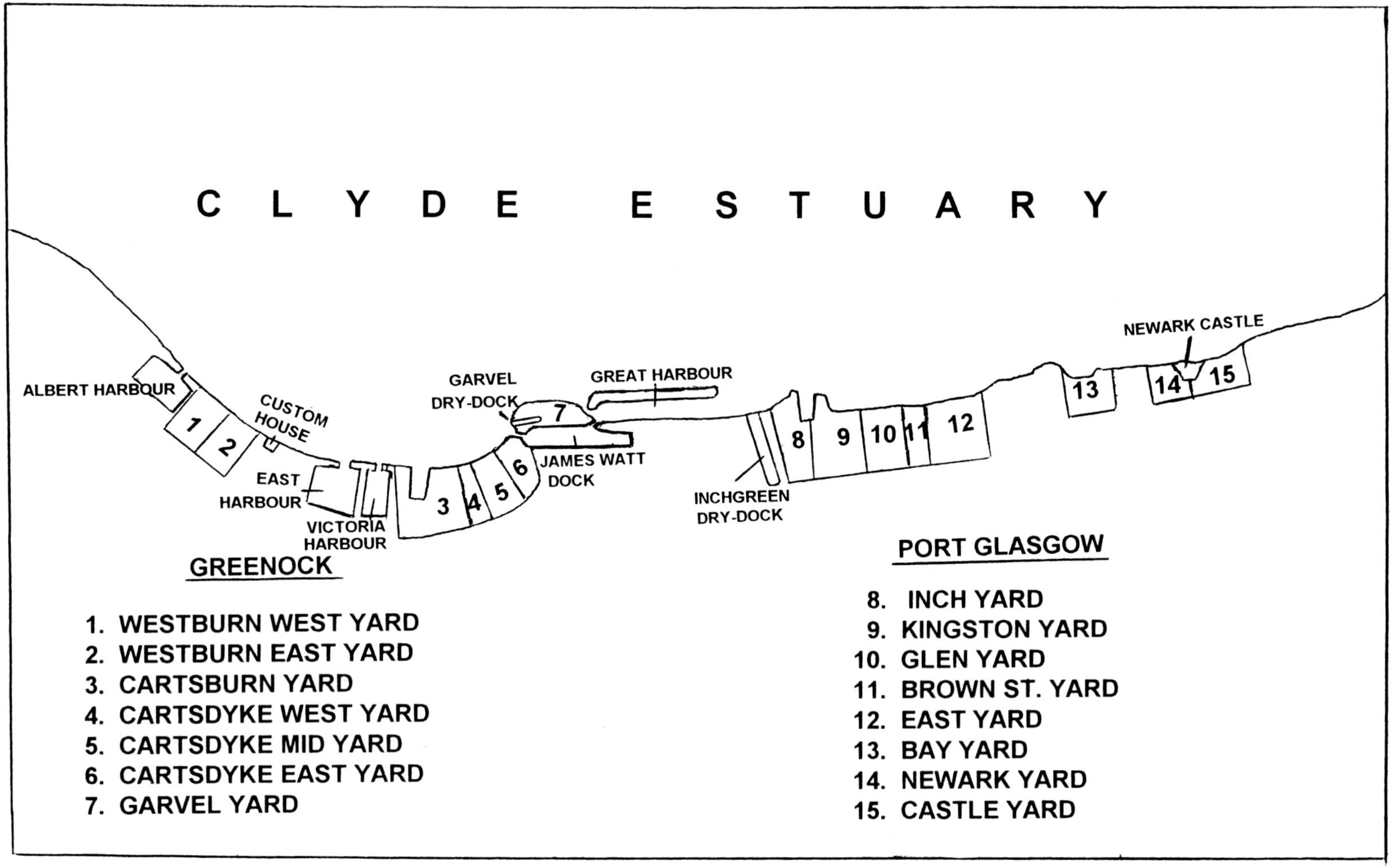
CLYDE ESTUARY
ALBERT HARBOUR
1
2
CUSTOM HOUSE
EAST HARBOUR
VICTORIA HARBOUR
3
4
5
6
GARVEL DRY-DOCK
7
JAMES WATT DOCK
GREAT HARBOUR
INCHGREEN DRY-DOCK
8
9
10
11
12
13
14
15
NEWARK CASTLE
GREENOCK
1. WESTBURN WEST YARD
2. WESTBURN EAST YARD
3. CARTSBURN YARD
4. CARTSDYKE WEST YARD
5. CARTSDYKE MID YARD
6. CARTSDYKE EAST YARD
7. GARVEL YARD
PORT GLASGOW
8. INCH YARD
9. KINGSTON YARD
10. GLEN YARD
11. BROWN ST. YARD
12. EAST YARD
13. BAY YARD
14. NEWARK YARD
15. CASTLE YARD

SCOTTS' of GREENOCK

The renowned Scotts' yards at Greenock had a very long history and became famous as builders of warships, as well as Chinese river steamers and cargo-liners for John Swire with 98 ships delivered, and 84 cargo-liners for the Far East service of Alfred Holt and his Blue Funnel Line. John Scott had founded a yard at Greenock as long ago as 1711 for the building of small fishing craft, and his son Charles Cunningham Scott first began building ships at the Cartsdyke Dockyard in 1850 under the style of Scott & Company. His sons, John Scott and Robert Sinclair Scott, completely reconstructed the Cartsdyke yard, and then acquired the nearby iron shipbuilding yard and graving dock of Robert Steele & Sons in 1883, on which they established the Cartsburn Dockyard, which was laid out for naval construction.

Interest in steam propulsion of ships and furthering James Watts' invention of the steam engine resulted in various experimental steamships on the Clyde, and in 1819 this yard then built the first steamer to trade between the Clyde and Liverpool. The Scott family purchased an engine works at Greenock in 1825 and then began to build steamers for the long trade routes out to the Middle East and Far East. They built the steamer *Tagus* in 1837 for the Gibraltar mail contract of the Peninsular Steam Navigation Company, which became the famous P & O company in 1839 when awarded the Egypt mail contract. *India* of 1206 tons was completed in 1839 as the largest steamer built to date on the Clyde, and transferred to P & O a few years later. *Dee* of 1848 tons was completed in 1841 for the new West Indies service of the Royal West India Mail Company. In 1865 Alfred Holt ordered his first three steamers from Scotts', *Ajax, Agamemnon* and *Achilles* of 2347 grt, and were the first long-haul ships to be fitted with compound steam engines, which made commercial trading possible with the Far East. It is interesting to note that the propellers of this trio were abaft the rudder !

The China Navigation Company was formed in 1873 by John Swire for river trading in China, and the first steamers built for him by Scotts' were the iron *Chefoo* 1087/76 and *Tientsin* 1987/76. A further 96 ships were to be built at Greenock, and in addition at the turn of the century Scotts' became technical advisers to John Swire, with Swire already having shares in the Scott yard, and Henry Scott being a senior partner in the Swire company. Scotts' were entrusted with the work of advising and preparing plans for the construction of a large graving dock, slipways, building berths and engine works at Hong Kong. This became the Taikoo Dockyard

& Engineering Co. Ltd owned by Swire with Scotts' remaining as advisers to the Swire Group of companies until the 1980s. The Scott family had around a quarter holding in Swire companies, with Scotts' sending drawings of all Swire ships from Greenock to the Taikoo Dockyard for construction there. The first of many twin-screw Swire steamers for navigating more than 1000 miles upon the fast-flowing Yangtsze river was completed at Greenock in 1878. The changeover to steel construction occurred in 1882 with the twin-screw sisters *Taiwan, Whampoa* and *Woosung* all 1734/82 and the smaller river sisters *Wuchang* and *Chung King*, both 1258/82.

In 1899 Scott & Company was incorporated as a limited liability company, Scotts' Shipbuilding & Engineering Co. Ltd, and absorbed the family engine works at Greenock in 1904. In the following year of 1905 they completed their last four-masted barque, *Archibald Russell* of 2048 tons for J. Hardie & Company of Glasgow, which survived until World War II in the famous Finnish grain fleet of Gustaf Erikson before being broken up at Gateshead in 1949. The two main customers remained as Blue Funnel Line with twenty ships built, and Swire had nineteen ships built between 1900 and 1905 of which only the largest are shown in the following list :-

MENELAUS	4672/95	YOCHOW	2127/01
GLAUCAS	5573/96	ANHUI	2209/03
CALCHAS	6748/99	FENGTIEN	1765/05
IDOMENEUS	6692/99	KANCHOW	2001/05
MACHAON	6738/99	KUEICHOW	2001/05
AJAX	7040/00	LIANGCHOW	2001/05
AGAMEMNON	7011/00	LUCHOW	2001/05
ALCINOUS	6743/00	YINGCHOW	2001/05
DEUCALION	7030/00		
PROMETHEUS	6894/03	and	
ASTYANAX	4872/06	smaller	
MEMNON	4870/06	craft	
GORGON	2885/08		
ATREUS	6700/11		
RHESUS	6704/11		
TALTHYBIUS	10254/12		
IXION	10263/12		
HELENUS	7366/13		
AGAPENOR	7392/14		
MENTOR	7555/14		

Booth Line of Liverpool ordered the small steamer *Banco* 2984/08 and 3140 dwt for their Amazon service, and she was followed by the larger *Hildebrand* 6991/11 for the tourist trade to Spain, Portugal and Madeira with accomodation for

674 passengers. British India Line ordered the twin-funnelled *Bharata* 4054/03, with the local Donaldson Line taking the passenger/cargo-liners *Cassandra* 8135/06 and *Letitia* 8991/12, the latter having accomodation for 1408 mostly steerage passengers and 8400 tons of cargo. Leyland Line also had a pair of passenger/cargo-liners from the yards in *Nessian* 6276/12 and *Orubian* 3876/14; and Ben Line of Leith ordered *Benmhor* 4887/11, with Strick Line taking three for Mediterranean and Persian Gulf services in *Afghanistan* 4443/05, *Gulistan* 4445/05 and *Bardistan* 3888/06.

Scotts' also acquired a good reputation for building large steam yachts with elegant bowsprits and raked funnels for private owners. Some twenty four luxurious yachts for the leisured wealthy were built in the yards between 1876 and 1908 of which the largest was *Margarita* completed in 1900. She displaced 2522 tons, had a length of 272 feet, breadth of 37 feet, was twin-screw and powered by two triple expansion steam engines with four cylinders in each engine to give 17 knots. Her owner was A. J. Drexel of Philadelphia and he designed her with thirteen large staterooms as well as dining, drawing and smoking rooms and a nursery. The last yacht completed was the twin-screw *Cassandra* of 1908 which displaced 1417 tons for another American owner, R. A. Rainy of New York. The elegant clipper-bowed yacht *Hinemoa* 542/76 was built as a parliamentary yacht for the Government of New Zealand and had a very long life until 1944, a testimony to her stout Scotts' construction.

Scotts' also built many tramps at this time, with the Clyde Shipping Co. Ltd, who named their ships after British lighthouses, ordering four. The first of these was taken on long-term charter by Anchor Line, who used a nomenclature ending in 'ia'. A British lighthouse with a name ending in 'ia' could not be found, thus a compromise was found in the North African lighthouse *Kalibia* 4930/02, and her sisters were completed as *Kish* 4928/02, *Beachy* 4718/09 and *Hurst* 4718/10. John M. Campbell & Son of Glasgow also had four tramps built in *Dalhanna* 4662/06, *Dalblair* 4661/06, *Daldorch* 4718/07 and *Dalmore* 4717/07; and James Gardiner of Glasgow took *Gleneden* and *Glenorchy*, both 4735/09.

Two tankers were completed for the Anglo-American Oil Co. Ltd as *Narragansett* 9196/03 and 12,000 dwt with engines and funnel amidships, and *Tatarrax* 6216/12 and 9614 dwt, the latter built on the Isherwood longitudinal system. Coastal vessels completed included *Lurcher* and *Setter*, both 993/06 for Burns Line of Glasgow for their service to Belfast, *Pladda* 1334/07 for the Clyde Shipping Co. Ltd and *Carron* 2351/09 for the Grangemouth to London service of the Carron Company. Many coastal steamers were built at the turn of the century for the Brazilian coastal services such as *Ondina* 993/91, as well as eight large sailing lighters of 500 tons built for service on the River Plate.

Scotts' completed their first Dreadnought battleship for the Royal Navy in 1909 as *Colossus* and followed her with *Ajax* in 1912. However the yard had a longer history of naval work than any other Clyde yard, stretching back to the sail-powered *Prince of Wales* of 1803. The first iron frigate was completed as Greenock in 1849, and then a large amount of development work was done at the Scotts engine works on high-pressure water-tube boilers. These were incorporated in the elegant three-masted gunboats *Thrush* and *Sparrow* of 1888/89, and the Greenock engine works then went on to build the boilers and engines of the battleships *Barfleur* (1894), *Canopus* (1900) - the first battleship to be fitted with water-tube boilers, *Prince of Wales* (1902) and the Dreadnought *St. Vincent* (1910) all built by other yards, as well as those of *Colossus* and *Ajax* from the Greenock yards. The trials of the four-funnelled armoured cruiser *Argyll* were completed satisfactorily in 1906, as were those of her sister *Defence* with Greenock-built machinery from a Royal Dockyard in 1909. Development work was begun on Italian-designed submarines in 1909 when a licence was taken out on the Laurenti design, and the first submarine to be built in Scotland completed her diving trials in 1914 as *S1*. The Scotts improvements in submarine design and equipment kept their name in the forefront of naval thinking at the Admiralty, and two more submarines to this design *S2* and *S3* were then built during the Great War as well as the motor-driven submarines E31, E51 - fitted with minelaying capability, and G14, as well as the steam-powered submarine *Swordfish*. The submarine depot ship *Maidstone* was completed pre-war, and two high-speed light cruisers, *Caradoc* of 1917 and *Dragon* of 1917, with a sister *Durban* completed after the war, the monitor *Sir John Moore* of 1915, and a dozen torpedo boat destroyers and three sloops completed the naval war programme.

Cunard Line took delivery of three passenger liners just prior to the war. They ordered a twin-funnelled pair for their Canadian trade capable of carrying 2078 passengers, *Alaunia* and *Andania* both 13405/13 and propelled by quadruple-expansion steam engines to give 14 knots. The twin-funnelled *Transylvania* 14315/14 was ordered by Cunard in 1913 and was the first Transatlantic liner to be propelled by geared turbines, giving a service speed of 16.75 knots. However she was sold to the local Anchor Line shortly before her loss as a transport in 1915 when 413 people lost their lives. *Albania* 13060/17 for Cunard was a twin-screw liner powered by two Brown - Curtis turbines and coal-fired boilers, and could carry 500 passengers and 15,500 tons of cargo. The yard had thus built a mixture of naval and merchant ships during the war, with their main peace-time customers of

Blue Funnel Line taking *Tyndareus* 11361/16 and *Diomed* 7253/17, and Swire taking *Sinkiang* 2771/16. A war-standard tanker *War Angler* and the 'B' dry-cargo *War Duck* were also built.

Two emigrant carriers were built in 1919 for Lloyd Royal Belge capable of carrying 1100 emigrants and 8200 tons of cargo; and then two passenger/cargo-liners were built for the Valparaiso to New York service of Cia Sud Americana de Vapores, Chile as *Aconcagua* and *Teno*, both 7288/22. The local Donaldson Line ordered the turbine-powered *Corinaldo* 7131/21 and *Gracia* 5642/21 for their South American service. However the main customers remained as Blue Funnel Line and Swire for whom the following were built :-

ACHILLES	11404/20	KALGAN	2655/21
TROILUS	7422/21	KWEICHANG	2644/21
PHEMIUS	7405/21	KIUNGCHOW	2651/21
PHILOCTETES	11431/22	KINGYUAN	2635/21
PATROCLUS	11314/23	NANCHANG	2489/22
HECTOR	11198/24	NEWCHWANG	2482/22
ADRASTUS	7905/23	ANKING	3472/25
ASPHALION	6274/23	ANSHUN	3188/30
DOLIUS	5506/24	SHENKING	3001/31
CENTAUR	3222/24	HUNAN	2827/32
POLYDORUS	5922/26	YOCHOW	2812/33
PROMETHEUS	6095/26	YUNNAN	2812/34
ALCINOUS	6189/26		
EURYBATES	6276/28		
MYRMIDON	6278/30		
CLYTONEUS	6278/30		
POLYPHEMUS	6269/30		
AJAX	7540/31		

Dolius and *Eurybates* were powered by the unique Scott - Still oil engine, however Blue Funnel Line changed to North-Eastern Holt oil engines for the Myrmidon class. *Anshun* was the first motor vessel in the Swire fleet followed by *Yochow* and *Yunnan*, all powered by Scott two-cycle oil engines of 1500 bhp giving 12.5 knots service speed, and all had two-inch teak decks with hand rails also made of teak. Three large tankers were also built, two for Atlantic Refining of Philadelphia with bridges and diesel-electric engines all-aft in *Brunswick* 6546/28 and *Winkler* 6927/30, and one for Standard Oil with bridge amidships and quadruple-expansion steam engines, *Eclipse* 9767/31. The East Coast coastal liner *Royal Archer* 2266/28 was completed for the fast 15 knot service of the London & Edinburgh Shipping Co. Ltd, while the Straits Steamship Co. Ltd of Singapore took their second ship from the yard in *Lipis* 914/30, the first having been *Krian* 845/11. The following tramps were also built :-

ELDONPARK	5186/28	J. & J. Denholm,Glasgow
EARLSPARK	5186/29	"
LYLEPARK	5186/29	"
DALBLAIR	4607/26	John M. Campbell & Son,Glasgow
DALCAIRN	4607/27	"
DALMORE	5193/27	"
DALVEEN	5193/27	"
DALCROY	4557/30	"
DALFRAM	4557/30	"
DALCROSS	4557/30	"

Scotts' were helped through the Depression years by warship orders starting with the destroyers *Anthony* (1929), *Ardent* (1929), *Escapade* (1934), *Escort* (1934), cruiser *Galatea* launched on 5th August,1934 and completed a year later, submarines *Seawolf* (1933) and *Cachalot* (1938), and the destroyers *Hostile* (1936), *Hotspur* (1936), *Matabele* (1939) and *Punjabi* (1939). The six-inch gun 'Town' class cruiser *Glasgow* was launched on 20th June,1936 and commissioned in September,1937, while Scotts' also manufactured the propelling machinery for her sister *Gloucester*.

However while work was still slack in 1934 the opportunity was taken to exchange the company's East Cartsdyke yard with the Mid Cartsdyke yard owned by the Greenock Dockyard Co. Ltd. This unique deal included all of the machinery in each yard, and placed Scotts' in a much more favourable position with a continuous river frontage and an enlarged Cartsburn Dockyard, as the slipway of the Cartsdyke West yard of Ross & Marshall had been purchased in 1925. This yard had completed some 14 Clyde puffers between 1899 and 1925 for Ross & Marshall. Orders were then obtained from Elder,Dempster for four cargo-liners of 6000 dwt powered by Scott-Doxford oil engines of 3100 bhp to give 12.5 knot service speeds on the West African route, *Sobo* 4124/37, *Swedru* 4124/37, *Sansu* 4174/39 and *Sangara* 4124/39 . Alfred Holt preferred to register his next cargo-liner under Glen Line as *Glenroy* 8997/38.

The Cartsburn Dockyard was given over entirely to naval construction during World War II, with three cruisers completed as *Bonaventure* (1940), *Scylla* (1942) and *Royalist* (1943) and twenty destroyers and twelve submarines as well as the destroyer depot ship *Tyne* commissioned in 1941. A bitter blow to the yard was the complete destruction of the Head Office with all the valuable ship and engineering records in a bombing raid in May,1941. The engine and boiler works suffered a direct hit and were out of action for six months, and the force of the explosions blew a fully-plated destroyer nearing launch completely off her slipway, and she had to be painstakingly pulled apart and rebuilt at great delay. A submarine on the next berth had been moved bodily some inches on the blocks, but by means of jacks and willing workers was replaced without damage. A third bomb exploded under the stern of a cruiser on the building berth, it fortunately did no damage to the ship but damaged the roof of the plater's shed thirty yards away. Office staff were then housed in various buildings and huts for the duration of the war until a new Head Office was built in 1948, when a new shipyard time office and ambulance room were also completed. Two further war-design submarines were completed in 1947/48 as *Artemis* and *Artful*, and the yard also handled overhauls for seven similar war-design submarines.

The shipyard was switched back to merchant construction at the end of the war, largely for the main customers of Blue Funnel Line; Elder,Dempster and Swire:-

AGAPENOR	7664/47	Blue Funnel Line
ASTYANAX	8301/48	"
CYCLOPS	7709/48	"
SINKIANG	3029/46	China Nav. Co. Ltd (Swire)
SHANSI	3152/46	"
CHANGSHA	7412/49	"
TAIYUAN	7412/49	"
ANKING	6124/49	"
CHUNGKING	9393/50	"
CHANGCHOW	9403/51	"
SHONGA	4810/46	Elder,Dempster
SULIMA	4810/48	"
SWEDRU	4809/48	"
EBOE	9397/52	"
EBANI	9396/52	"
EGORI	8586/57	"
PATANI	6183/54	"
DARU	6168/58	"
DUNKWA	8254/60	"
DEIDO	8254/61	"
FOURAH BAY	7704/61	"
FALABA	7703/62	"

The four larger passenger/cargo-liners for Swire were all powered by Scott-Doxford oil engines, however the trade for which *Chungking* and *Changchow* were designed failed to materialise and they were sold to the Government as supply ships. *Chungking* was renamed *Retainer* after a few months trading, but *Changchow* did not even leave the yard under that name, being painted grey and renamed *Resurgent*. Two cargo-liners were also built for British India Line as

Nowshera 8516/55 and *Nyanza* 8513/56, as well as the mini-liner *Fort Avalon* 3484/49 with accomodation for 100 passengers and 4010 tons of cargo on the St. John's(NF) to Halifax (NS) and New York service of Furness,Withy & Co. Ltd. The yard and engine works then built a series of tankers in the range 17260 to 19750 dwt for Norwegian, British and Greek owners :-

BUSEN ROLLO	11301/50	Hval. Tonsberg A/S,Tonsberg
LINDE	11347/51	"
JARABELLA	11317/50	Jahre A/S, Norway
LORD CANNING	11347/51	Northern S.S. Co. Ltd,London
NIMERTIS	11267/52	Andreadis,Greece
LADY DOROTHY	11261/52	"
BORDER REGIMENT	11311/53	Lowland Tanker Co. Ltd,Newcastle
BORDER HUNTER	11301/54	"
MARIETTA NOMIKOS	11577/54	Markos P. Nomikos,Greece
SPERVIK	11497/55	Skibs A/S Spervik,Norway
CALTEX EDINBURGH	12492/56	Texaco Overseas Tankship
ANGELOS LUSIS	11414/57	A. Lusi, Greece
N. GEORGIOS	13152/58	G. Nicolaou,Greece
BRITISH SWIFT	10922/59	British Tanker Co. Ltd
QUEDA	12898/59	British India Line
QUILOA	13506/60	"

In 1955 the yard began to use a new 360 feet long welding shed at the east end of the yard with two bays 80 feet wide, and with a height of 45 feet. The tanker programme above had given the impetus to all-welded ships, and *Caltex Edinburgh* was the first all-welded ship from the yard. *N. Georgios* was the first bridge and engines-aft tanker since the American diesel-electric pair of *Brunswick* and *Winkler*, built thirty years earlier. *N. Georgios* was powered by two steam turbines each of 9100 shp built at Greenock to give a service speed of 15 knots under her full load of 19726 tons of oil.

Greenock had a very long history of sugar refining for the Lyle family, and it was very fitting that the first sugar bulk carrier should be built at the yard in 1955 as *Crystal Cube* 8680/55. She could carry 9740 tons of sugar in five holds with a raised quarterdeck, and a Scott-Doxford oil engine gave a service speed of 12 knots. Two general cargo ships of 13000 dwt and two of 15500 dwt were completed for Ships Finance & Management with Scott-Doxford oil engines to give a service speed of 15 knots as *Lord Byron* 9364/57, *Lord Codrington* 9364/58, *Lord Gladstone* 11299/59 and *Lord Canning* 11299/59. Two ore-carriers were then completed for the Vallum Shipping Co. Ltd, Newcastle managed by Common Brothers and on ten-year charter to BISCO as *Iron Horse* 11125/60 and *Iron Crown* 11128/60.

The yard was then modernised for prefabrication between 1959 and 1961 (See Shipyard plan) to allow construction of tankers and bulk carriers up to 40,000 dwt. A crane pier was laid down the middle of the yard and two 60-ton cranes installed, and on the west of this pier a reinforced concreted berth was laid, which could either build one ship of 40,000 dwt or two ships of around 19,000 dwt . On the east side of the crane pier, ships of up to 24,000 dwt could be built, with a smaller berth for warships to the east of the main berths. Considerable modification was also made to the plate and section working bays, stockyard, blacksmith shop and joiners store with new burning machines and optical lofting installed. Ships could now be launched with engines and propeller shafts aboard and then moved to the fitting-out basin, which had dimensions of length 655 feet and width 160 feet with a 100-ton hammerhead crane on the west side and a 25-ton crane on the east side.

The first bulker from Cartsburn after modernisation was built to the order of the Government of Guinea as their first deep-sea ship and completed as *Simandou* 10764/63. She was followed by the Greek bulker *Kapetan Georgios* 17059/63 for the Andreadis family, and *Graigwerdd* 18618/64 for the Graig Steamship Co. Ltd of Cardiff managed by Idwal Williams, and *British Monarch* 16903/65 for the locally-owned Harrisons (Clyde) Ltd. The warship berth had not been affected by the modernisation programme, but had only built two new surface warships in post-war years, the frigates *Puma* (1957) and *Euralyus* (1964). The submarines *Cachalot* (1959) and *Walrus* (1961), the latter launched by the Duchess of Gloucester in 1959, had been followed by the similar *Otter*, launched by the wife of the Chairman in May,1961 and completed during 1962, and followed by *Otus* (1963) and *Opportune* (1964). An order for six submarines of the same class was then obtained from Australia, and completed as *Oxley* (1967), *Otway* (1968), *Onslow* (1969) and launched by Princess Alexandra, *Ovens* (1969), *Orion* (1977) and *Otama* (1978) with two similar submarines for Chile as *Hyatt* (1976) - damaged by an expolsion aboard while fitting-out on 27th January,1976 - and *O'Brien* (1976). The last submarine to be launched by Scotts' was *Otama* in December,1975 by Princess Anne.

The family-owned yard now had as Chairman Michael Sinclair Scott, grandson of Robert Sinclair Scott who had reconstructed the Cartsdyke East yard a century earlier and son of Cedric C. Sinclair Scott. He had been appointed in 1957, and other directors included John Swire Scott. It was thus very fitting that the Chairman should announce the merger of Scotts Cartsburn Dockyard with the Cartsdyke shipyard of the Greenock Dockyard Co. Ltd on 21st December,1965. In June of that year he had also announced that Scott & Sons (Bowling) Ltd (q.v.) was to be taken over. The merger of the Cartsburn and Carstdyke yards took effect

Aerial view of the Cartsburn Dockyard in 1968 with the Welsh bulk carrier GRAIGFFION in the fitting - out basin.
(Scott - Lithgow Ltd)

The drill ship BEN OCEAN LANCER of 1977 completed for Ben Odeco Ltd.

from 1st April,1966 while Cartsburn was building the bulkers *Binsnes* 10961/66 and *Bolnes* 11100/66 for Kristian Jebsen A/S,Norway. The Cartsdyke yard had been the same yard that Scotts had exchanged with the Greenock Dockyard Co. Ltd in 1934, and now at last the dream of a continuous shipyard was fulfilled. The Cartsdyke Dockyard had built the vast majority of the extensive Clan Line fleet of cargo-liners, and there was one Clan Line ship left on the order book when the yard was taken over, completed as *Clan Alpine* 8713/67. The reefer *Geestcape* 8042/66 was the last launch from Cartsdyke before the merger, and her sister *Geesthaven* 8042/66 for Geest was the first ship launched after the take-over.

The Geddes Report recommended mergers, and on the Lower Clyde the giants of Scotts' and Lithgows agreed to merge in 1968 by setting-up a holding company Scott - Lithgow Ltd, and two separate operating companies Scotts Shipbuilding Co.(1969) Ltd and Lithgows (1969) Ltd. to run the yards. It is perhaps easier to understand the Scotts' output of ships from 1966 if they are listed separately under the two shipyards :-

CARTSBURN DOCKYARD		CARTSDYKE DOCKYARD	
BINSNES	10961/66	GEESTCAPE (reefer)	8042/66
BOLNES	11100/66	GEESTHAVEN "	8042/66
CLYDESDALE	24024/67	CLAN ALPINE	8713/67
RESOURCE (R.F.A)	18029/67	PADUA (reefer)	5590/67
GRAIGFFION	18453/68	PARMA "	5590/67
GAS LION (l.p.g.)	8168/68	WORLD PRESIDENT	12341/69
ERISKAY	12489/69	WORLD HONG KONG	12341/69
GRECIAN LEGEND	22998/69	BAKNES	11524/70
GRECIAN SPIRIT	22992/70	BINSNES	11524/70
INGEREN	12636/70	BULKNES	13234/70
CUMBRIA	18570/71	GEEST-TIDE (reefer)	5865/71
IRON BANBURY	11388/71	GEESTLAND "	5881/72
BRITISH AVON	15540/72	GEESTSTAR "	5871/73
BRITISH KENNET	15540/73	BRITISH TWEED	15540/73
BRITISH FORTH	15540/73	SUGAR CARRIER	17792/74
JAG PRAKASH	15849/74	SUGAR TRADER	17801/74
JAG PRIYA	20416/75	BEN OCEAN LANCER	10823/77
NEWTON (R.A.M.S.)	2779/76	CLYDENES	2351/77
FORT GRANGE (R.F.A.)	16049/78	PACNORSE 1	9871/79
FORT AUSTIN (R.F.A.)	16049/79	MARON	16482/80
MYRMIDON	16482/80	MENTOR	16482/80
CHALLENGER (Seabed ops)	5100/84		

The two main traditional customers of Scotts' were represented in the above list by the three 'M' class cargo-liners of Ocean Transport & Trading (formerly Blue

Funnel Line) *Maron, Mentor* and *Myrmidon*. These in fact were built for the West African trade of subsidiary Elder,Dempster and fitted with five high goalpost masts on raised cargo working platforms, and could carry 21180 tons of cargo at 18 knots. The other main Scotts' customer was Swire and was represented by the bulker *Eriskay* of 19500 dwt, and who also purchased in 1972 her two sisterships *World President* and *World Hong Kong* renaming them *Erisort* and *Eriboll*, all three being designed to be able to trade to the Canadian Great Lakes.

Gas Lion (11528 cu. m.) for Leif Erichsens Rederi A/S of Oslo was very similar to the Houlder Brothers liquid gas tanker *Clerk-Maxwell* (11751 cu. m.) of 1967 and built on the Tyne, each having three rectangular tanks. The three largest bulkers from Scotts' were *Clydesdale* of Hadley Shipping Co. Ltd and 42820 dwt, and *Grecian Legend* and *Grecian Spirit* of 42280 dwt and owned by Goulandris of Greece. Construction started in 1975 in the Cartsdyke yard of the first of two self-propelled dynamically positioned drilling ships. She was launched on 2nd February,1976 as *Ben Ocean Lancer* for Ben Odeco Ltd, a subsidiary of Ben Line of Leith and completed in March,1977. Her tall drilling structure was positioned amidships with five diesel-electric motors aft driving twin propellers and with bridge right forward over her bow, and was capable of drilling down to 20,000 feet in depths of water as great as 3,000 feet. Construction started after her launch on the same berth of a sister and she was launched on 7th April,1977 as *Pacnorse 1* for the Pacnorse Group and completed in early 1979.

The launch on 9th December,1976 from the Cartsburn yard of the naval replenishment ship *Fort Grange* recalled the launch of the *Resource* of ten years earlier from the yard. However *Resource* with a length of 640 feet was 40 feet longer than *Fort Grange* and of different appearance with engines-aft and bridge forward and fitted with four sets of goalpost masts for replenishment transfers. *Resouce* had cost only £5.5M compared to double that for *Fort Grange*, which was completed in April,1978, and for her sister *Fort Austin*, launched on 9th March,1978 and completed in June,1979. The new sisters could each carry 3500 tons of armament, victualling and naval stores and were more efficient than *Resource* in that pallets and fork-lift trucks were used to bring the stores up from the four holds. They were equipped with a Sea King helicopter, operated from a helideck and hangar aft, and were propelled by an 8-cylinder Scott-Sulzer oil engine driving a controllable pitch propeller.

The Cartsburn and Cartsdyke yards were nationalised on 1st July,1977 but unfortunately soon began to run out of orders, with *Mentor* the last ship launched from Cartsdyke on 8th August,1979, and *Myrmidon* the last merchant ship launched from Cartsburn on 19th February,1980. However Cartsburn had one more ship left to build - the deep-diving seabed operations ship *Challenger* - launched on 19th May,1981 and accepted into naval service at Greenock in July,1984. Her features included a stern ramp for launching deep-diving submersibles, and a moonpool in the centre of the ship through which diving chambers could be operated by crane, and also a large goalpost mast abaft the bridge. Her delivery had been delayed by twenty months by having to rewire the entire ship, which escalated her cost, and after only being used twice for seabed operations she was laid-up, and eventually sold for commercial operation in 1993.

The Cartsburn and Cartsdyke yards were sold along with the Lithgow yards to the Trafalgar House consortium on 28th March,1984, and then lay forlornly for nearly four years until demolished to make way for redevelopment. A concrete promenade has been built along the waterfront, with offices for American-owned Crusader Insurance, and a new roundabout has been built on the main road to Port Glasgow on the site of the historic Cartsdyke slipways which launched ships for more than 150 years.

The site of the Cartsburn and Cartsdyke Dockyards today, with a newly built promenade and offices for an insurance company (right). The Garvel dry-dock and entrance to the James Watt Dock are on the left, and centre is the now closed Clark - Kincaid engine shops. (Author)

GREENOCK DOCKYARD CO. LTD.

The period from 1918 to 1966 when the Greenock Dockyard was owned by The Clan Line Steamers Ltd of Glasgow saw one of the greatest shipbuilder/owner associations in British shipyard history, producing some 65 Clan Line cargo-liners. The Cartsdyke Mid yard had been purchased from Russell & Company in 1900 by the Grangemouth Dockyard Company, which then amended its name to the Grangemouth & Greenock Dockyard Company. In its early days the yard was more commonly known as the 'klondyke' yard, in reference to the then recent Alaskan gold rush of 1894. One of the first ships built by the new company at Greenock was *Maria Goriainova* 1843/00, fitted with a triple expansion engine supplied by Hutson & Sons Ltd. Six ships were then built in 1901 of which the largest were *Nadia* 2422/01 for E.L. Weighall of London and *Jupiter* 2124/01 for the Hessler Shipping Co. Ltd, Hartlepool and *Restormel* 2118/01 for John Cory of Cardiff, with the others for Spanish,Dutch and German owners. J. Roy of Rouen took delivery of *Baltique* 2457/02 during a year in which the Great Lakes steamer *Wobun* 1551/02 was built, and the yard also built two more for the Great Lakes with engines aft and bridge forward in *Neepawah* 1799/03 and *Carleton* 1451/07.

The German barques *Beethoven* 2003/04 and *Mozart* 2005/04 for A.C. de Freitas, Hamburg were followed by ever-increasing sizes of triple-expansion steam tramps e.g. *Gretavale* 3124/05 and *Gryfevale* 4437/06 for Andrew Crawford of Glasgow as well as *Kyleakin* 3073/05 and *Luchana* 3051/04 for other local owners. William Burrell had ordered twenty tramps from five Port Glasgow and Greenock yards in 1906 including eight from this yard all with 'Strath' names e.g. *Strathclyde* 4417/06 in a time of bad slump when shipyards were desperate for orders and willing to take 'rock-bottom' prices. He was later to order four more from the Greenock Dockyard in the continuing slump for delivery between 1909 and 1912. An order was placed by Furness,Withy & Co. Ltd for four colliers of 3000 dwt with engines amidships, of which *Cramlington* 1824/07 and *Castle Eden* 1844/08 were built at Greenock, and the other pair at Grangemouth. In 1908 the company recognised the importance of the larger berths at Greenock, and reversed the yard names in the title, becoming the Greenock & Grangemouth Dockyard Co. Ltd.

The first tanker had been built by the yard in 1903 as *Pennoil* 4434/03 for the Pennsylvania Oil Company although registered in Germany, and she was followed by more tankers :-

PURELIGHT	4489/08	Purelight Trading Co.,U.S.A.
H.C. HENRY	4219/09	H.C. Henry, Seattle

MINA BREA	4145/09	London & Pacific Pet. Co. Ltd
IMPOCO	1683/10	Imperial Oil, Canada
BURMA	1832/11	Admiralty
HERA	4705/12	Deutsche-American Pet. Co. Ltd
UNCAS	4722/13	Tank Storage & Carriage Co. Ltd
CASSIS	4792/14	Anglo-Saxon Pet. Co. Ltd
SAXONIAN	4850/14	Lane & Macandrews, London
CUYAHOGA	4586/14	Anglo-American Oil Co. Ltd

as well as the following triple-expansion powered steam tramps :-

STRATHESK	4336/09	William Burrell, Greenock
STRATHDENE	4385/10	"
ESSEX ABBEY	3595/11	Meldrum & Swinson, London
RIVER ORONTES	4351/12	S. & J. Thompson
STRATHCARRON	4337/12	William Burrell, Greenock
STRATHMORE	4337/12	"
SAINT CECILIA	4411/13	A. Mackay, Glasgow
SAINT KENTIGERN	4411/14	"

The engines-amidships collier *Broompark* 1325/10 for J. & J. Denholm, Glasgow was the first ship from the yard for this owner, who placed many more orders for sisterships with the Grangemouth yard during the Great War, as well as larger tramps from the Greenock yard. An interesting coastal ship fitted with awning decks had earlier set sail from Greenock for the Brazilian coastal trade of Cia Navegacao of Rio de Janeiro as *Guahyba* 1891/08.

World War I saw the yard building steam tramps and two small Admiralty oilers, *Slavol* 2623/16 and *Thermol* 1902/17, and the standard coaster *Cambronne*. Tramps completed included *Beechpark* 4763/17 for Denholm, and *Gogovale* 5388/16 and *Gretavale* 5388/17 for Andrew Crawford of Glasgow. Five standard 'A' type tramps were completed as *War Briton* 5193/18, *Leapark* 5173/19 completed in April for Denholm, *Beechpark* 5135/19 completed in July, *Grangepark* 5132/19 completed in November and *Elmpark* 5800/20 completed in May,1920 and *Oakpark* 5800/20, which was sold on completion to the Union Steamship Co. Ltd of New Zealand and renamed *Orowaiti*.

In 1918 the yard was purchased by Cayzer,Irvine & Co. Ltd, owners and managers of The Clan Line Steamers Ltd of Glasgow with services to India and South Africa, and went on to build some 65 Clan Line cargo-liners starting with *Clan Alpine* 5442/18 and *Clan Macwilliam* 6086/18. Lord Cayzer then changed the title of the yard in 1920 to the Greenock Dockyard Co. Ltd. Orders were hard to find in the great slump of 1920/21, with *Mont Agel* 4572/20 completing for the French S.G.T.M. of Marseilles followed by the Dutch passenger ship *Staur* 4484/20 and the Norwegian steam tramp *Nordkyn II* 4902/21 for A. Harloff. J. & J. Denholm then took delivery of their first tanker *Cedarpark* 5087/22, however no ships were launched from the yard in 1923 with only *Clan Macilwraith* 4839/24 and two sailing barges *Mirasol* and *Garza Azul* during 1924. A series of tankers was built from 1925 including :-

MOBILOIL	5090/25	Vacuum Oil Company, U.S.A.
VALETTA	4903/25	Gow & Harrison, Glasgow
VIRGILIA	5728/27	"
VANCOUVER	5729/28	"
VOREDA	7216/35	" (Delivery delayed by Depression)
BRITISH RELIANCE	7000/28	British Tanker Co. Ltd
BRITISH RESOURCE	7209/31	"
BRITISH ENERGY	7209/31	"

as well as two coasters for the General Steam Navigation Co. Ltd, London in *Hirondelle* 1346/25 and *Woodcock* 1827/27, and the tramps *Barrdale* 5072/25, *Barrwhin* 4998/29 and *Melmay* 5413/30. The Clan Line Steamers Ltd then started to build up their fleet with ships from the Dockyard, with their first motor cargo-liners *Clan Macdonald* 6022/28 launched on 21st February, 1928 and completed in June of that year and *Clan Macdougall* 6843/29 launched on 28th September, 1928 and completed in January, 1929 - both propelled by 8-cylinder B & W oil engines built by Kincaid of Greenock. However the next pair were propelled by a triple expansion engine boosted by a low pressure exhaust turbine as *Clan Macpherson* 6940/29 and *Clan Macalister* 6795/30 for comparison purposes with the motorships.

The Depression hit the Dockyard hard with the yard closed from 1931 to 1935 with construction stopped on the tanker *Voreda*. A unique opportunity presented itself in 1934 to exchange the Cartsdyke Mid yard of Greenock Dockyard with the Cartsdyke East yard of Scotts' (q.v.). The deal included all of the machinery in the yards, although this had been supplemented by cheap second-hand machinery purchased from other redundant Clyde yards. The workforce returned to the Cartsdyke East yard in the Spring of 1935 to start construction of the next Clan liner, launched on 14th October, 1935 as *Clan Macarthur* 10488/36 and completed in January, 1936. She was twin-screw and powered by two triple expansion engines built by the North Eastern Engineering Co. Ltd at Wallsend, as were the similar engines for her sisters *Clan Macaulay* 10448/36 and *Perthshire* 10496/36, the latter owned by the Scottish Shire Line, an associate company of the Clan Line. A further eleven Clan Line cargo-liners were completed by the start of World War II with the same type of machinery although this time built by Kincaid of Greenock :-

CLAN CAMERON	7243/37	The Clan Line Steamers Ltd
CLAN CAMPBELL	7255/37	"

CLAN CHATTAN	7262/37	"
CLAN CHISHOLM	7256/37	"
CLAN CUMMING	7264/38	"
CLAN BUCHANAN	7266/38	"
CLAN FERGUSON	7347/38	"
CLAN MENZIES	7336/38	"
CLAN FORBES	7529/38	"
CLAN FRASER	7529/39	"
CLAN LAMONT	7673/39	"

The yard was just as busy during World War II, completing ten cargo-liners for the Clan Line, although two were requisitioned for Admiralty use with *Clan Brodie* completing as the aircraft transport ship *Athene* in 1941 with room for forty aircraft, and *Clan Davidson* in use from completion in 1943 as the midget submarine depot ship *Bonaventure*. *Clan Lamont* also served from 1942 as an Infantry Landing Ship able to carry twenty landing craft and 800 marines. *Lanarkshire* 8167/40 was completed for the associated Scottish Shire Line, and the Government placed orders for five standard 'Empire' tramps and three standard refrigerated 'Empire' cargo-liners. Four engines-aft bridge amidships heavy lift ships were built during 1945/46 with three holds, each served by an 120-ton capacity heavy lift derrick. These were *Empire Byng* 7832/45, *Empire Marshal* 7836/45, *Empire Wallace* 7800/46 with the last completed as *Belocean* 7908/47 for Belships A/S owned by Christen Smith & Company of Oslo, which had pioneered this trade from the early 1920s. Vessels had their engines installed and completed their out-fitting in the nearby James Watt Dock, which also handled sugar imports for the Greenock sugar refineries of Lyle. Many repairs were done by the Dockyard workforce on badly damaged ships in this dock and the nearby Garvel dry-dock, and a new bow section was built in the yard in 1941 and fitted to the tramp *Blairspey* 4248/29 built at Ardrossan and which had her bows blown off by torpedo on 18th October,1940, and she resumed her valuable war service in 1942 as *Empire Spey*. At the end of the war there were four berths in the yard, although this was later reduced to three, capable of building ships up to six hundred feet in length.

The yard returned to commercial use and continued to build cargo-liners for The Clan Line Steamers Ltd, and for Union-Castle Line from 1956 when the two rivals on the South Africa run merged into the British & Commonwealth Shipping Group. A series of very good-looking cargo-liners of the 'S' class for Clan Line and five for Pacific Steam Navigation Company had funnels topped by a 'helmet' to ensure efficient smoke dispersal away from the bridge structure, which also had accomodation for twelve passengers. The full list of post-war cargo-liners from the Dockyard is now given :-

CLAN MACLAREN	6389/46	The Clan Line Steamers Ltd
CLAN MACLACHLAN	6365/47	"
CLAN MACLEAN	6009/47	"
CLAN MACLENNAN	6366/47	"
CLAN MACLEOD	5997/48	"
CLAN MACLAY	6388/49	"
CLAN MACTAGGART	8035/49	"
CLAN MACTAVISH	8035/49	"
CLAN SHAW	8101/49	"
CLAN SINCLAIR	8386/50	"
KENUTA	8494/50	Pacific Steam Navigation Co.
FLAMENCO	8491/50	"
CLAN SUTHERLAND	8436/51	The Clan Line Steamers Ltd
CLAN MACINNES	6517/52	"
CLAN STEWART	8163/54	"
CLAN ROBERTSON	7878/54	"
COTOPAXI	8559/54	Pacific Steam Navigation Co.
POTOSI	8564/55	"
PIZARRO	8564/55	"
CLAN ROSS	7775/56	The Clan Line Steamers Ltd
ARGYLLSHIRE	9299/56	Scottish Shire Line
AYRSHIRE	9360/57	"
CLAN MALCOLM	7326/57	The Clan Line Steamers Ltd
CLAN MATHESON	7315/57	"
CLAN MENZIES	7315/58	"
CLAN MACIVER	7105/58	"
SWAN RIVER	9637/59	Houlder Bros.
ROTHERWICK CASTLE	9650/59	Union-Castle Line
ROTHESAY CASTLE	9650/60	"
CLAN MACILWRAITH	6894/60	The Clan Line Steamers Ltd
CLAN MACNAB	9169/61	"
CLAN GRAHAM	9022/62	"
CLAN GRANT	9022/62	"
CLAN MACGILLIVRAY	8811/62	"
CLAN MACGREGOR	8811/62	"
CLAN MACGOWAN	8811/63	"
LETABA	6827/63	Safmarine, South Africa
DRAKENSTEIN	6837/64	"
TZANEEN	6837/64	"
CLAN RAMSAY	7955/65	The Clan Line Steamers Ltd
CLAN RANALD	7955/65	"
CLAN ROBERTSON	7955/65	"
CLAN ROSS	7955/56	"

Clan Maciver presented the greatest problems for Dockyard staff when she listed some 35 degrees at her fitting-out berth beneath the hammerhead crane in the James Watt Dock in September,1958. A full capsize was averted by running some

ARGYLLSHIRE (above) on trials in 1956, and CLAN MATHESON (below) on trials in 1957 (Clansman).

(Previous page) ARGYLLSHIRE slides down the ways after being launched by Countess Jellicoe on 23rd May, 1956; and CLAN ROSS of 1956 on trials. (Clansman)

CLAN MACGILLIVRAY shortly before her launch in May, 1962 with a good general view of the Cartsdyke yard. (Clansman).

The launch of the last Clan Line cargo-liner CLAN ALPINE on 1st December,1966. (Clansman)

water out of the dock so that she lay on the bottom of the dock on her port bilge, and was eventually restored to an even keel with the help of Admiralty divers. A series of tankers of 16000 dwt was also built by the Dockyard in the early 1950s including *Thorskog* 11325/51 for Thor Dahl A/S, Norway; *Corato* 11387/52 for the Hadley Shipping Co. Ltd, London; *Imperial Transport* 11365/53 for Houlder Brothers; *Alva Cape* 11252/53 for Alva Steamship Co. Ltd, London and *Scottish Hawk* 11148/55 for the Scottish Tanker Co. Ltd. The latter had the misfortune to run aground on a sandbank near the entrance to the James Watt Dock after her launch.

The Cartsdyke East yard was modernised between 1958 and 1964 with the provision of two raised concrete crane piers at the sides of the two widened berths, instead of the previous three. Four new cranes of 25-ton capacity were installed, and this allowed the lifting of welded assemblies of this capacity on to ships of up to 25000 dwt. The last two ships built by the yard while still owned by the British & Commonwealth Shipping Group (Clan Line & Union-Castle Line) were two reefers for Geest Line, with *Geestcape* 8042/66 being the last launch before the yard was merged with the adjacent Cartsburn yard of Scotts' on 1st April,1966. *Geesthaven* 8042/66 was the first ship launched from Cartsdyke after the take-over, and there was still one Clan Line cargo-liner left to build, launched as *Clan Alpine* on 1st December,1966 by Miss Elizabeth Cayzer and completed in April,1967. The take-over of the yard by Scotts' included a ship price adjustment on *Clan Alpine*. The reader is now referred to the section on Scotts' for the subsequent history of the Cartsdyke yard.

CLAN RANALD being launched at the Cartsdyke yard on 21st December,1964 (Clansman).

CAIRD & CO. LTD.

This famous Greenock company was established as an engineering business initially by John Caird, who obtained an order in 1828 to re-engine the Clyde paddle tug *Industry*. His relative James Tennant Caird joined the business in 1831 and after further experience with Randolph, Elder & Company in Glasgow, James returned to the family business in 1838. In 1839 side-lever engines were built for the *Achilles* owned by P & O, and in the following year an order was won for four ships for the Royal Mail Steam Packet with the hulls being sub-contracted. Shipbuilding began under the Caird name in the Cartsdyke Mid yard in 1840, with large paddlers built for P & O as *Euxine* 1168/47 and *Malta* 1218/48, and for Cunard with *Etna* 2215/55 and Royal Mail Line with *Atrato* 3127/53, as well as many small Clyde paddlers. James Caird expanded into the two-berth Westburn East yard when he took over in 1863, followed by the two-berth Westburn West yard in 1871, vacating the Carstdyke Mid yard in 1867. The two Westburn yards were separated by a narrow dock basin and a dry-dock, and the main customer from 1870 was P & O with 85 ships being constructed with the yard having a monopoly on newbuildings for the famous liner company, starting with *Australia* 3664/70, *Khedive* 3742/71, *Mirzapore* 3763/71, *Pekin* 3777/71 and *Peshawur* 3749/71. Other important customers were the North German Lloyd Company with several ships built e.g. *Bremen* and *New York*, both 2794/58; and for Hamburg-Amerika Line e.g. *Borussia* and *Hammonia*; both 3035/67; and Royal Mail Line with *Eider* 1564/64, *Douro* 2824/65, *Arno* 1038/65 and *Neva* 3000/64 ; and Inman Line with *City of Chester* 4566/73 and *City of Berlin* 5491/74. The yard did not build many sailing ships, however the iron *Caperace* was an splendid example, and they also turned out some first-class steam yachts in the 1880s.

James Caird brought his four sons Patrick, William, Arthur and Robert into the business and on his death in 1888 they turned the company into one of limited liability. Numerous ships were built for the Gulf Line Association of Greenock e.g. *Gulf of Bothnia* 3452/91, *Gulf of Genoa* 3448/91, *Gulf of Siam* 3433/92 and *Gulf of Taranto* 3431/92; and for Hall Line e.g. *Rydal Hall* 3315/89, *Netherby Hall* 3316/90 and *Wistow Hall* 3314/90. Important milestones among P & O liners from the yard were the *Ballaarat* 4752/82 and her three twin-funnelled sisters built for the Australian mail service with accomodation for two hundred passengers, the sisters *Victoria* and *Britannia*, both 6525/87, and the fast yacht-like sisters *Peninsular* 5294/88 and *Oriental* 5284/88, and another pair in *Himalaya* and *Australia*, both 6901/92. The famous pair of 22 knot packets *Osiris* and *Isis*, both 1730/98, were

HARLAND & WOLFF LTD. GREENOCK YARD IN 1925

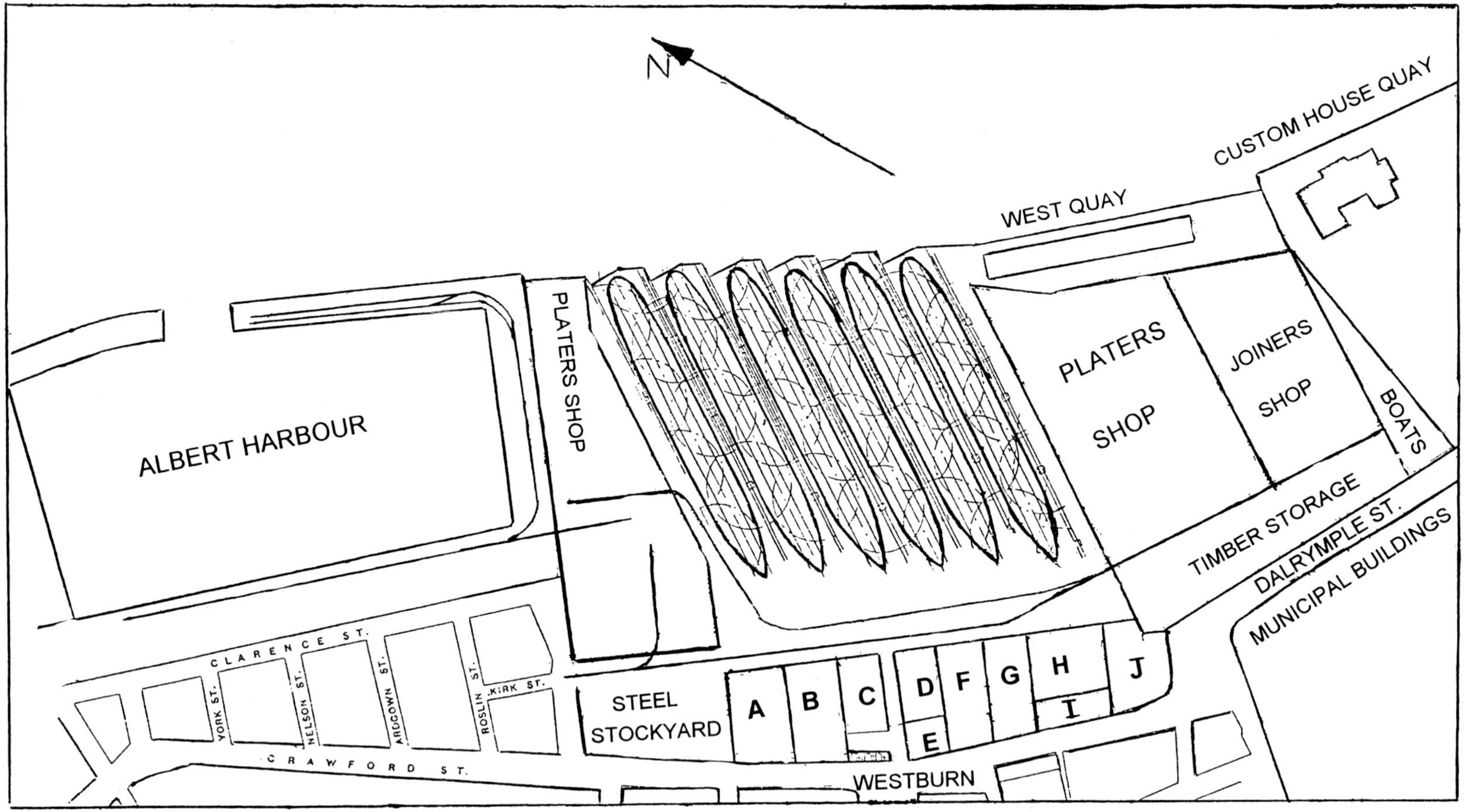

A. PLUMBERS / TINSMITHS / SHEET METAL WORKERS
B. BLACKSMITHS SHOP
C. PAINT STORE
D. GENERAL STORE
E. OFFICES
F. CARPENTERS SHOP
G. ENGINEERS SHOP
H. ELECTRICIANS SHOP
I. POWER STATION
J. DRAWING OFFICES

built by the yard to run the mail service between Brindisi and Port Said in connection with the Indian and Australian mails for P & O, who also ordered the 20 knot twin-funnelled *Salsette* 5842/08 for the shuttle service between Aden and Bombay connecting with the weekly Australian steamer. The Greenock yard built all the leading P & O liners around the turn of the century for their long-haul routes with the following :-

CALEDONIA	7558/94	NAGOYA	6874/13
INDIA	7911/96	NELLORE	6856/13
CHINA	7947/97	MOLDAVIA	9505/03
EGYPT	7971/98	MONGOLIA	9505/03
ARABIA	7930/98	DELHI	8090/05
PERSIA	7951/00	DEVANHA	8090/06
ASSAYE (Hospital ship)	7376/99	MALWA	10883/08
SOBRAON "	7382/00	MANTUA	10885/09
PLASSY "	7405/00	MEDINA	12350/11
SOMALI	6696/01	BALLARAT	11120/11
NILE	6694/06	BELTANA	11120/12
NAMUR	6694/06	BENALLA	11118/13
NYANZA	6698/07	BERRIMA	11137/13
NORE	6696/07	BORDA	11136/14
NANKIN	6846/12	KAISAR-I-HIND	11430/14
NOUARA	6875/12		

The yard carried out a number of repair and conversion contracts at the start of the Great War, as well as building fast patrol boats and other small vessels for the Admiralty. The yard obtained an order from P & O in late 1913 for the passenger liner *Naldera* and work was well advanced by the outbreak of war to launch stage but was suspended shortly afterwards. The uncompleted hull lay idle for over three years but was launched on 29th December,1917 with the Admiralty deciding to complete her as a cargo ship. Plans were then changed shortly before completion to that of an armed merchant cruiser, however with the end of the war these were cancelled and she completed her trials in March,1920 as a passenger liner capable of carrying 426 first and 247 second class passengers. Ten war standard ships were also built, comprising three 'A' types, *War Bracken, War Alyssum* and *War Anchusa*, and five 'B' types, *War Emu, Biafra, Siris, Dromore Castle* and *Dundrum Castle* with the last pair modified for Union-Castle Line by having an extra 'tween deck in no. 1 hold and three extra pairs of kingposts, and two 'AO' type tankers, *War Malayan* and *War Burman*.

Robert Caird, who managed the engineering department, died in December,1915 and at the end of 1916 the company was taken over by Harland &

Wolff Ltd for £432,493, with Arthur and Patrick Caird remaining as directors of the company, which traded under the Caird name until 1922. The Arthur Street engine works was sold to John G. Kincaid & Co. Ltd, Greenock in 1919. Approval was given by Greenock Harbour Trust in August,1919 for Harland & Wolff Ltd to lease the West Harbour for a scheme of extension and development of the combined yard, and considerable ground in the vicinity of the yard was acquired including a church and graveyard together with old buildings which were pulled down. The West Harbour was filled up and used for yard extension, and construction started of six longer berths (See Shipyard plan), with the old ones being scrapped. Four of the new berths were designed to accomodate ships up to 650 feet in length with the remaining two for ships up to 750 feet in length. The workforce in 1919 stood at 2000 workers and this was planned to increase, however the slump in orders after 1921 meant that only part of the plan was put into being with the remainder discontinued. The building berths that were completed were served by overhead tower cranes as in the Govan yard of Harland & Wolff Ltd, as were the cofferdams and concrete slipways. Some £350,000 was spent by the company on the yard in 1919 on these, with a further £114,000 on new shops and equipment, and the contractor was Sir William Arrol & Co. Ltd.

The yard was now able to build larger liners for P & O and completed *Ballarat* 13033/21, *Balranald* 13039/22 and *Bendigo* 13039/22, and went on to complete the twin-funnelled *Rawalpindi* 16618/25 and *Rajputana* 16568/25 for the Indian route, as well as *Razmak* 10602/25. The Pacific Steam Navigation Co. Ltd took *Lobos* 6479/21, Holland - Amerika Line took *Drechdyk* 9324/23, and Elder, Dempster the motorship *Adda* 7816/22. However no ships were launched during 1926, with only four during 1927 as *Grantleyhall* 4761/27 for West Hartlepool S.N. Co. Ltd, *Kheti* 2650/27 for James Moss & Co. Ltd, Liverpool, *Saugor* 6303/28 for Nourse Line and *Nimoda* 6303/28. The latter was the first of a pair from the yard ordered by P & O for their subsidiary Hain Steamship Co. Ltd, with the second of the pair the only launch of 1928 as *Behar* 6100/28, with *Behar* then being towed up to the Govan yard of Harland & Wolff Ltd at the end of 1928 for fitting-out. The yard then ceased shipbuilding and was sold to National Shipbuilders Security Ltd in 1935, with the Caird company being liquidated in 1937. The platers shed on the north-western side of the yard remains in existence today, as a warehouse for Greenock Container Terminal.

GEORGE BROWN & CO.(MARINE) LTD.

This five-berth yard was known locally as the 'Siberia' yard on account of its extremely exposed position near the Great Harbour of Greenock, open to the cold north wind and prone to hazardous icy deck working conditions. The Garvel dry-dock and James Watt Dock were neighbours, and the yard had been operated for two years from 1898 by Taylor & Mitchell and had built four ships. George Brown (1859 - 1933) had served his apprenticeship at the Stephen yard, and then been assistant manager for Denny before he started on his own account in 1900 with yard number 5. This was the cutter *Princess Beara* 212/01 for service in Bantry Bay, and was followed by the similar fast cutter *Lampo* 250/03, and the family-owned yard went on to build 275 small ships of all types including coasters, trawlers, tugs, grab dredgers, steam yachts and minesweepers. One of the early steamers was the coastal passenger ship *Lady Sybil* 676/08 for service in the Magdalen Islands in Nova Scotia. (See profile drawing). Other typical yard products were the steam yachts *Maretanza III* and *Maretanza V*, the Brazilian engines-amidships coaster *Campista* 1309/13, the engines-aft coaster *Ardgour* 779/14, and the local coasters *Starling* 212/05 and *Lintie* 172/09 for Steel & Bennie.

Twin-funnelled paddle minesweepers were built during the Great War, followed by the larger timber carriers *Terneuzen* of 4170 dwt and *Ustaritz* of 1663 dwt. Fred. T. Everard & Sons Ltd then became the main customer of the yard, with the coastal tankers *Prowess* 207/26 and *Authority* 616/28 and then a dozen dry-cargo coasters during the 1930s e.g. *Assiduity* 350/30 and *Sincerity* 635/36. After the death of the founder in 1933 the yard continued under the control of his two sons and later under his grandson. In 1937 the company was renamed George Brown & Co.(Marine) Ltd, and went on to build three coastal tankers of 800 dwt, four dry-cargo coasters of 1360 dwt, one tug, as well as *Serenity* 557/41 for Everard during World War II.

Peace-time saw the yard complete *Jacob Kjode* 1759/48 of 3010 dwt for the Bergen shipowner of the same name. Coasters included *Iberian Coast* 1188/50, *Netherlands Coast* 867/53 and *Yorkshire Coast* 988/59 for Tyne-Tees Steam Shipping Co. Ltd, as well as *Brentfield* 1262/55 for the Zillah Steamship Co. Ltd (W.A. Savage), and *Ballyhill* and *Ballyhaft* both 847/54 for John Kelly Ltd, and coastal tanker *Atonality* 1221/50 for Everard. The yard ran out of orders in the 1960s with a dredger for Ceylon, a car ferry for Canada and a coaster with the last ship built being the twin-screw tug *Vasabha* of 275 grt for Colombo Port Commission completed in June,1963. Part of the yard continued in business as a manufacturer of cargo-handling equipment under licence from a Norwegian company, and made a brief return to shipbuilding in 1981 when a £1M order was accepted for two tug/buoy tenders for Mexico. A third was ordered for the Tees, but in 1983 liquidation of the company took place with the yard plant sold by auction and the buoy lifter *Wilton* 388/83 completed on the Tees by her owners Tees & Hartlepool Port Authority.

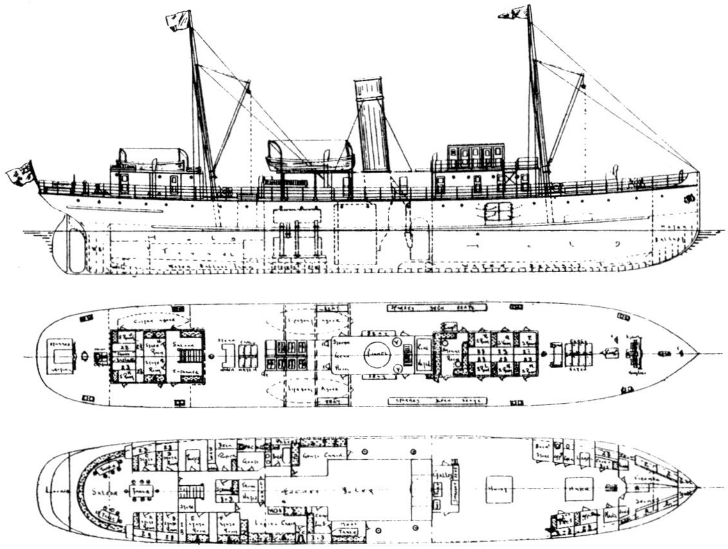

Nova Scotian cutter LADY SYBIL of 1908.

Company advertisement of 1959 showing NETHERLANDS COAST of 1953.

LITHGOWS LTD.

This prolific shipbuilding company was known as Russell & Company until 1918, and from beginnings in one small yard, was eventually to take over all of the other large Port Glasgow shipyards. Joseph Russell was born in London in 1833 the son of a Baptist minister, and began his apprenticeship with J. W. Hoby & Company, Renfrew, later William Simons & Company, and then joined Lawrence Hill in his Inch yard at Port Glasgow. When the Inch yard was sold to Cunliffe & Dunlop in 1869 Joseph Russell returned to London, but an opportunity arose in 1874 for him to form a partnership with Anderson Rodger (born 1843) and William Todd Lithgow (born 1854) to lease the Bay yard in east Port Glasgow. W. T. Lithgow had been apprenticed to John Reid in 1872 at the Glen yard, and this was the start of an exceptional shipbuilding legend which encompassed over a century of Port Glasgow shipbuilding history.

The three partners succeeded in making a profit of just under £10,000 in the two years to the end of 1876, with each partner having withdrawn £380. They then built in their Bay yard the famous barque *Falls of Clyde* in 1878, which is still preserved today in Honolulu, and then in 1879 expanded by purchasing the Cartsdyke Mid yard at Greenock. In 1881 they acquired their third and most important yard from Henry Murray, the Kingston yard at Port Glasgow. The six-berth Kingston yard was rebuilt and enlarged under its manager Alexander Lambie, and the partners Russell, Rodger and Lithgow then exploited the market for large capacity sailing ships, which were the only practical way of carrying bulk cargoes around the world at this time until the triple expansion engine was further developed for the steam tramp. Fast clippers were not built, but a determined policy of standardisation as used by Connell at Scotstoun at the same time, reaped its reward in productivity. During the ten years from 1882 to 1892 the three yards with 14 berths were head of the river with some 271 ships built, and in 1890 they captured the world output record with a total of 70,370 tons in 26 sailing ships and eight steam tramps.

The standardisation policy was carried through to such an extent that only sailing ships were built at the Kingston yard, with standard tramp hulls at the Bay and Greenock yards. A financial interest was taken by the partners in many of the ships, and some were built 'on spec', and as with Christopher Furness and his yards at West Hartlepool, if a buyer could not be found then it was traded by the partners e.g. the barques *Heathfield* 1643/95 and *Renfield* 1112/95. Regular customers for barques included Andrew Weir of Glasgow with 14 built, the last of which was *Thornliebank* 2105/96; James Nourse with eight including the famous *Clyde* 1813/94; Bruusgaard Kjosterud of Drammen in Norway with several including *Vildanden* 1598/91 and *Nordlyset* 1599/91; and a whole fleet for Crawford & Rowat of Glasgow including *Port Logan* 1988/95 as well as the big four-masted barque *Liverpool* 3407/90 for Leyland and the big locally-owned barques *Bermuda* 2846/93 and *Falls of Ettrick* 2264/95. These large sailing ships were used in the coal out trades, returning with grain from Australia, sugar from Java, nitrates from Chile, phosphates from the Pacific, case oil from America and Java, and all the other worldwide bulk trades of the time.

The partnership between Russell, Rodger and Lithgow was broken up in November,1891 when Russell retired, with Rodger taking the Bay yard and building under his own name (q.v.), and Lithgow taking the Kingston and Greenock yards while still using the title Russell & Company. Joseph Russell loaned Lithgow £122,965 at this time, and agreed to assist him by preparing the annual accounts and in purchasing timber. In the mid-1890s Lithgow began building through-deck standard triple-expansion steam powered tramps in the 4000/5000 g.r.t range. Some of the last sailing ships built by the Kingston yard were *Inverclyde* 1634/98 for G. Milne of Aberdeen, *Australian* 2103/97 for Lang & Fulton of Greenock, and the case-oil carriers *Brilliant* 3765/01 and *Daylight* 3756/02 for the Anglo-American Oil Co. Ltd. This last pair had an overall length of 352 feet, breadth of 49 feet and moulded depth of 28 feet, and carried a crew of 46 to handle the sails. Three steam-powered case-oil carriers were built for this same owner as *Seneca* 4848/01, *Kennebec* 5077/02 and *Schuylkill* 5176/03.

The Mid Cartsdyke yard was sold to the Greenock & Grangemouth Dockyard Co. Ltd in 1900, leaving William T. Lithgow with the Kingston yard. His trading profit for 1900 was a considerable £123,600, with steam tramps for local owners then becoming the bread and butter of the yard with eighteen for Gow,Harrison starting with *Ventnor* 3961/01 and ending with *Virgilia* 5697/18 and including the tankers *Vitruvia* 4573/13 and *Vallejo* 4781/18; nineteen for Andrew Weir starting with *Elleric* 3570/97 and ending with *Orteric* 6535/11; eight for Sir William Burrell who always ordered at the bottom of the periodic slumps; four for Raeburn & Verel; two for Maclay & McIntyre; and others for the Clyde Shipping Co. Ltd, Thomas Dunlop, Charles Barrie, A. Mackay, and the aptly-named *River Clyde* 3913/05 for Ormond, Cook of Glasgow. Liner shipowners also patronised the yard with a dozen ships for the Nelson Line with services to South America e.g. *Highland Enterprise* 5201/03 and *Highland Glen* 7472/10; ten ships for the Saint Line of Liverpool starting with

Saint Bede 4940/12; and *Socrates* 4979/13 and *Plutarch* 5613/13 for another Mersey shipowner - Lamport & Holt Ltd.

William T. Lithgow had married in 1879 Agnes Birkmyre, the daughter of Henry Birkmyre, owner of Gourock ropeworks, and grand-daughter of John Birkmyre, a wealthy Lower Clyde merchant and major investor in the Burrell fleet of tramps. Their first child was a daughter, Margaret, then their first son James was born on 27th January,1883 followed by Henry in 1886, the latter at a house called Drums some six miles in the hills south of Port Glasgow. The couple had rented Drums from late 1883 but as they became more prosperous the house was purchased and also by 1900 William had paid off half of the loan from Russell. In 1902 he bought the Ormsary estate at the mouth of Loch Caolisport, just south of Loch Sween in Argyllshire, and hired an architect to enhance its romantic appearance in the 'Scottish baronial' style. Their elder son James started as an apprentice at the Kingston yard in 1901 and both James and Henry were taken into partnership in 1907. On 7th June,1908 William T. Lithgow died leaving over £1M in his will with £102,000 invested in ships. He had withdrawn £1.24M from the business since the formation of the partnership in 1874, and had turned his original investment of just under £10,000 into almost £2M !

James was aged 25 years and Henry 22 years when they assumed full ownership of the Kingston yard on the death of their millionaire father in 1908. The brothers had a secure family and financial background to draw upon, and expanded in 1911 by acquiring the Bay yard after the death of Anderson Rodger in 1909. Family sentiment coupled with hard-headed business acumen to prevent new competition entering the Port Glasgow yards had influenced their decision. In 1911 James was appointed Vice-President of the Clyde Shipbuilders Association, and served as their President during 1912/13. He made the first contacts at this time with two men who later were valuable colleagues: Andrew Duncan (later Sir), an industrial lawyer and later secretary to the Shipbuilders Employers Federation, director and industrial adviser to the Bank of England and Chairman of the CEGB; and Alexander Belch, later Controller of the Shipbuilding Conference.

Russell & Company entered the Great War with the Kingston and Bay yards, and in 1915 the East yard of Robert Duncan & Co. Ltd (q.v.) was purchased but continued to build under its own name, and in 1917 the Lithgow brothers bought into the Glasgow marine engineers David Rowan & Co. Ltd. World War I production from the yards came to the huge total of 315,141 tons and included cargo-liners for Lamport & Holt, *Meissonier* 7206/15, *Murillo* 7206/15 and *Moliere* 7206/16, and for Blue Star Line *Rubiera* 5594/17 and *Montilla* 5595/17. The only naval vessel ever completed by Lithgows was the fast patrol boat P21 of 1916. Henry Lithgow ran the yards while his brother James served as Director of Merchant Shipbuilding on his return from France in May,1917, having reached the rank of Colonel after fifteen months at the battlefront. The Port Glasgow yards had been building standard ships of their own design for years, and during the war no attempt was made to replace such successful designs with those laid down by the Shipping Controller, as this would only have delayed production. Finally at the end of the war came the overdue renaming of Russell & Company into Lithgows Ltd.

The last ship launched under the Russell name was the standard 'H' type *War Ermine* in 1918 and she was completed as *Crossbill* 4565/19 as one of six similar ships. Five standard 'Z' type tankers with engines amidships were also built, *War Shikari, War Diwan, War Gaekwar, War Brahmin* and *War Pindari*. The Inch yard of Dunlop, Bremner & Co. Ltd was purchased in 1919 but continued to build under its own name (q.v.) until closure in 1926. The Glen yard of William Hamilton & Co. Ltd (q.v.) was purchased in 1919, and with the closure of the small yard of Murdoch & Murray in 1923 the Lithgow brothers then owned all of the Port Glasgow yards along the waterfront stretching from the Kingston to Bay yards inclusive. The steel stockists James Dunlop & Co. Ltd was purchased in 1920 to ensure steel supplies, and the Greenock marine engineers Rankin,Blackmore & Co. Ltd in 1923 for a supply of engines. A number of ships were also built 'on-spec' at the Irvine yard of the Ayrshire Dockyard Co. Ltd (q.v.) after purchase in 1928.

The Kingston and Bay yards under the Lithgow name during the 1920s produced some ninety cargo-liners and tramps, and a dozen oil tankers. Their best customers were the Asiatic Steam Navigation Co. Ltd,London with seven cargo-liners; H. Hogarth of Ardrossan with six tramps; Kaye,Son of London with six ships; as well as four cargo-liners each for Brocklebank Line, Bombay & Persia Steam Navigation Co. Ltd and Blue Star Line. The turbine-powered *Doricstar* 10098/21, *Rodneystar* 11803/27 and *Napierstar* 10116/27 had extensive passenger accomodation for Blue Star Line. The twin-screw *Northern Prince* 10917/29 and *Southern Prince* 10917/29 for the New York to South America service of Prince Line had accomodation for 101 passengers, and oil engines manufactured by J.G. Kincaid & Co. Ltd,Greenock. The Dutch turbine-powered *Tjibesar* 10836/22 was built for the service from Batavia in Java to China and Japan, and other Dutch-flag ships included *Salawati* 6643/20, *Saleier* 6563/20 for Nederland Line and *Springfontein* 6406/21 for United Netherlands Navigation and *Stad Haarlem* 4518/28 for Halcyon Line. French owners took the cargo-liner *Phenix* 5907/20, while Nippon Yusen Kaisha of Japan took *Atago Maru* 7543/24, and Westfal-Larsen of Bergen took *Leikanger* and *Hardanger*, both 4004/24; and Scindia Line of India took their first newbuildings *Jalabala* , *Jalaveera* and *Jaladuta*, all 3610/27. Two pilgrim ships were built for the Mogul Line of India as *Rahmani* 5463/28 and *Rizwani* 5448/30, while three passenger ships were built for Yugoslavia as *Aleksandar I* 6048/27, *Sveti Vlaho* 6001/28 and *Princ Andrej* 5092/30. *Tolten* 5348/30 was never delivered to her owners Cia Sud Americana of Chile, and had to be traded by Lithgows under the management of Lowden,Connell & Co. Ltd,Liverpool. The North Coast Steam Navigation Co. Ltd ordered the coastal passenger ship *Wollongbar* 2239/22 and four coasters of 500 tons each.

The majority of the forty tramps built by Lithgows during the 1920s were for local owners with six for H. Hogarth of Ardrossan; three each for Glen & Company, Lyle Shipping Co. Ltd, J. & J. Denholm, Andrew Crawford, Bell McConnell; two for P.D. Hendry and single ships for William S. Miller, T.L. Duff, Douglas & Ramsey and Grove Line. During 1929/30 three ships were built for the Larrinaga Steamship Co. Ltd of Liverpool while Pardoe-Thomas of Cardiff took delivery of four tramps with *'Knight'* names and Ambrose,Davies & Matthews of Swansea took the Welsh tramp *Ael-y-Bryn* 4458/28. A joint venture partnership was set-up by Lithgows and Kaye, Son to form the Walmer Steamship Co. Ltd to own their ships, and other tramps were similarly financed including the three motortramps completed for the Lyle Shipping Co. Ltd. When the gaunt frames of a fifth tramp for Pardoe-Thomas was left on the stocks for six years from 1930 due to the Depression it was financed for completion by Lithgows by a loan of £50,000 over five years at 3% interest for the Lyle Shipping Co. Ltd as *Cape Sable* 4398/36.

Tankers had also been built during the 1920s, and the engines-aft coastal tanker *British Tommy* 1411/21 was followed by four deep-sea tankers for the British Tanker Co. Ltd: *British Valour* 6952/27, *British Courage* 6952/28, *British Fortune* 4696/30 and *British Venture* 4696/30; and four for Standard Oil of America: *Ahamo* 8621/26, *Voco* 8629/27, *Pulpit Point* 8621/26 and *Yarraville* 8627/30; *Vacuoline* 8760/29 for Socony Vacuum of America; and *Atheltemplar* 8939/30 for Athel Line. Two further tankers were then delivered to the British Tanker Co. Ltd as *British Pride* and *British Prestige*, both 7106/31.

When James Lithgow had acquired the Glen yard from William Hamilton in 1919 he made the Glen offices his working headquarters, with Henry having his offices in the East yard, and both men used the same car to work from their home Drums. At lunch-time they walked to the Kingston yard to have lunch with yard manager John Muirhead and sort out any problems there. James was knighted in 1925, shortly after his marriage in September,1924 to Gwendolyn Amy Harrison daughter of a Glasgow shipowner who had previously ordered ships from his new son-in-law. Lady Lithgow laid the keystone for their new home at Gleddoch, one mile west of Drums, on 12th June,1925, and the couple were subsequently to have

LITHGOWS LTD.
KINGSTON SHIPBUILDING YARD
PORT GLASGOW
1932

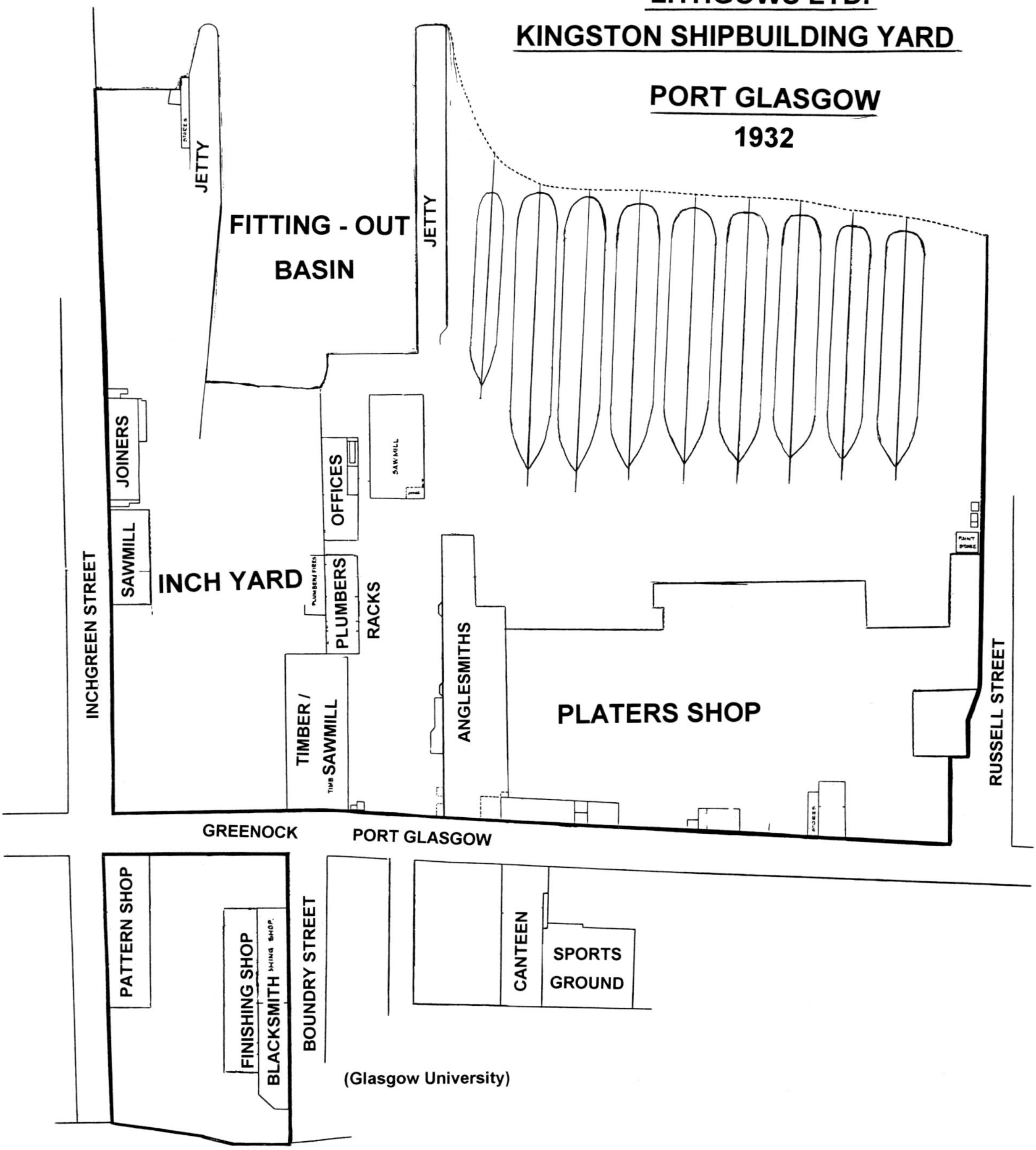

three children, the eldest Margaret, then Ann and finally the youngest a son named William.

In the five years from 1931 to 1935 the reasonably full Lithgow order book allowed work to continue at both the Kingston and Bay yards when most other British shipyards were closed for lack of work. Dividends had been kept low, and keeping resources within the company had enabled them to undercut competitors by as much as £10,000 on a £80,000 standard tramp. Some 30 ships were delivered representing 6% of world output at this time, and the workforce suffered comparatively less unemployment than in any other British shipyard. Twelve tramps were ordered at the rock bottom price of around £80,000 each by J. & C. Harrison of London and given names beginning with *'Har'*; two for Kaye, Son as *Marton* 4969/33 and *Marina* 5088/35 along with four West Indies banana boats in *Jamaica Pioneer* 5349/31, *Jamaica Progress* 5351/32, *Jamaica Producer* 5325/34 and *Jamaica Planter* 4098/36; the tramps *Baron Douglas* 3899/32, *Loch Maddy* 4996/4, *River Afton* 5479/35 and the Isherwood-designed 'Arcform' tramp *Arcgow* 4075/34. Booker Brothers with South American services took *Arakaka* 2379/33, British Phosphate Commissioners took the phosphates carrier *Triaster* 6032/35 for Pacific service, and a further pilgrim ship was built for the Mogul Line of India as *Islami* 5879/33, as well as the Brazilian passenger ship *Pedrinhas* 3666/35, and the Yugoslav *Kralj Aleksandar* 2463/32.

Sir James Lithgow approached Montagu Norman, Governor of the Bank of England, to set-up National Shipbuilders Security Ltd in 1930 with Sir James as Chairman, during the necessary rationalisation of yard capacity of that time. NSS Ltd was formed to secure a core price for the building rights of any yard going into liquidation, and was financed by shares taken up by shipbuilders participating in the company and by a 1% levy on the value of tonnage launched. Between 1931 and 1937 the company acquired all or part of the building rights on nine Clyde yards, with the Lithgow brothers having interests in five of these. They effectively used NSS Ltd to extend they own process of rationalisation at Port Glasgow, and in particular received considerable compensation when the Lithgow-owned Inch yard was sold to NSS Ltd in 1933 and the site sterilised for forty years. Public opinion was outraged, however the money was put to good use when the Lithgow brothers purchased the famous Fairfield yard (q.v.) at Govan in 1935 and saved it from closure.

The Bay yard was closed at the end of the Depression in 1935 and demolished. The six-berth East yard, formerly that of Robert Duncan & Co. Ltd although owned by Lithgow since 1915, had closed due to the Depression in 1931 but re-opened in April,1937 under the Lithgow name. The Kingston yard now had nine berths and the East yard with six now made a total of fifteen berths available, which then built four tankers for Eagle Oil, five tankers for the Anglo-Saxon Petroleum Co. Ltd, and the Admiralty oiler *Bishopdale* 8406/37. T. & J. Harrison Ltd of Liverpool had bought a ship on the stocks for £50,000 and had her completed as *Merchant* 4615/35, and then went on to order five more cargo-liners before World War II. Four iron-ore carriers were completed for the Broken Hill Pty. Co. Ltd of Australia as well as four tramps each for Lambert Brothers and Hain Line, two each for Hogarth and Denholm, one each for Lyle Shipping Co. Ltd and Mungo Campbell, three for Scindia Line of India as well as their pilgrim ship *El Hind* 5319/38. The fine passenger ship *Dubrovnik* 5156/38 was completed for Splosna Plovidba of Yugoslavia, as well as two phosphate carriers *Triadic* and *Trienza* both 6378/38 for Pacific service.

A huge total of 97 ships of over 1.2 million tons was completed during World War II, with 33 standard 'Empire' tramps, two fast cargo-liners *Empire Haig* and *Empire Rawlinson*, two merchant aircraft-carriers *Empire Macrae* and *Empire MacCallum*, three short-sea traders, three transport ferries and some 54 merchant ships for private owners. These latter included cargo-liners for the Asiatic Steam Navigation Co. Ltd (8), T. & J. Harrison (3), Anchor Line (2), and tramps for Lyle Shipping Co. Ltd (5), Crest Shipping Co. Ltd (5), Lambert Brothers (4), Hogarth (2), Hain (3) and Bolton (2). As in the Great War, Henry Lithgow ran the yards while his brother Sir James became Controller of Merchant Shipbuilding & Repairs. The fastest construction times for standard tramps achieved by the yard were nowhere comparable to the record five days achieved for similar ships in the U.S.A, however keel to trials times averaged five months, which was faster than most British yards. At the conclusion of the war there were nine berths in the Kingston yard for ships up to 550 feet in length, and six berths in the East yard for ships up to 700 feet in length. The yards then returned to what they had been good at in the inter-war years, the building of tankers, cargo-liners and tramps.

John Muirhead, Managing Director of the Port Glasgow yards, retired in 1946 after spending all of his life working for the Lithgow brothers. Henry Lithgow had never married, but before his death on 28th May,1948 at his home of Drums this cautious, genial, pipe-smoking man sketched out some early plans for prefabrication production at the Kingston yard, which unfortunately were not implemented until 1960. His brother Sir James Lithgow suffered a thrombosis in September,1948 near Gleddoch, and was to remain struggling to walk and regain his health for the remaining three and a half years of his life. In 1949 he relinquished responsibilty for the redevelopment of the Beardmore yard, and set-up Scottish Ore Carriers Ltd to ensure ore supplies reached Scottish smelters in Port Glasgow - built ships. He died on 23rd February,1952 at Gleddoch, having been in control of the greatest Scottish shipbuilding Group for a continuous 44 years. He was buried at Ormsary, from where he had often sailed for hunting on Islay and Jura in his yacht *Carraig*, and on his gravestone was etched 'Continuing the work of their father, he and his brother Henry built ships at Port Glasgow'.

Welding had been used throughout the war to build standard tramps, and then new post-war welding shops were built and partial prefabrication of up to 25-ton units, the limit of berth cranes, was introduced on the following tanker programme :-

ANDREA BROVIG	8988/48	Th. Brovig, Farsund
BISCOE	9313/49	Hektor Whaling A/S,Norway
BONNY	8997/49	A. Johannson, Finland
HEKTORIA	9027/50	N. Bugge, Norway
ISFONN	9044/50	Sig Bergesen, Bergen
KORSFJORD	9100/50	K. Olsen, Stavanger
BRITISH ADVOCATE	8573/48	British Tanker Co. Ltd
BRITISH COUNCILLOR	8573/48	"
BRITISH PATRIOT	8661/49	"
BRITISH PEER	8661/50	"
BRITISH PREMIER	8663/51	"
ALTNES	9025/49	Jebsen, Bergen
TELNES	11006/51	"
WAZIRISTAN	9113/50	Common Bros., Newcastle
LARISTAN	12446/52	"
ATLANTIC EAGLE	10054/51	Livanos, Greece
NEWBURY	11199/51	Houlder Bros.
ALAGOAS	11354/51	Petroleos Brasileiro
MATO GROSSO	11346/52	"
SYDHAV	10946/52	Per Lodding, Norway
SILVERDALE	11289/52	Silver Line, London
BEDFORD	12578/53	Blandford Shpg. (Fred Olsen)
LLANDAFF	12501/53	Evan Thomas Radcliffe,Cardiff
OAKWOOD	11360/54	J. I. Jacobs,London
TUAREG	11480/53	W. Wilhelmsen, Oslo
BRITISH GUARDIAN	11359/53	British Tanker Co. Ltd
BRITISH HERO	11358/54	"
BRITISH TRUST	11211/59	"
BRITISH ROBIN	11211/60	"
HYALA	12164/55	Shell Tankers Ltd
HYDATINA	12161/56	"
HYGROMIA	12161/56	"
HYRIA	12132/54	"
AXINA	12283/58	"
BENGUELA	13969/55	N. Bugge, Norway
ATHELCREST	7548/57	Athel Line

BORDER LAIRD	11366/55	Lowland Tanker Co. Ltd
KALDFONN	12566/55	Sig Bergesen, Bergen
SIR JAMES LITHGOW	12698/54	A.F. Klaveness, Oslo
DAVANGER	11827/54	Westfal-Larsen, Bergen
ORKANGER	11817/55	"
BORDER SHEPHERD	13606/60	Lowland Tanker Co. Ltd
ORLANDO	13969/60	Bowring

The best customers of the yards for cargo-liners in the twenty post-war years from 1946 were Henderson Line of Glasgow with thirteen ships; Elder,Dempster with eight ships and the Asiatic Steam Navigation Co. Ltd with eight ships; A.F. Klaveness of Oslo with four ships, while fellow Norwegians Morlands Rederi A/S took two more. Canadian Pacific and T.& J. Harrison took three cargo-liners each, and *Kongsfjord* 5934/51 with split-profile and five holds was built for the Norwegian-Amerika Line, and *Highland* 7689/63 for Currie Line. Scindia Line were a valued former customer and took three more ships, *Jalarajan, Jalarashmi* and *Jalaratna*, all 11323/66, while there was plenty of fitting-out work on the three Mogul Line pilgrim ships *Mohammedi* 7026/47, *Mozaffari* 7024/58 and *Saudi* 5973/56. Two banana boats were completed also for Kaye, Son as *Jamaica Planter* 6159/59 and *Jamaica Producer* 5781/62.

The Mogul Line pilgrim carrier SAUDI of 1956 with accomodation for 900 pilgrims and 12 first-class passengers. She was powered by a triple-expansion steam reciprocating engine boosted by an exhaust turbine by Rankin & Blackmore Ltd, Greenock.

Tramp customers included Lyle Shipping Co. Ltd (5); Lambert Bros. (3), H. Clarkson (2); Trader Navigation (1); Galbraith Pembroke (1); Graig Shipping Co. Ltd (1); J. & C. Harrison (1) and Hogarth (1). Ore-carriers had also featured in the post-war yard lists with fourteen built, of which eight were for Scottish Ore Carriers Ltd managed by J. & J. Denholm Ltd of Glasgow. The most significant of these was the gas-turbine powered *Morar* 6584/59 with her revolutionary engine built by the Lithgow subsidiary Rankin & Blackmore in Greenock, and others were named after the Lithgow estates of *Gleddoch* 6859/53 and *Ormsary* 6859/52, and their great friend *Sir Andrew Duncan* 10687/58.

Management structure after the deaths of the Lithgow brothers was simple and straightforward, consisting of three executive directors with a shipyard manager and two assistant managers in each yard. In 1959 with the company having six berths at the Kingston yard and five berths in the East yard and half-ownership of the Glen yard, an ambitious reconstruction of the Kingston yard was begun. A feature was a large number of long prefabrication shops running parallel to the Clyde, and improved cranage on the reduced number of berths to allow the assembly of larger and heavier sections. Some ships were fitted out at the Kingston fitting-out basin, while others were completed at Finnieston, where Rowan-built engines were installed, or in the James Watt Dock at Greenock, where Rankin & Blackmore engines were installed. The East yard was then merged with the Glen yard of William Hamilton & Co. Ltd in 1963, with *Freetown* of Elder,Dempster being the last launch under the Hamilton name in 1963 with completion as a Lithgow ship in 1964. The Glen / East yard was then modernised for the prefabrication of large tankers and bulk carriers by the erection of a high 225-ton capacity Arrol gantry crane over the berths for lifting large assemblies.

The Geddes Report recommended mergers of British shipyards to beat international competition, and the Lower Clyde giants of Scotts (q.v.) and Lithgow agreed to merge in 1968 by setting-up a holding company Scott-Lithgow Ltd, and two separate operating companies Scotts' Shipbuilding Co.(1969) Ltd and Lithgows (1969) Ltd to run the yards. The small yards of Ferguson Brothers (q.v.), acquired by Lithgows in 1961, and Scott & Sons of Bowling (q.v.) were also included but Fergusons later withdrew to join forces with Ailsa Shipbuilding Co. Ltd. The Lithgow engine building subsidiary of Rankin & Blackmore Ltd at Greenock was closed in 1964. Campbeltown Shipyard Ltd was purchased in 1970.

The large Inchgreen dry-dock was purchased from the Firth of Clyde Drydock Co. Ltd in 1966. It had been built on the site of the old Inch shipyard and had been opened in 1964 with the first ship docked being the Fairfield-built *Devonia* 11300/39, which had suffered a collision in the river. The dock was subsequently used to dry-dock the Clydebank-built Cunarder *Queen Elizabeth* when she was refurbished in 1966 by John Brown & Co. Ltd.

Kristian Jebsen A/S of Bergen were good customers of both the Lithgow yards and the Scotts yards at Greenock at this time, with orders for twenty bulkers of which fifteen were built by Lithgows. The following large ore-carriers, bulk carriers and tankers were built by the Lithgow yards :-

GOTHLAND	16708/61	Currie, Leith
MYLLA	15548/61	Interessenskaper A/S, Norway
CAPE NELSON	12351/61	Lyle Shipping Co. Ltd,Glasgow
CAPE HOWE	19032/62	"
CAPE RODNEY	12104/65	"
BRUNES	10485/62	Kristian Jebsen A/S, Bergen
BERNES	10485/62	"
BRIMNES	10594/63	"
BIRKNES	12456/67	"
BAYNES	12404/68	"
BORGNES	12404/68	"
BELLNES	12404/68	"
BAUGNES	13124/69	"
BRUNES	13124/69	"
BRISKNES	13124/70	"
BROOKNES	13098/70	"
BLIDNES	13100/71	"
BERNES	22961/72	"
BRIMNES	22901/72	"
BRAVENES	22904/73	Completed as SILVERDON
BRITISH FERN	13252/64	British Tanker Co. Ltd
BRITISH HOLLY	13271/65	"
BRITISH IVY	13271/65	"
THORSHAMMER	31685/63	Thor Dahl A/S, Norway
ORAMA	38982/64	P & O
ORISSA	39035/65	"
LARISTAN	37900/65	Common Brothers, Newcastle
JERSEY BRIDGE	22490/66	H. Clarkson, London
NAESS TALISMAN	40769/67	Anglo-Norness Shpg. Co. Ltd
GALLIC BRIDGE	42774/67	H. Clarkson, London
WESTMINSTER BRIDGE	42202/68	Watts,Watts & Co. Ltd
SUGAR CRYSTAL	13894/68	Sugar Line Ltd
SUGAR PRODUCER	13894/68	"
SUGAR TRANSPORTER	13907/70	"
SUGAR REFINER	13907/71	"
NAESS ENTERPRISE	65300/70	Anglo-Norness Shpg. Co. Ltd
GOLD STAR	73730/70	Samyang Nav. Co. Ltd, Korea
KING STAR	73730/71	"

The 225-ton Arrol gantry (top), aerial view of the Kingston / Glen / East complex in the 1970s showing two halves of a VLCC under construction (centre), and the Kingston yard offices and prefabrication shops (bottom).

The Common Brothers tanker *Laristan* and the P & O tankers *Orama* and *Orissa* were fitted with a Lithgow-designed ram-bow for better fuel consumption. The Korean tankers *Gold Star* and *King Star* were of 900 feet length and were the largest tankers that could be built in one piece in the yard. In marked contrast to these enormous giants, a replica of the pioneer Clyde paddle steamer *Comet* of 1812 was built in the yard in 1967, and stands today at the front of Port Glasgow shopping centre. The original *Comet* had been launched on 24th July,1812 in a yard owned by John Wood on the site of the East yard.

The Glen / East yard was then absorbed into the Kingston yard in 1972 to form one 'super' yard with three wide berths suitable for the construction of very large bulk carriers and crude oil tankers of around 250,000 dwt. The crude oil tankers, of which four were built, were built in two halves, and joined together afloat by welding in an ingenious water-tight underwater cofferdam. The bow halves were always launched with the bulbous bow pointing down the berth to give a cleaner launch, and they were completed as *Nordic Commander* and *Nordic Clansman* in 1974/75, and *World Score* and *World Scholar* in 1978/79. Three large bulkers of Panamax size were also built during 1975/76 for Indian owners as *Jalavihar, Jhansi kiRani*, and *Kasturba*, and were notable for being launched with engine, funnel and fully-painted superstructure aboard !

The Scott-Lithgow Ltd yards at Port Glasgow and Greenock came under state ownership as part of British Shipbuilders Ltd on 1st July,1977. Two cargo-liners were on order by the Furness, Withy Group for their west coast of South America trade formerly that of the Pacific Steam Navigation Co. Ltd. This pair of engines-aft semi-container ships had capacity for 536 containers in the five holds as well as stacked on the deck. *Oroya* and *Oropesa*, both 14275/78, had nine sets of electric derrick cranes, eight of 22 tons capacity and one of 100 tons capacity, and the weather and 'tween deck hatch covers were electro-hydraulic folding - all at the touch of a button. They were also the last conventional ships built by the Lithgow yards, as Scott-Lithgow Ltd at the end of 1979 had only one segregated ballast tanker with double skin to build for British Petroleum, as well as an oil-rig type support ship for joint ownership by British Petroleum/British National Oil Corporation. The former was launched as *British Spirit* on 26th March,1982 and completed in March,1983; and the latter was launched as *Iolair* on 6th April,1981 and moved out to the North Sea oilfields under her diesel-electric propulsion later that year.

Iolair was a foretaste of what was to come, for with no further orders for shipping forthcoming, the Lithgow yard turned to oil-rig construction, forming Scott-Lithgow (Offshore) Ltd for this purpose. A large dynamically-positioned oil rig was ordered by Lloyds Leasing for lease to St. Vincent Drilling Ltd, a company jointly formed by Britoil and Ben - Odeco Ltd for delivery in April,1984. However with some £40M paid by the owner and the rig only 30% complete by Christmas, 1983 the order was cancelled, and lay in an incomplete state at Port Glasgow until the Scott-Lithgow yards were sold to a consortium of Trafalgar House and Howard Doris Ltd for £12M on 28th March,1984. Trafalgar House held 75% of the equity, and completed the self-propelled, semi-submersible rig in February,1985 as *Sea Explorer*, and a similar rig was then completed for Ben - Odeco Ltd in 1988 as *Ocean Alliance*. An additional cargo-section was fitted in September,1987 into the Swan Hunter-built container ship *Atlantic Conveyor* in the Inchgreen dry-dock.

A huge total of over 1200 ships has been built by the Lithgow yards under the Russell and Lithgow names, with several hundred more by subsidiaries under their own names. The Lithgow family diversified their interests into electronics by setting-up Lithgow Electronics Ltd, and into hotels by purchasing the Tontine Hotel of 1805 at Greenock in 1971.

The oil - rig support ship IOLAIR (Y1200) being launched on 6th April, 1981 for joint ownership by BP and BNOC (later Britoil). (Scott - Lithgow Ltd)

WILLIAM HAMILTON & CO. LTD.

William and John Hamilton completed two ships in 1867 at the Bay yard in Port Glasgow, formerly owned by Kirkpatrick & McIntyre. They then began shipbuilding in 1873 in the Newark yard at Port Glasgow, building sailing ships such as *Glen Afton* 1109/84 for the Dundee Shipowners Company, *Semantha* for J. R. Haws of Liverpool and the more famous *Grace Hawar* 1816/89 for W. Montgomery of London, as well as coasters and trawlers. *Grace Hawar* later joined the grain fleet of Gustaf Erikson of Finland and sailed on until broken up in 1935. Their first steel ship was the steamer *Colonsay* 1132/82, and one of the last by Hamilton from the Newark yard was the French steamer *Vauban* 1553/90. The twin-screw ferry *Macassa* 459/88 was built for service on Lake Ontario to the order of the like-named Hamilton Steamboat Co. Ltd. William Hamilton, now on his own, then in 1891 purchased the yard which was to make him famous, the Glen yard at Port Glasgow from the bankrupt John Reid. One of the first ships from the Glen yard under Hamilton was the sailing ship *David Morgan* of 1566 grt and delivered in October,1891 to H.O. Morgan of Liverpool, and sailing ships continued to be built until 1904. Three-masted barques such as *Eva Montgomery* 1944/01, *Fitzjames* 1951/02 and *Ladye Doris* 1947/02 were completed for W. Montgomery of London; and four-masted barques designed to carry case-oil such as *Comet* and *Nonpareil*, both 3014/01, for the Anglo-American Oil Co. Ltd, with the last four-masted barques from the yard being *Hans* and *Kurt*, both 3107/04, for G. Siemers of Hamburg. *Kurt* was launched last in April,1904 and is still afloat today as the *Moshulu* on the American eastern seaboard.

The Glen yard launched on average six ships each year from its four berths during the best years, although no ships were built at all during the year of 1903 due to a slump in orders. Local customers for tramps included William Burrell (8), Andrew Weir (4), Glen & Company (2), John Hardie & Company (1), and Robertson,Paterson & Company (1). Testimony to the soundness of Hamilton construction is shown by *Borneo* 3722/00, built for the Soc. Ungherese di Oriente, Fiume, and with a career of well over sixty years under other flags, and other overseas ships which gave long service included the Australian steamer *Kooringa* 3174/02 for McIlwraith, McEachearn of Melbourne, and the Cuban coastal steamer *Habana* 1494/06 for S. Herreras.

William Hamilton had converted his company into one of limited liabilty in 1904, and he was to retire at the end of the Great War in 1919 when he sold out to the Lithgow brothers (q.v.). He had built up a significant customer base of liner shipowners including Elder,Dempster; Bucknall Line; Strick Line; Saint Line of Liverpool; James Chambers and Charles G. Dunn of Liverpool; T. & J. Harrison Ltd of Liverpool; Lamport & Holt Ltd of Liverpool, and overseas liner customers included Rotterdam Lloyd (Ruys & Zonen); Nederland Line; Union Steamship Co. Ltd,New Zealand; East Asiatic Company of Copenhagen; D/S Norden of Copenhagen and D/S Argo of Bremen. However the most significant of these associations was that of Thomas and Jno. Brocklebank, who although they were taken over by Cunard in 1919 had no fewer than 31 cargo-liners built by the yard for their Brocklebank Line, which ultimately owned almost 50% of the shares in the yard alongside Lithgows. Their first ship from the Glen yard was launched in 1912 as *Maidan* 8205/12, which was wrecked in the Red Sea in 1923 and by which time two more Brocklebank cargo-liners had been built by the Glen yard. One of the most impressive cargo-liners of this period from the yard was the twin-funnelled *Howick Hall* 4821/10 built for the New York and South America Line service managed by Charles G. Dunn of Liverpool. She was launched on 1st October,1910 as a shelter-decker with a well-deck aft and was powered by a triple-expansion steam engine supplied by David Rowan & Co. Ltd of Glasgow.

The yard produced more than a dozen warships usually sloops such as *Spey* during the Great War together with 36 'X' craft lighters, as well as merchant ships to private order e.g. *Chronos* 4364/15 for Howard Smith Ltd of Melbourne and *Ardgowan* 5344/18 for Lang & Fulton of Greenock, . Two standard 'Z' type tankers were completed in 1919 as *War Dogra* and *War Hindoo*, together with the 'AO' standard tanker *War Celt*, while a standard 'B' type became the second cargo-liner completed for Brocklebank Line in 1920 as *Mandasor* 5144/20.

Orders were hard to come by during the lean 1920s, however a mixture of passenger ships, cargo-liners, tramps and tankers were built. A contract was signed on 3rd November,1925 with C.T. Bowring & Co. Ltd for the construction of a coastal passenger liner with accomodation for 200 passengers for their Red Cross Line service between St. John'S(NF) to Halifax(NS) to New York service. The liner was to be ready within seven months, and she was launched as *Nerissa* 5583/26 on time on 31st March,1926 and was ready to sail to New York at the end of May after very fast work by the yard. The following cargo-liners, coastal liners and tramps were completed by the Glen yard during the 1920s :-

CORNWALL	10606/20	Federal S.N. Co. Ltd
ERA	3148/21	Howard Smith Ltd, Melbourne
TURAKINA	8565/23	N. Zealand Shpg. Co. Ltd
TONGARIRO	8879/25	"
MALIA	3752/21	Brocklebank Line, Liverpool

MAHRONDA	7880/25	"
MAHOUT	8089/25	"
MATRA	7911/26	"
MARKHOR	8036/29	"
BARON DALMENY	3536/24	H. Hogarth, Glasgow
GOLDEN SEA	4555/24	Howard Tenens Ltd, London
LIMERICK	8675/25	Union S.S. of New Zealand
NERISSA	5583/26	Red Cross Line (Bowring)
SANDVIKEN	2916/26	H.J. Wallem, Bergen
DAVIKEN	2922/26	"
NORVIKEN	2924/26	"
NIKOLA PASIC	4984/27	Dubrovacka Plovidba, Yugoslavia
DARSHIEL	5197/27	Douglas & Ramsey, Glasgow
TEMPLE BAR	4291/28	Lambert Bros., London
TEMPLE LANE	4289/28	"
TEMPLE PIER	4312/28	"
WINTON	4388/28	Avenue Shpg. Co. Ltd, London
BIO-BIO	4316/30	Cia Sud Americana de Vapores,Chile
CAUTIN	4316/30	"
PUDETO	4321/30	"

Malia was an experimental motorship and was one of the first ships fitted with Cammell, Laird - Fullagar oil engines and was twin-screw. However she had to be re-engined in 1923 by Cammell, Laird and was sold in 1927, and Brocklebanks stayed with steam for the next forty years. The following tankers were built :-

DAVANGER	7102/22	Westfal-Larsen, Bergen
LUNULA	6363/27	H.E. Moss, Liverpool
CYMBELINE	6317/27	Bowring, London
EL ALETO	7703/27	"
ATHELMONARCH	8995/28	Athel Line, London
ATHELPRINCESS	8882/29	"
ATHELSULTAN	8882/29	"
ATHELDUCHESS	8940/29	"
ATHELEMPRESS	8941/30	"
VALVERDA	8817/34	Gow, Harrison, Glasgow

with the last tanker *Valverda* left on the stocks throughout the Depression, with completion delayed for four years until November,1934 while the yard was closed. The next ship for Brocklebanks was thoroughly tank-tested and many alterations in her specifications were made to her design by her owners before the contract was signed in 1933 and the yard re-opened to build her as *Marwarri* 8063/35, and she was also the first company ship to have refrigerated capacity. Orders were also received from United Africa Co. Ltd, Prince Line and the local tramp owners Douglas

& Ramsey, Glasgow who in those cost-effective days fitted an economical exhaust turbine to the triple expansion engine fitted to their pair of tramps.

DARCOLM	4297/35	Douglas & Ramsey, Glasgow
DARLENY	5402/37	"
ASHANTIAN	4917/35	United Africa Co. Ltd
KUMASIAN	4922/35	"
PALESTINIAN PRINCE	2001/36	Prince Line
ARABIAN PRINCE	2001/36	"
NEREUS	5205/37	E.E. Hadjilias, Syros
MALANCHA	8288/37	Brocklebank Line
MACHARDA	8117/38	"
ARCSCOTT	4202/38	Completed as MOUNT IDA
WRAY CASTLE	4253/38	Lancs. Shpg. Co. Ltd (J. Chambers)
MARTAND	8007/39	Brocklebank Line
SAINT BERNARD	5183/39	Mitchell,Cotts, London

The yard during World War II built six standard 'Empire' tramps and five to private order for Counties Ship Management managed by London Greeks Kulukundis & Rethymnis, as well as five cargo-liners for Brocklebank Line, half owners of the Glen yard. In addition, a new fore half was built for the Houlder Brothers tanker *Imperial Transport* in June,1941 and joined to the stern half, which had been sailed in by her crew in February,1940 after a torpedo attack.

In post-war years half of the Glen yard output was for cargo-liners, especially for Brocklebank Line with twelve ships, with another five for the parent company Cunard Line for which three ships were built for their Mediterranean services as *Pavia, Lycia* and *Phrygia*. The other half of production was for tankers :-

CIS BROVIG	8996/48	Th. Brovig, Farsund
NORDBO	9064/49	H. Kuhnle, Bergen
BERGLJOT	8930/49	Gill - Johanessen A/S, Norway
ERLING BORTHEN	8977/50	Harry Borthen A/S, Norway
KATARINA	9013/51	H.E. Hansen - Tangen, Kristiansand
DEA BROVIG	10917/51	Th. Brovig, Farsund
G.C. BROVIG	10917/51	"
PARA	11218/52	Petroleos Brasileiros
BRIS	9061/53	M. Thorvik, Oslo
ALVA BAY	11340/53	Alva S.S. Co. Ltd,London
PACIFIC STAR	11218/54	Blue Star Line, London
BRITISH OFFICER	11362/55	British Tanker Co. Ltd
GEROLDA	11430/55	Gerrards Rederi A/S, Kristiansand
NORDNES	11470/56	H. Kuhnle, Bergen
TOBIAS U. BORTHEN	9041/56	Harry Borthen A/S, Norway
HOLMGAR	9001/57	Stamers Rederi A/S, Bergen
MELITI	11691/57	Andreadis, Greece

SAGONA	11850/58	H.E. Hansen - Tangen, Kristiansand
BRITISH KESTREL	11171/62	British Tanker Co. Ltd

and yard production included the following cargo-liners :-

MAIDAN	8566/46	Brocklebank Line
MAHRONDA	8537/47	"
POSEIDON	2529/47	N.V. Koninlijke NSM, Amsterdam
AGAMEMNON	2515/47	"
HELICON	2515/47	"
OBERON	2515/47	"
JAL-AZAD	8521/48	Scindia Line. Launched as EL HIND
MAHSEER	8945/48	Brocklebank Line
MATRA	8954/49	"
MANAAR	8996/50	"
AJANA	5627/50	Australind S.S. Co. Ltd,London
TREGLISSON	5270/49	Hain S.S. Co. Ltd
TREMAYNE	5608/52	"
TREMORVAH	5605/54	"
PAVIA	3411/53	Cunard Line
LYCIA	3534/54	"
PHRYGIA	3534/55	"
HELLENIC GLORY	7510/56	Hellenic Lines, Greece
HELLENIC TORCH	7510/56	"
MASKELIYA	7350/54	Brocklebank Line
MATURATA	7365/55	"
TREMEADOW	6504/57	Hain S.S. Co. Ltd
TRECARRELL	6499/59	"
TRECARNE	6499/59	
MAKRANA	8771/57	Brocklebank Line
MASIRAH	8773/57	"
MAWANA	8744/58	"
MANGLA	8805/59	"
MATHURA	8674/60	"
ALAUNIA	8717/60	Cunard Line
ANDANIA	8717/60	"
NORDHOLM	7187/61	H. Kuhnle, Bergen
TREVALGAN	6706/61	Hain S.S. Co. Ltd
HALLFAX	5780/62	Hall Corporation of Canada
BENTE BROVIG	12086/63	Th. Brovig, Norway
TRENEGLOS	9976/63	Hain S.S. Co. Ltd
FREETOWN	7869/64	Elder, Dempster

Jal-Azad had sizable passenger accomodation for Scindia Line, and Cunard gave *Alaunia* and *Andania* of 1960 accomodation for twelve first-class passengers. The last class of five ships for Brocklebank Line completed between 1957 and 1960 were well equipped with cargo gear on bipod masts with a heavy 100-ton derrick on the foremast. The yard by way of variety also built a small coaster for Osborn & Wallis and completed as *Colston* 550/55. In 1960 the paid-up capital of William Hamilton & Co. Ltd was £170,000 and shared equally between T. & J. Brocklebank and Lithgows Ltd. The Hall Corporation of Canada then placed an order for an engines-aft bulker of 8160 dwt and completed in June,1962 as *Hallfax*. The only other bulker built at the Glen yard by Hamilton was the engines-aft *Bente Brovig* of 16868 dwt and fitted with a Kincaid oil engine to give a service speed of 15.5 knots.

Treneglos was the last ship completed by the Glen yard in August,1963, and *Freetown* the last ship launched at the Glen yard on 19th September,1963 with her completion under the Lithgow name in February,1964. The Glen yard was then merged with the East yard of Lithgow, with the Glen slipways being replaced by a new long platers shop at right angles to the Clyde, and the Glen/East yard was then modernised for the prefabrication of very large bulkers and supertankers after the erection of a high 225-ton capacity Arrol gantry crane for lifting large assemblies.

The Greek cargo-liner HELLENIC GLORY of 1956 owned by Hellenic Lines.

ROBERT DUNCAN & CO. LTD.

Robert Duncan served his apprenticeship in Robert Steele's yard at Greenock, and then gained further shipbuilding experience in his father's Greenock yard and other neighbouring yards before setting-up on his own in 1862 in the East yard at Port Glasgow to build in iron. He was aged 35 years when he purchased the East yard from John Wood, and he built sailing ships for many owners including John Kerr of Greenock and his 'Diamond K' fleet of sugar traders e.g. *Colombo* 1199/68 and *Sinde* 1200/68, and for the New Zealand trade of the Albion Line of Paddy Henderson e.g. *Auckland, Canterbury, Dunedin, Invercargill, Nelson* and *Wellington* all 1247/74, and *Lyttelton* and *Westland*, both 1186/78, and the very successful sailing ship *MacCallum More* in 1873. Iron steamers were built for the Anchor Line of Henderson Brothers e.g. *Victoria* 3358/72, with one of the last iron steamers being *Lamington* 1958/81 for Raeburn & Verel of Glasgow. Steel replaced iron in 1882 for both steamers e.g. *Torch* for Clyde Lighthouse Trustees and sailing ships, the latter continuing to be built until the 1890s for local customers e.g. the four-masted barques *Cape Clear* 2129/92 and *Cape Wrath* 2140/92 for Lyle of Greenock; *Achnashie* 2476/92 for Thom & Cameron; *East Indian* 1745/94 and *East African* 1731/95 for Lang & Fulton; *Inverness-shire* 2307/94 for Thomas Law; *Glenbreck* and *Morven* , both 2150/93 for J. G. Thorburn,Greenock; and *Pass of Killiecrankie* 1746/93 for Gibson & Clark, Glasgow. The last sailing ship from the East yard was the barquentine *Alta* 1379/00 for A.P. Lorentzen of Chile.

Robert Duncan died in 1889, having also been closely associated with the Barrow Shipbuilding Company founded in 1871 with Henderson and Cavendish money and building ships for charter to Anchor Line. He left the East yard in the capable hands of his three sons, who had entered the business in 1883, and one of the last ships he oversaw at the yard was the steamer *Holyrood* 2712/89 for Raeburn & Verel. The yard continued to build ever larger steel steamers such as *Italiana* 2763/98 for the Transatlantic trade of Furness,Withy & Co. Ltd, *Highland Laird* 4123/99 for the Nelson Line service to South America, *Domingo de Larrinaga* for Larrinaga of Liverpool for their service to the West Indies, *Ontarian* 4309/00 for Allan Line Transatlantic service, *Melville* 4439/02 for the Elder,Dempster service to West Africa, *Kalomo* 5019/07 for the Bucknall Line service to South Africa. A regular customer at this time was William S. Miller of Glasgow with 14 tramps built between 1903 and 1925 including *Iriston* 3782/12 and *Mariston* 3793/12, and other tramps were completed for local owners such as Thomas Dunlop , William Burrell, James Bruce and John Little. Greek shipowner Alexandros Michalinos from Chios ordered two of his first new tramps from the yard in *Aeolus* and *Bacchus*, both 3078/02. A small steel-hulled ship which has proved the strength of Duncan construction was the twin-screw steamer *Flying Serpent* of 260 tons built in 1886 for the Clyde Shipping Co. Ltd with a two-cylinder compound engine by Rankin & Blackmore, which after fitting a new diesel engine is still sailing today around Turkish coasts as *Mehlika* some 108 years later !

The yard continued to build steam tramps with the similarly-named *Agnes Duncan* 2514/12 built for a Cardiff shipowner, J.T. Duncan, and *Queen Margaret* 4972/12 for Thomas Dunlop of Glasgow and *Ardgorm* 5065/13, *Ardmore* 5131/13 and *Ardgair* 5119/13 for Lang & Fulton of Greenock. The yard was taken over by the Lithgow brothers in 1915 but continued to build under its own name, with war output including tramps for William S. Miller in *Wilston* and *Iriston*, both 3218/16, and *War Fantail* 4453/18 and *Trafalgar* 5021/18 for Glen & Co. with her sister launched as *Camperdown* 5038/18 but completed as *Montezuma* for Canadian Pacific. Brocklebank Line took two cargo-liners in *Mahratta* 6690/17 and *Makalla* 6781/18, and a standard 'C' type was completed as *Granicos* 3108/19, and three standard 'Z' tankers were completed as *War Mogul, War Afridi* and *War Wazir.* After the war tankers were built fitted with cylindrical tanks e.g. *Gobeo* 3365/21.

The yard then continued to build for both liner and tramp customers throughout the lean 1920s:-

TELESFORA DE LARRINAGA	6072/20	Larrinaga S.S.,Liverpool
RAMON DE LARRINAGA	5791/20	"
TJIKANDI	7979/21	Java - China - Japan Line
DURENDA	7241/22	British India Line
LUCISTON	5017/24	William S. Miller, Glasgow
GRETASTON	5008/24	"
LORNASTON	4934/25	"
DUNROBIN	5041/24	Glen & Company, Glasgow
VARNA	1514/24	"
JUTLAND	6153/28	"
SAINT OSWALD	5030/25	Saint Line, Liverpool
BENICIA	5050/25	J. Edgar & Co., Liverpool
ALOE	5047/25	S. African Govt.
GRAIG	3683/24	Graig Shpg. Co. Ltd,Cardiff
GRAIGWEN	3697/26	"
SHAKESPEAR	5029/26	Glover Bros, London
CHAUCER	5792/29	"
REYNOLDS	5024/27	Bolton Shpg. Co. Ltd, London
ROMNEY	5840/29	"
RAMSAY	4855/30	"
CAPE ST. ANDREW	5094/28	Mitchell Cotts, London

CAPE ST. GEORGE	5112/28	"
NEWBURY	5102/27	Capper, Alexander , London
MALMESBURY	5173/28	"
BIBURY	4616/29	"
BONNINGTON COURT	4909/29	Court Line, London
ARICA	4540/31	Cia Chilena Interoceanica, Chile
DALIA	5188/31	Union Govt. of South Africa (Railways & Harbours),Durban

Durenda was the first motorship built by the yard, with *Bonnington Court* also motor-driven and fitted with a Kincaid oil engine. The Dutch liner *Tjikandi* was turbine-powered, whereas most tramps and the Clyde steamer *Dalriada* 758/26 were triple-expansion powered. The engine of the latter had four cylinders and gave over 17 knots enabling this new steamer, launched on 16th March,1926 for the centenary of the Campbeltown & Glasgow Steam Packet Co. Ltd, to reach Campbeltown from Gourock in under three hours. The following tankers were also built :-

RONALD	6249/20	A/S Hektor (N. Bugge),Tonsberg
SANTA MARIA	8088/22	Union Oil of California
VANDUARA	4870/25	Gow, Harrison, Glasgow
VITRUVIA	4870/26	"
VENETIA	5728/27	"
VIMEIRO	5586/28	"
VALLEJO	5586/28	"
ATHELVISCOUNT	8882/29	Athel Line, London
ATHELDUKE	8966/29	"
ATHELKNIGHT	8940/30	"
LANGANGER	9178/30	Westfal-Larsen, Bergen
STORANGER	9223/30	"
VALLDEMOSA	7223/35	Gow, Harrison, Glasgow

The East yard closed in 1931 leaving the tanker *Valldemosa* on the stocks, and she was launched and completed during 1935. The yard re-opened under the Lithgow name in April,1937 after some four hundred ships had been built under the Duncan name at the East yard.

DUNLOP, BREMNER & CO. LTD.

In 1871 David J. Dunlop and James L. Cunliffe took over the Inch yard at Port Glasgow from Lawrence Hill, trading as Cunliffe & Dunlop, with both men having had shipbuilding experience with John Elder at the Fairfield yard. Dunlop was the leading partner and the son of a merchant in Mexico City, where he was born in 1838. He was sent home to be educated at Glasgow and after some civil engineering experience his first shipyard experience was to help John Elder lay out his new Fairfield yard at Govan. He left the Fairfield yard in 1869 after the death of Elder, and decided to start shipbuilding on his own account. Many shallow-draft craft were the first products of Cunliffe & Dunlop as well as several cable ships including *Retriever* of the 1870s. Cunliffe retired in 1881 and David J. Dunlop continued alone until 1911 building over one hundred ships of varied types. Customers included Trinity House with the tender *Satellite*; Booth Line with *Amazonense* 2828/99; the local Glen & Company with *Dunolly* 3281/01; *Zafiro* 2539/01 for the China & Manila Steamship Co. Ltd, Hong Kong ; and Woermann Line of Hamburg with *Hans Woermann* 4059/00 and *Ernst Woermann* 4065/00 for their African services; and the Union Steamship Co. Ltd of New Zealand with *Atua* 3444/06.

The Inch yard is best remembered for a number of large tankers, large for the time, built from 1889 e.g. *Manhattan* 3384/89 of 4000 dwt, *Delaware* 3855/93 and *Lackawanna* 3855/94 of 4700 dwt and *Chesapeake* 4557/95 of 5200 dwt for the Anglo-American Oil Co. Ltd; and the larger *Phoebus* 6268/03 for the Deutsch - American Petroleum Co. Ltd. In 1911 David Dunlop died and Donald Bremner took over the Inch yard, retaining the Dunlop name as Dunlop, Bremner & Co. Ltd and building for local owners such as J. & J. Denholm with *Mountpark* 1376/12.

Output during the Great War included three 'Flower' class sloops, four paddle minesweepers and six twin-screw minesweepers, and dumb barges for the Admiralty, and five coastal liners for Wilson Line of Hull. Standard ships included four 'H' type standard coasters, completed as *Backworth* 2481/19, *Coatsworth* 2555/19, *Roseworth* 2555/19 and *Knebworth* 2555/19 for R.S. Dalgleish Ltd of Newcastle. Largest ships built at this time were *Camana* 5574/18 and *Almeda* 6817/19 for Blue Star Line, the latter being renamed *Norman Star*. The yard was taken over by the Lithgow brothers in 1919 but continued under its own name until work ran out in 1926 with :-

DIDO	3574/20	Ellerman Lines
DESTRO	3574/20	"
FAUSANG	2256/21	Indo-China S.N. Co. Ltd

PABJUNE	1859/23	Gt. Lakes trader
LYCIA	2338/24	(motorship) T. & J. Brocklebank
BARON RUTHVEN	3178/25	H. Hogarth, Ardrossan
BARON CARNEGIE	3178/25	"
BARON WEMYSS	2996/24	"
QUERCUS	2695/26	Arbor Shpg. (Howard Tenens)
ULMUS	2697/26	"

The last two ships were built as speculations, and when the yard closed in 1926 it had six berths for ships up to 450 feet in length with its own fitting-out basin and covered around nine acres. Some three hundred ships had been built at the Inch yard by the various owners. The yard was purchased in March,1933 by National Shipbuilders Security Ltd with a restrictive convenant prohibiting shipbuilding for forty years.

A. RODGER & COMPANY

After the dissolution of the partnership of Russell, Lithgow and Rodger of Russell & Company in 1891, Anderson Rodger took the Bay yard in east Port Glasgow and started building three-masted barques under his own name. The first (Y298) was *Beacon Rock* 1789/91 followed by *Ballachulish* (Y299), with some twenty ships out of the 120 built by Rodger to 1912 being sailing ships. These included *Glenlee* 1613/96 for Sterling & Company, Glasgow which is still afloat after spending many years as a Spanish Navy training ship at El Ferrol, and has recently been returned to the Clyde as a museum ship and is lying at Yorkhill Quay. The largest were the case-oil carriers *Eclipse* 3090/02 and *Arrow* 3071/02 for the Anglo-American Oil Co. Ltd, followed by *Radiant* and *Alacrita*, both 1974/03, for the same owner.

The biggest customers for tramps were the local owners of Hogarth (13), Craig Line (7), Maclay & McIntyre (3), Burrell (3), Kyle Shpg. Co. Ltd (1), Andrew Crawford (1), Glen & Company (1) and Miller & Richards (1). Liner customers included the local Glen Line with three ships, *Glenfruin* 3096/04, *Glenfinlas* 3095/06 and *Glenmorag* 3535/06; with *Mariana* 4147/05 for Furness,Withy & Co. Ltd; and *Bessie Dollar* 4329/05 and *Hazel Dollar* 4304/05 for the Dollar Line of Vancouver with other exports being *Heros* 2745/99 to Finland and *Arciduchessa Maria Theresa* 2886/01 and *Francesco Musner* 3225/08 to Austro-Hungary. Anderson Rodger died in 1909 and his Bay yard then reverted to Lithgow control in 1912 under the Russell name.

MURDOCH & MURRAY LTD.

Henry Murray served his apprenticeship as a joiner and then worked at the Castle yard (q.v.) of Blackwood & Gordon before setting-up under his own name at the Kingston yard in 1866. He left to team up with James Murdoch as Murdoch & Murray at this Brown Street yard in 1875. A mixture of small iron schooners and barques e.g. *Norman Macleod* 860/76 for William Rankin was built as well as steamers e.g. *Miramar* 1198/80 and *Iolani* 1543/82 for Raeburn & Verel, Glasgow, and *Cassia* and *Claudia*, both 1163/83 for Stephens & Mawson, Newcastle, together with the Clyde tug *Flying Foam* 150/77. A change to steel construction was then made with the steamer *Naranja* 975/84 for Goodyear & Company of Liverpool. The yard specialised in shallow-draft passenger/cargo steamers for the Amazon, of which seventy were built, as well as small steamers for Australian and New Zealand services e.g. *Jessie Darling* 232/84 and *Claymore* 210/02, the latter for Auckland owners. The last three-masted schooners were the Swedish *Halvar* 911/91, and *America* 767/06 and *India* 738/06 for service on the Plate in Argentina.

In 1895 John Murray, son of the founder, established the coaster company of Murray,McNab & Co.,Glasgow and ordered two coasters from the yard completed as *Rossbank* and *Rosslyn*. In the same year of 1895 the yard was closed for a few months during a slump in orders but re-opened to build two Amazon steamers. Henry Murray continued to run the yard after the death of James Murdoch until his retirement in 1909, when Murdoch & Murray was made into a limited liability company, with his two sons James and George Murray as directors with James also yard manager.

Steel tramp steamers were also built e.g. *Lochgiel* 2111/88 and *Rannoch* 2005/89 for James Gardiner of Glasgow, *Baron Elibank* 1772/89 for Hogarth, *Rosneath* 1779/90 and *Valetta* 3017/99 for Gow & Harrison of Glasgow, and then a series of steamers of 3000 dwt for Swedish owners e.g. *Atlanten* 2133/02, *O.H. Wiens* 2363/05, *Gerd* 2065/07 and *Vidar* 2074/07. Small steamers at the turn of the century included four pilot tenders for the Mersey, two Newfoundland coastal liners for Bowring *Portia* and *Prospero* of 1904, and also the hull of the paddler *Queen-Empress* 411/13 for the Williamson fleet on the Clyde, and the Anchor Line tender *Paladin* 332/13 for Moville, and *Linmere* 1595/13 for Lever Bros. of Manchester.

The yard at the start of the Great War had five berths capable of building ships up to 350 feet in length, and output included minesweepers of both the paddle and tunnel-screw types, two tugs for Mesopotamia, four rescue tugs of the Saint class, several trawlers, the coaster *Grangetown* 1574/17, and the Russian ice-breaking tug *Ledokol V,* and Mersey pilot cutter *Walter J. Chambers*. A number of conversions of small merchantmen into naval auxiliaries was also undertaken. The yard and that of the neighbouring Newark and Castle yards was purchased by the London group of John Slater Ltd at the end of the war, with the directors then being James and George Murray and John Slater and his wife Mrs. A.E. Slater. A final flurry of ships included :-

PAIGNTON	1514/19	London & Edinburgh Shipping Co. Ltd
BEAUMANOIR	2328/20	Soc.Chargeurs de l'Ouest, Nantes
SPERO	1960/20	Pelton Steamship Co. Ltd,Newcastle
MOTO	2693/20	"
WINDERMERE	2815/21	Balls & Stansfield, North Shields
ANNAVORE	3324/21	A/S Vore, Farsund
PACIFIC	2816/23	Walter Cockerline, Hull

Pacific was the last ship launched in March,1923 with the yard finally closed in October,1927 and soon after the yard was demolished and made into a public recreation ground, the land later being reused by Lithgows.

FERGUSON BROTHERS LTD.

The Newark yard just downstream of Newark Castle had been used by William Hamilton until he moved to the Glen yard in 1891. In 1903 four brothers named Ferguson left the yard of Fleming & Ferguson in Paisley to set-up on their own in the Newark yard. They obtained orders for three tugs for the Clyde Shipping Co. Ltd and completed as *Flying Falcon, Flying Linnet* and *Flying Swallow*, all 185/04; as well as for hoppers and dredgers e.g. *Vulcan* 790/04 to work on the Mersey; *Pioneer* 543/05 to work in Victoria(Australia); *Shieldhill* 787/06 to work on the Clyde and *Fleetwood* 479/06 to work in the port of the same name, and several for the port of Preston. The larger hopper dredger *Lord Desborough* 2965/07 was then completed for service on the Thames, and in the same year the tug *Canterbury* 292/07 was completed for the Lyttleton Harbour Board in New Zealand. Further hopper dredgers were completed e.g. *Cowpen* 1122/13 for Blyth Harbour Commissioners, tugs for the Clyde Shipping Co. Ltd, and ferries for the Clyde Navigation Trust. A limited liability company Ferguson Brothers (Port Glasgow) Ltd was set-up in 1912.

At the end of the Great War the yard was purchased by the John Slater Ltd group of London, and built the cargo ships *Elizabeth Ann Slater* 2088/21 for the owners, *Bothal* 2109/20 for Det Danske Kulkompagni, *Ellen Stubb* 2630/20 for German owners. The suction dredger *Oceanus* 2115/22 was built for the Union Government of South Africa, Durban; and the hopper dredger *Carronwater* 1232/26 for service on the Firth of Forth. The Antarctic scientific and exploration ship *Discovery II* was built and sent to the Falkland Isles in 1929, by which time the yard was back in Ferguson family hands.

During World War II the yard built trawlers, corvettes, boom defence vessels, naval tugs and the twin-screw suction/trailing dredger *Empire Sorcerer* 2594/46, the hopper *Empire Hartland* 683/46, and four passenger and vehicle ferries for Turkey with ramps at both ends. The yard stayed in its traditional markets for bucket and grab dredgers in post-war years with three for Mersey Docks & Harbour Board e g. *Mersey Engineer* 887/49, as well as *J.P. Webb* 967/54 and one for Clyde service as *Blythswood* 786/63 and one for Brazil as *Brazilia* 885/72, as well as the larger suction dredgers *Baglan* 1889/66, *Abbotsgrange* 1864/67, *Lavernock* 1837/67, *Aberavon* 2246/69, *Marinex V* 2825/71, *Consortium* 2549/72, *Cambrae* 3896/73 and *Sand Weaver* 3366/74, and the sludge carriers *Percy Dawson* 1525/68, *Gilbert J. Fowler* 2548/71, *Gardyloo* 1952/76 and *Thames* 2663/77.

Many tugs have also come from the Newark yard through the years including three fire-fighting tugs for the Abeille fleet at Le Havre in 1950, *Abeille X, Abeille XI* and *Abeille XII*, and the BP fire-fighting tug *Faramand* 362/60 for Persian Gulf duties, *Holmgarth* 204/79 for Cardiff service, *Flying Phantom* 287/81 for Clyde service of the Clyde Shipping Co. Ltd, *Shalder* and *Tirrick* both 482/83 for Shetland Towage Co. Ltd, and *Mwokozi* 672/84 and *Simba II* 672/84 for Kenya Port Authority for service at Mombasa. The pilot tender *Wyuna* 1313/53 was built for distant Australian duties, while the lighthouse tender *Granuaile* 2003/70 serves the Irish Light Commissioners. Several stern trawlers were also built including *St. Jason* 1343/67, *St. Jerome* 1254/68, *St. Jasper* 1254/68, *St. Benedict* 1313/70, *Roman* 1154/74 and *Goth* 1169/74, and the fishery research vessels *Cirolana* 1731/70 and *Scotia* 1521/71.

In 1955 Lithgows purchased a minority interest in the yard and then obtained full control in 1961, with their directors Sir William J. Lithgow and Ross Belch (later Sir) replacing Ferguson family directors. As part of the Scott - Lithgow Group it became a member of British Shipbuilders in July,1977 and was then associated with the Troon yard of Ailsa Shipbuilding Co. Ltd from 1980, a full merger as Ferguson - Ailsa Ltd occurring in 1983. However in October,1986 this was disbanded after the sale of the Ailsa yard, and the yard was then merged with Appledore Shipbuilders

The Garston dredger BAGLAN of 1966 (top), oil-rig supply vessel SEAFORTH HIGHLANDER of 1976 (centre) and Polish mini - bulker ZGORZELEC of 1980. (Ferguson - Ailsa Ltd)

The Isle of Wight double - ended car ferry RED OSPREY under construction by Ferguson at the Newark Yard during 1994. A good panoramic view of the Port Glasgow waterfront (below) with Newark Castle on the left. (Author).

The twin-screw oil-rig supply vessel STAR PEGASUS on trials in April, 1992. (Ferguson Shipbuilders Ltd).

Ltd to form Appledore - Ferguson Shipbuilders Ltd. In September,1989 the yard was sold by British Shipbuilders to the HLD Group, which came under the control of Kvaerner A/S of Norway shortly afterwards, and the yard traded as Ferguson Shipbuilders Ltd. In 1991 the yard was sold privately again becoming Ferguson Marine Ltd.

Despite these changes of ownership the yard is still very much in operation producing quality small ships such as oil rig supply ships e.g. *Seaforth Jarl* and *Seaforth Highlander*, both 1376/76, *Seaforth Earl* and *Seaforth Baronet*, both 850/86, *Star Capella* 1599/83, *Fort Resolution* and *Fort Reliance* both 1371/86 and *Star Pegasus* 2145/92, the Scottish fishery protection cruisers *Sulisker* and *Vigilant* of 1982, and the Admiralty trials vessel *Auricula*. The mini-bulker *Clarknes* 2351/78 of 3600 dwt was followed by two mini-bulkers of 4400 dwt for Poland as *Zgorzelec* and *Mlawa* of 1980, and the large Arran ferry *Isle of Arran* 3296/84 and Western Isles ferries *Isle of Mull* 4331/88 and *Lord of the Isles* 3504/89 for Caledonian Macbrayne Ltd. Two Isle of Wight double-ended ferries for Red Funnel Ferries are the latest products with *Red Falcon* 2881/93 having accomodation for 890 passengers and 140 cars and 16 coaches, with the sister *Red Osprey* under construction during 1994 and due to be delivered in November. The yard has work for some time to come, including a £15M order for a ferry from Caledonian Macbrayne Ltd.

CLYDE SHIPBUILDING CO. LTD.
JAMES LAMONT & CO. LTD.

The Castle yard just upstream of Newark Castle had a long history before operating under the above title from 1900. The yard was taken over in 1860 by Blackwood & Gordon in order to build larger ships than hitherto possible at their Paisley yard. Six iron steamers were built for George Gibson of Leith, the largest being *Redgauntlet* 1437/71, and eight steamers were built for Burrell & Son with the last being the steel-hulled *Adria* 1039/80, the first from the yard. Steel steamers were turned out quickly and cheaply e.g. *Ardancorrach* 1432/82 for Clark & Service of Glasgow, with several built for Italy e.g. *Polcevera* 2207/82 and *Entella* 2258/83, and *Baron Douglas* 2700/88 for Hugh Hogarth of Ardrossan, two for Lloyd Brazileiro as *Satellite* 1412/90 and *Iris* 1430/91. The City of Dublin Steam Packet Co. Ltd had a number of steamers built by the yard in the last decade of the century as *Louth* 1273/94, *Carlow* 1235/96, *Kerry* 1299/97 and *Cork* 1280/99.

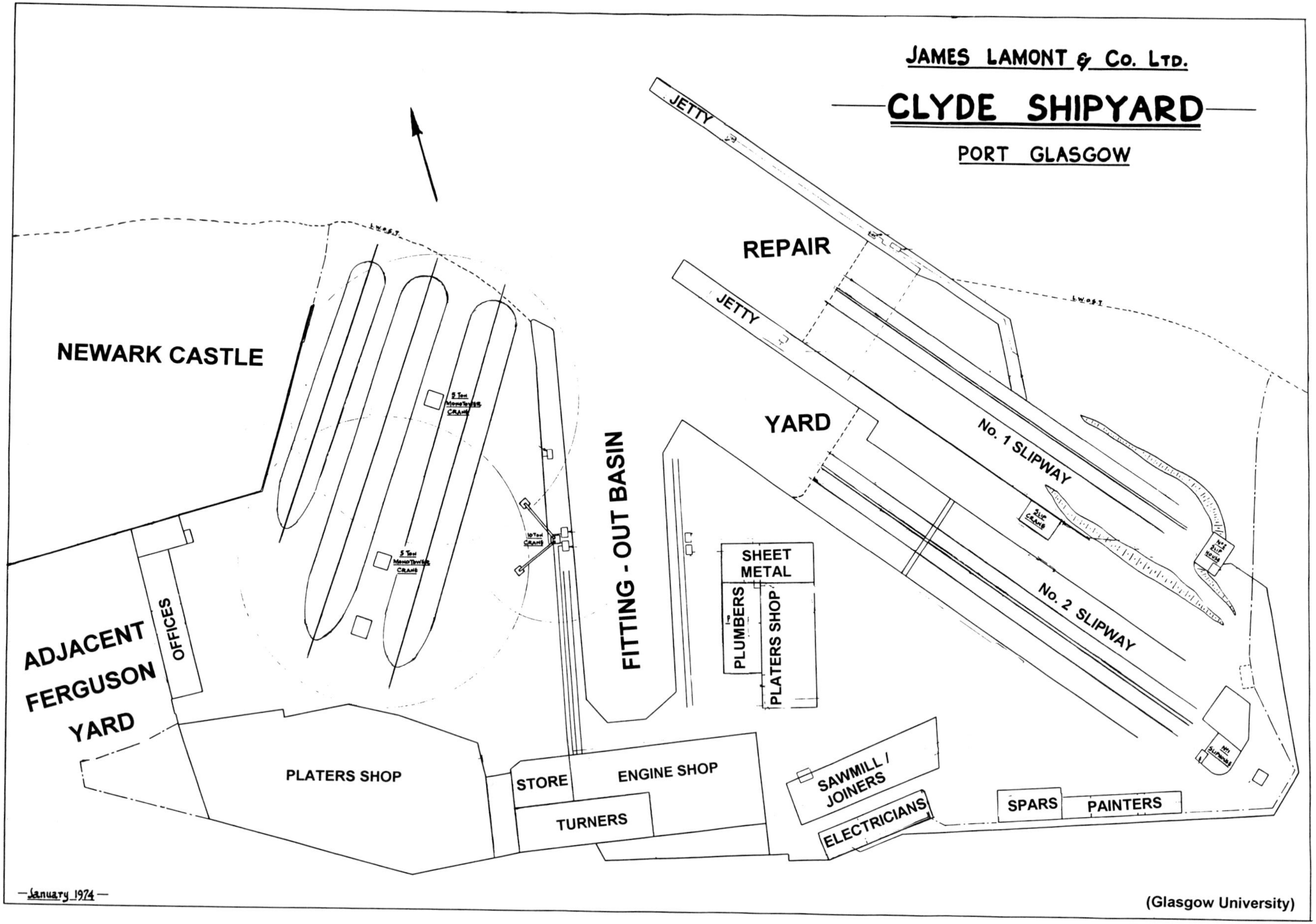

(Glasgow University)

The yard had been closed between 1887 and 1889 after financial difficulties, and was restarted by Blackwood and three new partners, but further financial difficulties after the completion of *Clan Macfadyen* 2816/99 led to the take-over of the yard in 1900 by the Clyde Shipbuilding Co. Ltd, set-up with a capital of £30,000. Elder, Dempster then ordered *Egwanga* 2600/02, *Muraji* 3238/04 and *Zaria* 3243/05 J. Neil of Glasgow took *Hermia* 2050/03 and *Silvia* 2035/04; four were ordered by the Dansk-Russiske D/S of Copenhagen in *Generalconsul Pallisen, Helmer Morch, Wladimir Reitz* and *Michail Ontchoukoff*, all 2130/05; and three for Austro-Hungary as *Luna* 2808/07, *Sabbia* 2808/07 and *Onda* 3186/07;and *Kurdistan* and *Shahristan* both 2808/06 for Strick Line, London.

Coastal passenger ships were sent to Australia e.g. *Kooyong* 2296/07 for McIlwraith,McEachearn of Melbourne; *Mataram* 3331/09 and *Montoro* 4057/11 for Burns,Philp of Sydney. The British & Irish Steam Packet Co. Ltd of Dublin took *Lady Gwendolen* 2390/11, and another important customer was Blue Star Line with *Brodhurst* 3071/14. Standard ships were built during the Great War as well as four gunboats of 800 tons. In 1919 the yard was taken over by the John Slater Ltd group of London, and construction of larger still vessels commenced :-

MAINDY BRIDGE	2445/20	Maindy Shpg. Co. Ltd, Cardiff
GEORGIOS	3246/21	V.G. Mantacas, Andros
REMUS	4900/21	A.O. Lindvig, Oslo
HAULERWIJK	3278/24	N.V. Maats Noordwijk,Rotterdam
PERLA	5741/26	Nav.Libera Triestina SA, Venice
SABBIA	5787/26	"
ZVIR	5607/26	Prekomorska Plovidba DD,Yugoslavia
KALINGO	2047/27	Union Steamship Co. Ltd,New Zealand
PREDSEDNIK KOPAJTIC	1793/28	Jadranska Plovidba D.D.,Yugoslavia
FORTH	1058/28	Carron S.S. Co. Ltd, Grangemouth
ZONNEWYK	5605/28	Erhardt & Dekkers, Rotterdam

as well as several Great Lakes traders. In 1927 the John Slater Group crashed and one of the last ships built by the Clyde Shipbuilding Co. Ltd was the motor yacht *Migrant* 348/27 for K. Lee Guinness, who had her engined with 12-cylinder M.A.N. oil engines. The Castle yard was eventually sold to James Lamont, a shiprepairer in Greenock, who did not use the Castle yard for shiprepairing until 1938. The yard was a shiprepairer only during World War II, but began shipbuilding again in 1946.

Some seventy ships were then built by Lamont including *Benin* 2483/50 for the West African coastal services of Elder,Dempster; *Knut Jarl* 1026/49 and *Eystein Jarl* 1013/50 for coastal Norwegian services of Nordenfjeldske D/S and the similar *Tejo* and *Douro* both 1125/48 for E.A. Aaby Rederi A/S, Oslo; and six motor coasters for J. G. Stewart & Co. Ltd,Glasgow e.g. *Yewforest* 1097/58; *Darlington,*

Harrogate and *Selby* all 963/58 for Associated Humber Lines services to the Continent; and *Ballymoney* 1342/53 and *Ballymena* 1356/54 for John Kelly Ltd, Belfast; the sludge hoppers *Dalmarnoch* 2266/70 and *Garroch Head* 2808/77 for Glasgow Corporation.

The yard acquired a good reputation for the construction of tugs with *Campaigner* and *Wrestler* both 248/57 for the Clyde services of Steel & Bennie Ltd, and several for J. H. Lamey Ltd of Liverpool, as well as for Clyde ferries e.g. *Jupiter* 849/74 and several small double-ended car ferries. The last ship built was the sludge carrier *Divis II*, launched in 1978 for Belfast City Corporation. The three-berth Castle yard then closed and the company concentrated on shiprepair work at its two dry-docks in Greenock.

One of the disused Lamont dry-docks near the Custom House at Greenock, with an abandoned Clyde puffer at its head. (Author).

ARDROSSAN DOCKYARD LTD

John Barr and James Shearer commenced wooden shipbuilding at Ardrossan in 1842 as Barr & Shearer, and changed their business name in the 1870s to the Ardrossan Shipbuilding Company. They had three berths and a dry-dock of 340 feet in length, and the company became of limited liability in 1891. The yard was renamed in 1899 as the Ardrossan Dry Dock & Shipbuilding Co. Ltd, and ships were launched from the North yard into a non-tidal fitting-out basin with a restricted width entrance. A early motor coaster was completed as *Isleford* 414/13 for the Isleford Shipping Co. Ltd, Glasgow and powered by twin two-cylinder Bolinder oil engines. It was decided to construct a new South yard in 1916 launching from five berths of up to 500 feet in length directly into the sea, and the total yard area was then 33 acres with employees increased from 200 up to 2300 men. The manager of the yards was Aitken Quack, and he remained as manager after the yards were sold at the end of the war to Lamport & Holt Ltd. The latter company was part of the Royal Mail Group, which also included Harland & Wolff Ltd of Belfast. Lord and Lady Pirrie later visited the yard from Belfast in 1923 with Lady Pirrie launching *Lady Louth* 1084/23 for Burns-Laird Line as the only launch of 1923. This was one of the last launches attended by Lord Pirrie as Chairman of Harland & Wolff Ltd as he died in March,1924 while returning from South America. The company name was shortened to Ardrossan Dockyard Ltd in 1925.

Minesweepers and small warships had been built during the war, followed by two standard 'H' type colliers completed as *Hunstanworth* and *Glassford*, both 2579/19, and the smaller standard coasters *Ardgantock* and *Independence*. Two yards were then worked and completions included :-

POLJANA	3822/20	Cia Argentina, Argentina
DUNKERQUOIS	3150/21	Cie de Bateaux a Vap du Nord,Dunkirk
CAMBRAISIEN	3150/21	"
BAYESKIMO	1200/22	Hudsons Bay Co. Ltd, London
TROLDFOSS	1349/22	Iceland S.S. Co. Ltd, Iceland
LAATEFOSS	1349/21	"
LOUISIANA	6513/21	DFDS, Denmark
PENRITH CASTLE	4070/22	Lancs. Shpg. Co. Ltd (J. Chambers)
LADY LOUTH	1084/23	Burns-Laird Line, Glasgow
LADY LIMERICK	1084/24	"
ANTHEA	5186/24	Bowring, London
URLA	5186/24	"
FORESTROW	1548/24	Forest S.S. Co. Ltd, Newcastle
BARON DECHMONT	3675/29	H. Hogarth, Ardrossan

BLAIRSPEY	4155/29	Clydesdale Nav. Co. Ltd,Glasgow
BLAIRNEVIS	4155/30	"
DEIDO	3894/28	Elder, Dempster
HENRY STANLEY	4028/29	"
MARY KINGSLEY	4017/30	"
WAIMARINO	3067/30	Union Steamship Co. Ltd,New Zealand

Louisiana was a twin-screw cargo-liner for North American service and the first motorship built at Ardrossan, being supplied with two 6-cylinder B & W oil engines from the Danish works in Copenhagen. However after just over ten years of operation orders were now impossible to obtain and the new South yard was sold in 1931 to National Shipbuilders Security Ltd and closed with a forty-year prohibition on building in the yard.

The old North yard, which had completed coasters such as *Sardis* 1021/28 for Moss-Hutchinson Line and the David Macbrayne twin-screw motor ferries *Lochearn* and *Lochmor*, both 542/30, was sold to the joint ownership of Coast Lines Ltd and engine builders John G. Kincaid & Co. Ltd of Greenock. However the yard was restricted to building ships only up to 275 feet in length, and work resumed in a small way in 1933 to build *Arran* 208/33 for Clyde Cargo Steamers Ltd followed by *Lady Meath* 1598/34 for British & Irish Steam Packet Co. Ltd, Dublin, and then a series of coasters for yard owners Coast Lines Ltd e.g. *Pacific Coast* 1210/35, as well as the Kincaid oil-engined *Kindiesel* 350/36 for P. McCallum.

During the ensuing war eight coasters were built for the yard owners Coast Lines Ltd, and a number to standard design for Government account, including the refrigerated coaster *Empire Atoll* 692/42 laid down for Coast Lines but completed as the only refrigerated coaster built during the war-time emergency programme. Coast Lines Ltd purchased her in 1946 as *Hadrian Coast* and operated her as the first full reefer coaster. Trawlers and boom defence vessels were also built during the war for the Admiralty.

The yard continued to build mini-cargo liners in post-war years e.g. *Zambesia* 2625/48 and *Lurio* 2639/49 for Cia de Nacional, Lisbon, and coasters for yard owners Coast Lines Ltd and associated companies e.g. *Pacific Coast* 1188/47, *Lairdsglen* 1496/54, *Pointer* 907/56 and *Dorset Coast* 1225/59, as well as for other coaster owners e.g. the Zillah Steamship Co. Ltd, Liverpool with *Birchfield* 1265/56. The only Clyde ferry completed by Ardrossan Dockyard Ltd was the 500 passenger *Maid of Cumbrae* 508/53. The last ship from the yard was the engines-aft container ship *Buffalo* of 2163 grt delivered in January,1962 for the Link Line service of Coast Lines Ltd. The yard was then sold later in 1962 to shiprepairers and the old North yard and dry-dock finally closed in 1969.

AYRSHIRE DOCKYARD LTD.

Mackie & Thomson sold their Govan Old yard to Harland & Wolff Ltd (q.v.) in 1912 in return for a four-ship contract to be built at their new six-berth yard at Irvine on the coast. The yard was built one mile from the sea on the river Irvine above the junction with the Garnock estuary, and a Simons-built dredger was acquired to ensure depth of water at the foot of the slipways and in the approaches to the yard. The Harland & Wolff Ltd ships were completed as the passenger/cargo *Maryland* and *Missouri* both 4731/13 for the Atlantic Transport Co. Ltd, and motorships *Falstria* 4344/15 for the East Asiatic Co. of Denmark with her sister ship also laid down for this company but completed as *Kangaroo* 4348/15 for the Western Australian Government.

During the Great War the yard built fleet tugs for the Admiralty as well as merchant ships e.g. the motorship *Glenartney* 7237/16 and steamer *Glenamoy* 7269/16 for Glen Line; *Glennevis* and *Glencarron*, both 5119/17 for James Gardiner & Co. Ltd, Glasgow; *Clan Morrison* 5931/17 and *Clan Monroe* 5913/18 for The Clan Line Steamers Ltd; *Montezuma* 5500/15 for Elder,Dempster and *Baron Inchcape* 7005/17 for Hugh Hogarth of Ardrossan, as well as the Indian coastal passenger steamer *Bradfield* 769/18 for the Bombay Steam Navigation Co. Ltd. Six standard 'B' types were ordered of which only three were completed as *Harmodius, Harmonides* and *Halizones* for R.P. Houston & Co. Ltd, with *Halizones* not completing until April,1920. The main customers of the yard then became The Clan Line Steamers Ltd of Glasgow and Hogarth of Ardrossan :-

CLAN MURDOCH	5950/19	The Clan Line Steamers Ltd
CLAN MACTAGGART	7603/20	"
CLAN MACNAB	6076/20	"
CLAN MACTAVISH	7603/21	"
CLAN MACNAIR	6096/21	"
CLAN MACNAUGHTON	6110/21	"
CLAN MACNEIL	6111/22	"
CLAN MACFARLANE	6196/22	"
CLAN MACFADYEN	6191/23	"
METCALFE	1851/23	Canada S.S. Lines (Gt. Laker)
MEREL	1088/25	General Steam Nav. Co. Ltd
BARON INCHCAPE	7005/17	H. Hogarth, Ardrossan
BARON MACLAY	6317/24	"
BARON FAIRLIE	6706/25	"
BARON HAIG	3391/26	"
BARON OGILVY	3391/26	"

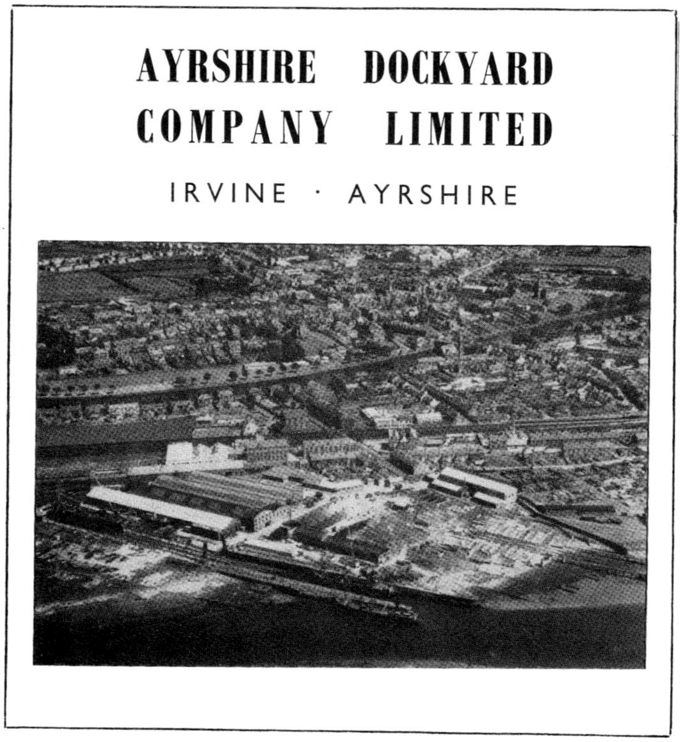

Two for Clan Line from Irvine in CLAN MACNAIR of 1922 (centre) and CLAN MURDOCH of 1919.

BARON LOVAT	3395/26	"
BARON PENTLAND	3410/27	"
BARON SALTOUN	3404/27	"
BARON COCHRANE	3385/27	"
BARON YARBOROUGH	3388/28	"
BARON NEWLANDS	3386/28	"
BLAIRMORE	4141/28	Clydesdale Nav. Co. Ltd,Glasgow
ALFONSO	3076/28	Menendez-Behety, Chile
KINDUR	1267/28	Newcastle & Hunter River S.S. Co. Pty, Australia

The yard was acquired by the Lithgow brothers in 1928 and a few tramps were built as speculations e.g. *Charterhurst* 4973/30, which was traded by Henry Lithgow under the management of Lewis and Grove Williams, Cardiff, and another which was eventually sold to Yugoslavia as *Trepca* 5051/30. Two futher hulls were laid down but construction was stopped in 1933 due to the Depression and they were not launched and completed until 1936 as *Coulmore* and *Coulbeg*, both 3670/36, for the Dornoch Shipping Co. Ltd (Lambert brothers). The yard was purchased by National Shipbuilders Security Ltd and closed for shipbuilding and became a shiprepairer only. Henry Lithgow then developed a flourishing trade in cold rolled steel sections, and some major shiprepair and conversion contracts were carried out during World War II.

Shiprepairing continued until 1959 when this ceased, and the yard was left with the production of cold rolled metal sections for Ayrshire Metal Products Ltd. This company is still in operation today on the site, with the old platers shed also used by the Scottish Maritime Musuem to house boats and engines. The engine shop from the Linthouse yard of Alexander Stephen & Sons Ltd has also been moved to a site at this old Irvine shipyard.

AILSA SHIPBUILDING CO. LTD, Ayr & Troon

Alexander McCreadie and Peter Wallace started a shipyard in 1883 at the Maidens to build small steamers, and in 1885 a three-berth yard at Troon was purchased jointly with the Marquis of Ailsa, who had experience of boatbuilding at his Culzean Castle. The yard was renamed with his family name as the Ailsa Shipbuilding Company, becoming of limited liability in 1901. In 1902 the six-berth yard of S. McKnight & Co. Ltd at Ayr was taken over, having previously built the Clyde paddlers *Madge Wildfire* 220/86 and *Lady Rowena* 332/91; and *Kyle* 543/85 for Ayr Harbour Commissioners. The Ayr yard then went on to build two hundred more ships under the Ailsa name including *Queen of the Lake* 152/07 for knock-

AILSA

SHIPBUILDING CO. LTD.

SHIPBUILDERS, SHIP-REPAIRERS AND MARINE ENGINEERS

M.V. "GLEN SANNOX," PASSENGER, VEHICLE AND CONTAINER FERRY

★ TWO DRY DOCKS — 400 FEET AND 289 FEET

★ BUILDERS UNDER LICENCE OF DOXFORD OPPOSED-PISTON OIL ENGINES UP TO A MAXIMUM OF 3,300 B.H.P. PER ENGINE

★ CHRISTIANSEN AND MEYER DOUBLE COMPOUND STEAM ENGINES UP TO 3,000 I.H.P.

★ MARINE STEAM RECIPROCATING ENGINES UP TO 3,000 I.H.P.

★ ALL TYPES OF VESSELS UP TO 350 FEET LONG

TELEPHONE:
TROON
38, 39 AND 58

TROON

SCLAND

TELEGRAMS:
"SHIPYARD"
TROON

Company advertisement featuring the Clyde car ferry GLEN SANNOX of 1957, and collier HUDSON FIRTH of 1949. (G.R. Scott).

down and re-erection at Loch Tay for service between Killin and Kenmore; and the coasters *Maple* 1276/14 for Laird Line; *Seamew* 1332/15, *Drake* 1597/20 and *Petrel* 1457/20 for the General Steam Navigation Co. Ltd before closing in 1929 after the completion of the twin-screw coastal steamer *Cobargo* 860/29 for the Illawarra & South Coast S.N. Co. Ltd, Sydney, and the Bristol Channel sand dredger *Durdham* 477/29. The Ayr yard re-opened only during World War II for repair work.

The Troon yard after take-over by the Marquis of Ailsa built sailing ships such as *Killoran* 1523/00 and *Kildalton* 1794/03 for John Hardie & Company, Glasgow, and steamers such as *Ailsa* for the service between Girvan and Ailsa Craig, the steam yacht *Hiniesta* 361/02, the coaster *Findnorn* 1064/03 for William Sloan of Glasgow, the paddler *Bournemouth Queen* 353/08, and paddlers *Glen Avon* 509/12 and *Glen Usk* 524/14 for P. & A. Campbell Ltd, Cardiff. An engine works was opened at Troon in 1907 and hulls from Ayr were then towed the six miles northward for machinery fitting. A series of seven Brazilian coastal ships for Cia Nacional de Nav. Costeira, Rio de Janeiro started with *Itapuca* 1849/09 and ended with *Itabera* 2162/16. The yard also built sloops, minesweepers and river gunboats for the Admiralty during the Great War.

The main customers of the Troon yard after the war were the General Steam Navigation Co. Ltd with a dozen coasters e.g. *Heron* 1314/22, *Starling* 1320/30 and *Crane* 785/37 with some having navigating bridges well forward e.g. *Falcon* 1025/27. J. Hay & Sons Ltd took seven coasters between 1927 and 1932 e.g. *The Duke* 820/27, with other coasters for William Sloan of Glasgow e.g. *Beauly* 1030/24 and *Orchy* 1090/30. The largest ship built by far at this time was the South American coastal liner *Jose Menendez* 4441/22 for the Patagonian Import & Export S.A., Argentina, having followed two similar sisters for the same owner *Alejandro* and *Asturiano*, both 2947/13, with other exports going to Egypt in the shape of the coasters *Zaafaran* and *Zamalek*, both 1566/21. The Bristol Channel paddler *Glen Gower* 553/22, the Thames paddler *Medway Queen* 316/24 and the Isles of Scilly steamer *Scillonian* 429/26 were other examples of the Troon yard skill.

World War II output included the small hospital ship *Magician* for the Admiralty, the turbine excursion ship *Empress Queen* 1781/40 which was used as a troopship during the war, the collier *Empire Pioneer* 2076/42 and two standard coasters of 300 dwt, eight standard engines-amidships 'Scandinavian' types of 4700 dwt with the last two completed as *Uskside* 2961/46 for R.W. Jones of Newport and *Greenland* 2958/45 for Currie Line of Leith, who also had privately built *Zealand* 1924/43 and *Rutland* 1907/46.

The facilities at Troon in immediate post-war years were four berths for ships up to 350 feet, and two dry-docks and an engine works capable of building steam reciprocating engines and Doxford oil engines under licence. The berths were later reduced to three and augmented by a very large prefabrication facility, which dominated Troon harbour. Five colliers for the Hudson Steamship Co. Ltd of London of up to 4500 dwt were some of the largest ships built at Troon in post-war years, *Hudson Strait* 3105/46, *Hudson Cape* 2524/46, *Hudson River* 3128/49, *Hudson Firth* 3117/49 and *Hudson Sound* 2577/50, all with coal-fired triple expansion engines except for *Hudson Firth* being oil-fired to enable her to spend the majority of her trading in the West Indian sugar trade. Cargo-liners of 4000 dwt were built for Ellerman Lines and associated Ellerman Wilson Line e.g. *Sicilian* 3351/48 and *Grecian* 3347/49, *Dago* 2302/47, *Domino* 2302/47 and *Borodino* 3206/50 Smaller colliers of around 2000 dwt included *Amber* 1596/56 and *Amethyst* 1548/58 for William Robertson Ltd of Glasgow, and *Irish Rose* and *Irish Willow*, both 1749/56 for Irish Line, and coasters included *Tynewood* 1495/57, *Thameswood* 1799/57 and *Eastwood* 1793/60 for Joseph Constantine of Middlesbrough, and *Whitewing* 1102/53 and *Ringdove* 1102/54 for General Steam Navigation Co. Ltd.

Large and small ferries were also built at Troon with *St. Clair* 2863/60 one of the largest with accomodation for 450 passengers on her Aberdeen to Shetland service, and she was given Sulzer oil engines to maintain her service speed of 16 knots. Another car ferry of this size was *Mona's Queen* 2998/72 for the Isle of Man Steam Packet Co. Ltd, capable of carrying 1600 passengers and 100 cars and fitted with Crossley - Pielstick diesel engines to give a service speed of 21 knots. The sister car ferry *Lady of Mann* 2990/76 followed from Troon, and the cargo-only *Fenella* 1019/51 and *Peveril* 1048/64 and *Ramsey* 446/65 were also built for this owner by the yard. The general purpose Clyde ferries *Cowal* and *Bute* , both 569/54, were the second and third of three new sisters to carry cars for the first time on Clyde service, and were followed by the larger *Glen Sannox* 1107/57 and *Saturn* 851/78, while *Iona* 1192/70 was built for the Western Isles service of David Macbrayne Ltd. Double-ended car ferries were also built e.g. *Freshwater* 363/59 for Isle of Wight service and *Isle of Cumbrae* 201/77 for Cumbrae service.

The Troon yard was not included in the list of yards for nationalisation in June,1977, but joined British Shipbuilders Ltd after a direct approach in June,1978. The yard was then linked with the Ferguson yard at Port Glasgow as Ferguson-Ailsa Ltd from 1981. An order for a 7230 dwt liquid gas carrier from Anchor Line via its subsidiary of George Gibson Ltd was too big to build in either yard, and the solution was to build the aft section at Troon and the forward section at Port Glasgow. The two sections were launched on the same day of 21st August,1981 and then joined together in the Inchgreen dry-dock at Port Glasgow, the resulting vessel being *Traquair* 5967/82. Another gas tanker of 1875 dwt was later completed at Troon as

Tarihiko 2169/84 for the Shipping Corporation of New Zealand, and the last ship completed at Troon was the research ship *Corystes* of 1280grt which left the yard in early 1987. The Troon yard currently trades as Ailsa - Perth Shipbuilders Ltd as a shiprepairer and small module builder but no new ships have been built by this Australian financed company.

CAMPBELTOWN SHIPBUILDING CO. LTD

This yard was founded in 1877 by Archibald MacEachern at Trench Point on the site of 17th century earth works at the entrance to Campbeltown loch to relieve local unemployment. The yard built small steamers for Glasgow shipowners e.g. *Kingswear* 374/83, *Elsa* 813/82, *Batley* 1300/83 and *Bramble* 1508/88, as well as the Queensland steamer *Gympic* 900/83 for Australian coastal services, with engines supplied by Kincaid & Company and Dunsmuir & Jackson of Glasgow. The first steamer in the large fleet of Andrew Weir was built at Campbeltown as *Duneric* 1878/96 as well as the steam yacht *Glenesta* in 1901. Some of the largest ships built at Campbeltown were *Mistor* 2989/06 for R.H. Holman, *Amphion* 2931/11 for Greek owners, *Progress III* for H. Kias, *Neuquen* 3583/13 for the Buenos Aires Southern Railway, the well-deckers *Lady Plymouth* 3521/15 and *Lady Charlotte* 3999/17 for the Redcroft S.N. Co. Ltd and *Roquelle* 4364/18 for the Imperial Direct Line. Two colliers were also built during the war as *Oxshott* 1241/15 and *Redriff* 1256/17, and two standard types as *War Rother* and *War Foyle*, both 1400/18.

The workforce had increased to 300 men during the war, but with the post-war slump in orders the yard had only three more ships to build - *Oceania* 3600/20 for Ditta Luigi Pittaluga, and *Hillbrook* 1262/21 and *Hillglen* 1262/22 for the Portsmouth Steamship Co. Ltd. After building 110 ships the yard closed down in 1922. In 1969 Campbeltown Shipyard Ltd opened on the site of the former yard as a subsidiary of Lithgows Ltd with a workforce of 22 to build fishing vessels, and some 150 men were employed in 1980 but unfortunately the yard again closed shortly afterwards.

LADY OF MANN being launched for the Isle of Man Steam Packet Co. Ltd in 1976. (G. E. Langmuir).

BIBLIOGRAPHY AND FURTHER READING

'FAIRFIELD SHIPBUILDING & ENG. CO. LTD. 1860 - 1960 published by the company in 1960.
'ALEXANDER STEPHEN & SONS LTD. - A SHIPBUILDING HISTORY 1750 - 1932 published by the company in 1932.
'STEPHEN OF LINTHOUSE' 1750 - 1950 published by the company in 1950.
'LAUNCHING WAYS' - History of Barclay, Curle & Co. Ltd - published by Swan, Hunter & Wigham Richardson Ltd in 1953.
'DEVELOPMENT OF SHIPBUILDING ON THE UPPER REACHES OF THE CLYDE & SOUVENIR OF JAMES GILCHRIST'S JUBILEE' published by Barclay, Curle & Co. Ltd in 1911.
'FOUR AND A HALF YEARS WORK 1914 - 1918' published by Barclay, Curle & Co. Ltd in 1919.
'SHIPS & SHIPBUILDING' published by Barclay, Curle & Co. Ltd in 1932.
'SHIPBUILDERS TO THE WORLD' - 125 YEARS OF HARLAND & WOLFF LTD by Michael Moss and John R. Hume published by Blackhall Press, Belfast in 1986.
'CLYDE SHIPBUILDING FROM OLD PHOTOGRAPHS' by Michael Moss and John R. Hume published by Batsford of London in 1975.
'YARROWS - the FIRST HUNDRED YEARS' published by the company in 1965.
'STEEL & SHIPS - THE STORY OF JOHN BROWN' by Sir Allan Grant published by Michael Joseph Ltd in 1950.
'INGLIS OF GLASGOW' by John G. Inglis published privately in 1977.
'BEARDMORE BUILT ' by Ian Johnston published by Clydebank District Libraries in 1993.
'SCOTTS' of GREENOCK 250 YEARS of SHIPBUILDING' published by the company in 1961.
'THE 4.15 TO CARTSDYKE' by Michael Dick published by Pentland Press Ltd in 1993.
'JAMES LITHGOW - MASTER OF WORK' by J.M. Reid published by Hutchinson of London in 1964.
'THE DENNY LIST Vols 1 - 4' compiled by D.J. Lyon published by the National Maritime Museum in 1975.
'SONG OF THE CLYDE' by Fred M. Walker published by Patrick Stephens Ltd in 1984.
'STEEL SHIPBUILDING' by Fred M. Walker published by Shire Publications Ltd in 1981.
'BETTER BY YARDS' by Colin M. Castle published by Murdoch Carberry in 1988.
'THE SHIPBUILDING INDUSTRY - A GUIDE TO HISTORICAL RECORDS' edited by L.A. Ritchie published by Manchester University Press in 1992.
'AT THE SHARP END' by George H. Parker published by Brown, Son & Ferguson Ltd in 1992.
'SHIPBUILDING IN BRITAIN' by Leslie Jones published by University of Wales Press in 1957.
'DICTIONARY OF SCOTTISH BUSINESS BIOGRAPHY' edited by A. Slaven & S. Checkland published in 1986.
'HISTORY OF BRITISH MOTORSHIPPING' by A.C. Hardy published in 1955.
'CLYDE BUILT' by J. Shields published in Glasgow in 1949.